THE SOCIAL FABRIC OF THE METROPOLIS

THE HERITAGE OF SOCIOLOGY

A Series Edited by Morris Janowitz

THE SOCIAL FABRIC
OF THE METROPOLIS

Contributions of the
Chicago School of Urban Sociology

Edited and with an Introduction by

JAMES F. SHORT, JR.

THE UNIVERSITY OF CHICAGO PRESS

CHICAGO AND LONDON

ISBN: 0–226–75466–9 (clothbound); *0–226–75467–7 (paperbound)*
Library of Congress Catalog Card Number: 75–129926

THE UNIVERSITY OF CHICAGO PRESS, CHICAGO 60637
The University of Chicago Press, Ltd., London

Contents

III. STRUCTURE, PROCESS, COMMUNICATION, AND CHANGE

IV. SOCIAL WORLDS

Acknowledgments

THE SUBTITLE OF THIS VOLUME could well be "An Appreciation," for that at least is what I intend it to be. The "Chicago School" has meant a great deal to me, both personally and professionally. I suppose I was one of the last Ph.D. candidates whose thesis committee consisted of William F. Ogburn and Ernest W. Burgess. Earlier, in that first traumatic year of graduate school— made all the more so because I was a small-town boy from "downstate" Illinois transplanted for the first time to the iniquitous big city—I had been sustained by the warmth and sheer human kindness of Samuel C. Kincheloe, and the friendly guiding hand of Ethel Shanus. "Dr. K." supervised my M.A. thesis, even to guiding me through the community I had chosen to study for the purpose of choosing a sampling of blocks for interviewing—literally a "purposive" sample. Everett Hughes was the second member of the M.A. committee (between visits to Frankfort on the Main), and I remain much indebted to him. I had in the meantime been much influenced especially by fellow student Andy Henry and by Clifford Shaw, who served on the staff of the Downtown College of the University of Chicago and of the Illinois Institute for Juvenile Research— where he introduced me to Henry McKay and Solomon Kobrin.

The department at Chicago was approaching the end of an era during those years; shortly after I completed graduate work, Ogburn and Burgess retired, Louis Wirth died, and Herbert Blumer left for Berkeley. Younger associates also departed after serving the university in a variety of capacities—Albert J. Reiss, Jr., Morris Janowitz, Ed Swanson, Tomatsu Shibutani, and others.

When I returned to my alma mater in 1959, as a visiting associate professor, only Hughes and Philip Hauser remained of the department as I had known it, and Dudley Duncan had come back. It was rumored that my coming back signified a resurgence of the spirit of the Chicago School, a rumor which met with very mixed reactions—great enthusiasm in some, at least a hint of scorn in others. I was puzzled by these reactions, for I had never considered Chicago the zenith of sociological accomplishment, but rather as representative of a special emphasis on field research and empiricism, pioneering at one time but now widely diffused in sociology. It is a tradition I am proud to be a part of. Hopefully this compilation is consistent with it. An attempt has been made to avoid repetition of material published in other volumes of the Heritage series, though some overlap is unavoidable. In some instances, selections constitute a distillation of virtually the entire sociological work of an author, in others but a small sampling. All are part and parcel of the Chicago School, which was comprised not alone of giants but of workers in the vinyard as well.

The reader will forgive, I hope, this brief personal reminiscence. I am especially grateful to Morris Janowitz, who first suggested the idea of such a volume and was helpful and patient beyond reasonable endurance, and to Albert K. Cohen, Howard S. Becker, R. E. L. Faris, Everett C. Hughes, Helen MacGill Hughes, Henry D. McKay, J. Clyde Mitchell, Albert J. Reiss, Jr., and Sol Tax, who gave the benefit of their counsel at various stages of the enterprise. Finally to the National Institute of Mental Health and the Center for Advanced Study in the Behavioral Sciences appreciation is due for their part in providing the "leisure" time in which to complete this long delayed project.

James F. Short, Jr.

Introduction

THIS BOOK IS ABOUT CITIES. It is about city people—their origins, their problems, and the social arrangements which sustain them. It deals in the hard facts the scientist musters to document and explain, and in accounts of personal experience which enliven and enrich with the humanist's touch. The book brings together selections from what has come to be known as the "Chicago School" of urban sociology.

Early in the 1920s, sociologists at Chicago began the painstaking task of gathering facts of urban life, guided by theoretical notions concerning the growth and structure of cities and the nature of man and his institutions. The integrating theme of the Chicago School was the *metropolis*, the great urban complex which plays so dominant a role in the social life of its inhabitants, and in the cultural, political, and economic life of nations the world over. While the specific focus of Chicago sociologists varied greatly in scope and interest, the general emphasis was on the metropolis as a "natural" phenomenon. As Ernest W. Burgess wrote,

The city has been the "happy hunting ground" of movements: the "better-government" movement, the social-work movement, the public-health movement, the playground movement, the social-center movement, the settlement movement, the Americanization movement. All these movements, lacking a basic understanding or conception of the city, have relied upon administrative devices, for the most part, to correct the evils of city life. Even the community organization movement, theoretically grounded upon a conception of the city as a unit, had the misfortune to stake its program upon an assumption of the supreme value of the revival of the neighborhood in the city instead of upon a pragmatic, experimental program guided by studies of actual conditions and trends in urban life.

The tendency at present is to think of the city as living, growing; as an organism, in short. This notion of the city in terms of growth and behavior gives the character of order and unity to the many concrete phenomena of the city which otherwise, no matter how interesting, seemed but meaningless flotsam and jetsam in the drift of urban life.[1]

These words, written in the 1920s, seem just as applicable to the period of the New Deal, and to the 1960s, which once more brought outbursts of social movements in urban settings.

To some it has seemed that the Chicago School of urban sociology was more interested (and certainly more successful) in describing "meaningless flotsam and jetsam in the drift of urban life" than in forging a generalized, comprehensive view of society and human behavior. It is the thesis of this introduction that this was not the case and that the Chicago sociologists sought, and in considerable measure were responsible for, a general perspective in terms of method, data, and theory.

On Science, Research Methods and Social Reform: The Heritage

Chicago sociologists of the 1920s and 30s devoted much effort to developing sociology as a science. In the paper quoted above, Burgess noted that study of "the many concrete phenomena of the city" was "just the course of development by which sociology is being transformed from a social philosophy into a science of society."[2] The old "Green Bible" of a generation of sociologists, Park and Burgess's *Introduction to the Science of Sociology*, pictured the discipline as "just now entering" the "period of investigation and research" which was to lift sociology from its former speculative, philosophical character.

---

[1]   Ernest W. Burgess, ed., *The Urban Community*, Selected Papers from the Proceedings of the Amrican Sociological Socity, 1925 (Chicago: University of Chicago Press, 1926), p. viii.
[2]   Ibid., p. ix.

Sociological research is at present [1921] in about the situation in
which psychology was before the introduction of laboratory methods,
in which medicine was before Pasteur and the germ theory of disease.
A great deal of social information has been collected merely for the
purpose of determining what to do in a given case. Facts have not been
collected to check social theories. Social problems have been defined in
terms of common sense, and facts have been collected, for the most
part, to support this or that doctrine, not to test it. In very few instances have investigations been made disinterestedly, to determine the
validity of a hypothesis.[3]

Such a formidable task demanded great enthusiasm and a multitude of interests and talents. In this respect, despite the small number of scholars involved, Chicago was fortunate.[4] The department
headed by Albion W. Small—in 1892, the first department of sociology in the United States—included also Charles R. Henderson,
W. I. Thomas, and George E. Vincent.[5] This group represented a
rich mixture of historical and classical scholarship, theological and
humanistic concern for the welfare of man. Small and Thomas, in
particular, were determined to build the new science of sociology,
and their impact on the field was considerable.[6] While his influence

[3]   Robert E. Park and Ernest W. Burgess, *Introduction to the Science of Sociology*, 2d ed. (Chicago: University of Chicago Press, 1924),
p. 44.
[4]   For a more thorough, and most entertaining, treatment of the
historical background of the department, and its development, see Robert
E. L. Faris, *Chicago Sociology 1920–1932* (San Francisco: Chandler Publishing Company, 1967; rev. ed., Chicago: University of Chicago Press,
1970). I am indebted to Professor Faris, and to the editors of other volumes in the Heritage Series for aid in choosing selections and in com-
posing this introduction.
[5]   George Herbert Mead joined the faculty of philosophy in 1894.
See Anselm Strauss, ed., *George Herbert Mead on Social Psychology*
(Chicago: University of Chicago Press, 1964).
[6]   Everett C. Hughes notes that Small also played an active role in
the early Chicago emphasis on studying the city. He says, in personal
correspondence, that "Small wrote a would-be novel. . . . It contained
scarcely concealed stores of early Chicago events and personalities. . . .
Leonard White told me of a famous meeting at which Small got all the
social science people together and suggested they all undertake study of
the city, starting with Chicago. Merriam (Charles E.) in Political Science
was part of it. Park was just getting things moving his way in sociology."

was not as apparent, and he appeared to be interested chiefly in humanitarian reform, Henderson was from the beginning interested in the city as a sociological laboratory, and university records indicate that he sought funds for systematic study of the city during this early period.[7] From the beginning there was great enthusiasm for the enterprise. "The atmosphere," as described by Faris, was one of "adventure, exploration, and responsibility for opening up new directions of sociological research."[8]

It was the "second generation" of Chicago sociologists that was chiefly responsible for the full flowering of the discipline in that university, and to a considerable extent throughout the United States. One of the most important factors permitting this development—in sharp contrast with the dominating influence at other universities of somewhat doctrinaire sociological scholars such as Sumner (Yale), Ward (Brown), Giddings (Columbia), and Ross (Stanford and Wisconsin)—was the *openness* with which sociology was viewed, both in substance and in method. There was no "party line," save for the admonition to "objectivity" and "disinterested investigation" in the interests of a developing science. In contrast with other sociological giants of the day, as Faris remarks, Small is remembered to have urged his graduate students "to proceed as quickly as possible to make everything he taught them out of date."[9] Of even greater importance "was the intelligent perception by Small, accepted enthusiastically by his colleagues and successors, of the inhibiting consequences of doctrines, schools of thought, and authoritative leaders."[10]

Chicago's "second generation" was even broader in its interests and methodological perspectives than was the first. When he joined the department in 1914, Robert E. Park had been a teacher, a newspaperman, and an aide to Booker T. Washington. He had studied philosophy at Harvard and sociology in Germany under Simmel and Windelband.[11] Ellsworth Faris was trained as an engineer and

[7]   My thanks to Vernon K. Dibble for bringing documentary evidence to this effect to my attention.
[8]   Faris, *Chicago Sociology*, p. 88.
[9]   Ibid., p. 12.
[10]   Ibid., p. 128.
[11]   See Ralph H. Turner, ed., *Robert E. Park on Social Control and Collective Behavior* (Chicago: University of Chicago Press, 1967).

had become a missionary before entering academic life in philosophy, psychology, and finally sociology. Only Burgess took his
degree in sociology (at Chicago) as his first career interest and
while still a young man.[12]

Park, Burgess, and Faris were joined in 1927 by Ogburn (who
came to sociology via his interest in social welfare and in other
social sciences, particularly economics and statistics).[13] The impact
of these men was great. Everett Hughes describes the department
at this time as consisting "of a mere handful of men, very different
from each other in background and temperament, but among whom
there was informal collaboration such that a student had a sense
of unity and of common enterprise."[14] The common enterprise was
shared by faculty and students alike. Louis Wirth, for example, who
completed his Ph.D. degree in 1926 returned to Chicago as associate professor in 1931 and remained throughout his professional
life.[15]

SURVEYS AND STATISTICS   There was great enthusiasm during this early period for the "social survey" as a method of investigation of urban environment. When the Chicago department was
founded, Charles Booth was in the midst of his monumental survey,
Life and Labour of the People in London, a study which in many
respects presaged the development of urban sociology.[16] In this
country the Pittsburgh Survey—published in six volumes between
1907 and 1914—set the tone for many similar, but less thorough,

---

[12]   See Everett C. Hughes, "The First Young Sociologist," *Ernest
Watson Burgess, 1886–1966: Four Talks Given at a Memorial Service.*
The University of Chicago, 1967.
[13]   See Otis Dudley Duncan, ed., *William F. Ogburn on Culture and
Social Change* (Chicago: University of Chicago Press, 1964).
[14]   Hughes, "The First Young Sociologist," p. 4.
[15]   For a list of some of the graduate students in the department in the
early 1920s, see Faris, *Chicago Sociology,* p. 32.
[16]   17 vols., London: Macmillan and Co., 1902–3). Publication of this
work began in 1891 as *Labour and Life of the People,* vol. 1, *East London.*
See Harold W. Pfautz, ed., *Charles Booth on the City: Physical Pattern
and Social Structure* (Chicago: University of Chicago Press, 1967). There
had been other "ecological studies," but none of such scope. See e.g., M. C.
Elmer, "Century-Old Ecological Studies in France," *American Journal of
Sociology* 39 (July 1933) : 63–70.

works of this type. And, closer to "home" for the Chicago sociologists, the Hull House Papers provided an early model for systematic
urban studies.[17]

Many of these early efforts were characterized by highly partisan purposes of immediate social reform. Those which were disinterested, as was the case with Booth's work, were unguided by
explicit theoretical premises and hence not productive of generalized, objective statements about urban structure and social life.
Urban sociologists soon moved away from the comprehensive social survey—with its "shotgun" approach to data gathering—and,
with Chicago taking the lead, undertook more detailed and conceptually guided studies of specific social phenomena. For many
sociologists the social survey was viewed as the primary tool for
building a science of contemporary society.[18]

At the same time, other methods were being developed and put
to the test of field studies. While Park was suspicious of those who
felt that all of the nuances of social life could be captured in quantitative methods, he recognized that systematic measurement was
necessary. Emory S. Bogardus credits Park for suggesting to him
that he develop a generally applicable device for the measurement
of social distance—a suggestion which resulted in a widely used
social distance scale.[19] Burgess was more quantitatively oriented
than Park and made significant contributions to statistical prediction of success and failure in marriage and on parole.[20] And while

[17]   Ernest W. Burgess and Donald Bogue, eds., *Contributions to
Urban Sociology* (Chicago: University of Chicago Press, 1964), p. 5.
[18]   See Carl C. Taylor, The Social Survey and the Science of Sociology," *American Journal of Sociology* 25 (May 1920): 731–56. Consistent with the historical concerns of Small and others, it was widely
believed that over time social surveys would provide extensive and objective evidence for historical analysis. The study of social trends, carried to
its fullest development by Ogburn, was recognized as important also by
Booth. See Pfautz, ed., *Booth on the City.*
[19]   Turner, ed., *Park on Social Control*, p. xix, referring to Emory S.
Bogardus, *Social Distance* (Yellow Springs, Ohio: Antioch Press, 1959),
p. 5.
[20]   Despite a late start in acquiring statistical competence. Writing
in memoriam, R. E. L. Faris, Leonard P. Cottrell, and Philip M. Hauser
independently recall that Burgess, already past forty, sat in on colleague

Wirth was not noted for his statistical research, or even competence, in statistics, he was the founder of the Chicago Community Inventory and coeditor of its first two "local community fact books."[21] Ogburn brought to Chicago its strongest statistical emphasis, and he, perhaps more than any other sociologist, is the intellectual godfather of modern statistical methods as applied to demography, human ecology, and the study of social change.[22] Healthy competition, not only among different methodological persuasions, but among the scholars who espoused them, contributed to the intellectual ferment of the department. Similarly, collaboration and competition among practitioners of different disciplines greatly stimulated work emanating from 1126 East Fifty-ninth Street, the most famous address in the history of American social science.[23]

Certainly the study of specific social problems such as crime and delinquency was enhanced greatly by the availability of statistical materials. Thus, Clifford Shaw, long an advocate of "the personal document and life history approach to sociological re-

---

Ogburn's statistics courses in 1929, after having defended case studies in debates concerning the efficacy of case study versus statistics. See *Ernest Watson Burgess, 1886–1966*. Cottrell recalls that "In the days of the Park and Burgess Research Seminar, Professor Park would sometimes hurl Jovian thunderbolts at the folly of the statisticians or the misguided Freudians. Professor Burgess, sitting beside him, would nod solemn approval, twinkling the while at those of us who knew of his assiduous study of those forbidden mysteries" (page 21).

21   See Albert J. Reiss, Jr., ed., *Louis Wirth on Cities and Social Life* (Chicago: University of Chicago Press, 1964); Louis Wirth and Margaret Furez, *Local Community Fact Book: 1938* (Chicago: Chicago Recreation Commission, 1938); Louis Wirth and Eleanor H. Bernert, *Local Community Fact Book of Chicago*, Chicago Community Inventory (Chicago: University of Chicago Press, 1949).

22   Ogburn did not think of himself as a methodologist, and his primary interest lay in the study and explanation of social change. See Duncan, ed., *Ogburn on Culture*.

23   For documentary evidence of the extraordinary degree of cross-fertilization of social science disciplines at Chicago during the period under review, see T. V. Smith and L. D. White, eds., *Chicago: An Experiment in Social Science* (Chicago: University of Chicago Press, 1929), and Louis Wirth, ed., *Eleven Twenty-Six: A Decade of Social Science Research* (Chicago: University of Chicago Press, 1940).

search," and "a central figure in the stormy controversy over 'qualitative versus quantitative' research methods," headed a department of the Institute for Juvenile Research which "calmly turned out more statistical research on sociological topics than most of his critics."[24] It is clear, also, that Shaw's use of case materials was intended to be cumulative, providing the basis for abstraction of factors which could be summarized and manipulated statistically.[25] The "life-history document"—in which an individual is encouraged to tell his "own story"—was viewed as a method of study meaningful also to the person being studied. As Rice points out, in discussion of Shaw's methods, "before units can be counted they must first be identified, and identification is a process more and more equivalent to case study as the units become more complex."[26]

ON THE JUSTIFICATION OF SOCIOLOGY   While there was common enthusiasm among the Chicago sociologists for their emerging science, there was much disagreement over such fundamental matters as the basic focus of the discipline.[27] And while there was general agreement on the justification of sociology in terms of its ultimate service to mankind, there were almost as many views concerning the means by which such service might properly be rendered by sociology as there were scholars to hold them. Ogburn became the most "pure" science-oriented of the group, but he came from a distinctly liberal—indeed, radical—background, and his scientific stance was based on the conviction that systematic

[24]   Burgess and Bogue, eds., *Contributions to Urban Sociology*, p. 591. Henry D. McKay was primarily responsible for the statistical output, but the two men worked together most compatibly and successfully for many years.

[25]   See Stuart A. Rice, "Hypotheses and Verifications in Clifford R. Shaw's Studies of Juvenile Delinquency," in *Methods in Social Science: A Case Book*, ed. Stuart A. Rice (Chicago: University of Chicago Press, 1931), p. 563.

[26]   Ibid.

[27]   Cf. the previously cited volumes in this series devoted to the works of Park, Ogburn, and Wirth; and Morris Janowitz, ed., *W. I. Thomas on Social Organization and Social Personality* (Chicago: University of Chicago Press, 1966); see also Faris, *Chicago Sociology*.

and objective study of social change was more efficacious than was social reform as an approach to human problems.[28] Ogburn remained active in a consultative capacity to such governmental policy agencies as the National Recovery Administration, the National Resources Committee, and the Bureau of the Census.

Park had participated in social reform as "a sort of secretary" to Booker T. Washington for seven years, but even this experience seems to have been related primarily to his belief "that Washington was able to face the subject (of race relations) with some realism and with less sentimentality than was customary in that period."[29] Park "saw sociology as ultimately useful and practical," but he demanded of his students "the same objectivity and detachment with which the zoologist dissects a potato bug."[30] "Applied sociology is not concerned with uncovering mechanisms and devices for reform, but with exposing the broad setting of social organization and human nature which policy-makers must take into account."[31]

In contrast to both Park and Ogburn, Burgess actively associated himself with organizations dedicated to social action and reform throughout his life, and he addressed himself in professional publications to such questions as "Is Prediction Feasible in Social Work?" (*Social Forces* 7 [June 1929]: 533–45). He also conducted extensive research and wrote persuasively on such topics as "The Value of Sociological Community Studies to the Work of Social Agencies" (*Social Forces* 8 [June 1930]: 481–91), "Protecting the Public by Parole and by Parole Prediction" (*Journal of Criminal Law and Criminology* 27 [November-December 1936]: 491–502), *Predicting Success or Failure in Marriage* (with Leonard S. Cottrell, New York: Prentice-Hall, 1939), and on the problems of the aged.

Wirth was even more involved than Burgess in efforts directed

[28]   Duncan, ed., *Ogburn on Culture*.
[29]   Faris, *Chicago Sociology*, p. 28.
[30]   Turner, ed., *Park on Social Control*, p. xvi. The latter part of the quote is from Ernest W. Burgess, "Social Planning and Race Relations," in *Race Relations: Problems and Theory: Essays in Honor of Robert E. Park*, ed. Jitsuiki Masuoka and Preston Valien (Chapel Hill: University of North Carolina Press, 1961), p. 17.
[31]   Turner, ed., *Park on Social Control*.

at social reform, but the two men had very different styles. Wirth began the quest for sociological knowledge with a question of fundamental philosophical significance, viz., "Can we do anything about social life, or do we live in a matrix of social forces that elude understanding? . . . Wirth's 'competent sociologist' was one who experiences the reality he investigates and assumes the full role of citizen as well as the role of scientist qua scientist. The professional sociologist he recommended should be a scholar in action."[32]

Robert E. L. Faris describes the "Chicago attitude" as "essentially that of pure science":

. . . that is, that while all knowledge is ultimately of potential value to human applications, it is worthwhile to pursue many intellectual questions without reference either to their immediate service or to the question of what particular applications the knowledge may have. In this view, the restriction of scholarly attention to the search for immediate alleviation of present problems may and generally does fail to solve such problems and also delays the development of the organized and tested knowledge which could be effective.[33]

Virtually the full range of positions with respect to science and social action has been followed by "third" and subsequent "generations" of Chicago students. Characteristically there has been no single "party line." All would probably agree with the underlying position, however, stated by Ellsworth Faris, that "the most objective research, if sufficiently successful, will pay its debt to the society which made it possible and will definitely contribute to the amelioration of our social life."[34]

"The nineteen-twenties were the greatest years of urban sociological study in the United States," wrote Shils in 1948.[35] This

[32]   Reiss, ed., *Wirth on Cities*, pp. xxvi-xxviii.
[33]   *Chicago Sociology*, p. 130. Faris elaborates this point of view in "The Discipline of Sociology," chap. 1 in Robert E. L. Faris, ed., *Handbook of Modern Sociology* (Chicago: Rand, McNally and Co., 1964).
[34]   "Foreword" to Ruth Shonle Cavan, *Suicide* (Chicago: University of Chicago Press, 1928), p. xvii. It should be noted that this, too, was a view widely shared by colleagues in other social science departments of the University.
[35]   Edward Shils, *The Present State of American Sociology* (Glencoe, Ill.: The Free Press, 1948), pp. 54–55.

activity centered in large part at Chicago. Shils criticized the Chicago sociologists for their failure to "set out to demonstrate any explicitly formulated sociological hypotheses." Park had "a unified and coherent vision of the main processes of social life [which] underlay the specific researches to which he set his students" but "in the course of time the original vision vanished and there was left behind a tendency towards the repetition of disconnected investigations." Shils was critical of Park for his failure to see "the need to relate concrete indices to general abstract definitions, and the indispensability of general and not just particular explanations." He acknowledged, however, that . . . "they have fulfilled a momentously important function in the development of social science by establishing an unbreakable tradition of first-hand observation, a circumspect and critical attitude towards sources of information, and the conviction that the way to the understanding of human behavior lies in the study of institutions in operation and of the concrete individuals through whom they operate."[36]

Others have been less harsh in their assessment, and on balance, the contributions acknowledged by Shils are not inconsiderable. A product of that school, O. D. Duncan, stresses the importance of the "insight that some social processes yield important but latent and unanticipated structural patterns."[37] This insight, and the concepts utilized for its empirical exploration, formed the basis for a more genuinely ecological approach to the study of social change and social organization.

The discovery that spacial patterns of cities varied greatly from that found in Chicago led many to question the basic processes hypothesized to account for these patterns. What has emerged more recently is a vigorous comparative urban sociology in which the early work of the Chicago school continues to play an important part.[38]

---

[36]   Ibid., pp. 9, 10, 11. For a similarly critical assessment and a somewhat different appreciation, see John Madge, *The Origins of Scientific Sociology*, New York: Free Press of Glencoe, 1962.
[37]   Otis Dudley Duncan, "Social Organization and the Ecosystem," Chapter 2 in Robert E. L. Faris, ed., *Handbook of Modern Sociology*, p. 77.
[38]   For an excellent review of the Chicago position, as represented by Burgess' zonal hypotheses of city growth, and subsequent studies, as well

While it was a basic emphasis at Chicago, human ecology languished for a time as a result of a widely held misconception which relegated it to the status of "an auxiliary research technique." Recent advances in method and substance have done much to dispel this image. The ecological approach to the study of human collective life with its stress upon social and environmental interdependence, assumes added—even urgent—importance in a period of deep concern over the uses and abuses of the environment, and collective disorders in the metropolis and its environs, and the birth and growing pains of developing nations. The new generation of ecologists and demographers owes much to the Chicago tradition.

The Social Fabric of the Metropolis: An Overview

The rationale for organizing this book is simple. The first paper, by Harvey W. Zorbaugh, was chosen because it tells a great deal about social life in Chicago in a manner which captures much of the spirit of the Chicago School. Part 2 presents outstanding examples of the basic perspectives of the Chicago sociologists, beginning with human ecology, then covering social organization, and social psychology. Part 3 illustrates the manner in which cultural heritages, urban structure, communication, and change were studied. Parts 4 and 5 present a sampling of the descriptive accounts and analyses of various social worlds and problems of the modern metropolis. The methods and perspectives of human ecology, social organization, and social psychology cut across each of the other areas and inform one another. Together they remain the mainstream of sociological thought and inquiry.

DEMOGRAPHY, ECOLOGY, AND TECHNOLOGY   Chicago ecologists have been criticized for overemphasizing an ecological perspective based on impersonal and technological forces, and for

---

as a prolegomenon for further research concerning a more general theory of urban land use, see Leo F. Schnore, "On the Spatial Structure of Cities in the Two Americas," in Philip M. Hauser and Leo F. Schnore, eds., *The Study of Urbanization* (New York: John Wiley and Sons, 1965), pp. 347–98.

regarding "the contemporary American metropolis as a universal climax formation."[39] The latter charge is hardly sustained by the record, as evidenced by the first paper in part 2 of this volume. Roderick D. McKenzie outlines the ecological perspective in a manner which reflected contemporary concern with—and foreshadowed later work on—the social impact of changes in the economy and in technology, of the development of new systems of transportation and communication, and of urban renewal and rapidly increasing urbanization.[40]

The comparative study of urbanism in different cultures has lagged. Indeed, sociology generally has been relatively culturebound, concerned far too exclusively with the United States, where the discipline has experienced its greatest development. However, the study of demography, human ecology, and technology is less vulnerable to this charge than are other fields in sociology.[41]

In part because the objects of study were relatively amenable to measurement, we know a great deal about the distribution of behavioral phenomena in the city and their relation to indices of physical and economic characteristics of the city, its environs, and rural areas. Less is known of relations between distributions of behavioral phenomena and cultural factors, such as belief and value systems, though significant beginnings were made in Chicago, as is evident in selections in parts 3, 4, and 5 of this volume.[42]

Fundamental research on the nature and extent of urbanization

39   Lewis Mumford, "The City: Forms and Functions," *International Encyclopedia of the Social Sciences* (New York: The Macmillan Company and The Free Press, 1968), 2: 448.

40   For a more comprehensive review of McKenzie's work see Amos H. Hawley, ed., *Roderick D. McKenzie on Human Ecology* (Chicago: University of Chicago Press, 1968).

41   See e.g., Otis Dudley Duncan, et al., *Metropolis and Region* (Baltimore: Johns Hopkins Press, 1960); and articles by Theodore R. Anderson and Gideon Sjoberg on "Comparative Urban Structure" and "The Modern City" in *International Encyclopedia of the Social Sciences*, 2:466–73 and 2:455–59.

42   See, more recently, Walter J. Firey, *Land Use in Central Boston* (Cambridge, Mass.: Harvard University Press, 1947); Maurice R. Stein, *The Eclipse of Community* (Princeton, N.J.: Princeton University Press, 1960); and Florence R. Kluckhohn and Fred L. Strodtbeck, *Variations in Value Orientations* (Evanston: Row, Peterson and Co., 1961).

and population distribution, on spatial patterns of cities and demographic and vital processes, on social stratification, institutional and organizational structure and process, has expanded greatly in recent years.[43] Here, again, ecological and demographic perspectives tend to merge with institutional and organizational analysis and with social-psychological concerns.

Cross-cultural research has been particularly important in modifying theoretical conclusions in each of these areas. Thus, anthropologists studying urbanization among contemporary primitive peoples have found that traditional forms of social organization sometimes remain relatively intact and effective among groups newly settled from rural to urban settings, and *local* identities are not always transformed into *nationalistic* identities. For example, migrant villagers moving into Indonesian cities tend to settle in patterns similar to their previous villages. Social control in their urban *kampongs* "does not differ much from that in the rural areas."[44] This is a very different situation from that documented for immigrants to the United States as described in the selection from "Old World Traits Transplanted," reprinted here in part 3. Frazier's own assessment of his classic work *The Negro Family in*

[43]   See, e.g., Morris Janowitz, *The Community Press in an Urban Setting* (1952; 2d ed., Chicago: University of Chicago Press, 1967); Philip M. Hauser and Otis Dudley Duncan, eds., *The Study of Populations: An Inventory and Appraisal* (Chicago: University of Chicago Press, 1959); Reinhard Bendix and Seymour A. Lipset, eds., *Class, Status and Power: A Reader in Social Stratification* (Glencoe, Ill.: The Free Press, 1953); Albert J. Reiss, Jr., et al., *Occupations and Social Status* (New York: Free Press, 1961); Natalie Rogoff, *Recent Trends in Occupational Mobility* (Glencoe, Ill.: The Free Press, 1953); and Peter M. Blau and O. Dudley Duncan, *The American Occupational Structure* (New York: John Wiley and Sons, 1967); Herbert J. Gans, *The Urban Villagers* (New York: The Free Press of Glencoe, 1962; Gerald D. Suttles, *The Social Order of the Slum* (Chicago: University of Chicago Press, 1968).
[44]   William R. Boscow, "Urbanization among the Yoruba," *American Journal of Sociology* 60 (March 1955): 446–53; see also, J. J. Panakal, *Prevention of Types of Criminality Resulting from Social Changes and Accompanying Economic Development in Less Developed Countries*, part 1 (New York: U.N., 1960), p. 16; A. L. Epstein, *Politics in an Urban African Community* (Manchester: Manchester University Press, 1958); Peter Marris, *Family and Social Change in an African City* (Evanston: Northwestern University Press, 1962).

Chicago reflects on these problems among developing countries in Africa and discusses similarities with the American Negro experience.

The important factor . . . in differentiating the pre-industrial and industrial city concerns the difference in social organization. In the pre-industrial cities of Africa, kinship and lineages and primary forms of social control played the chief role in the social organization. But as these cities acquire the character of industrial cities, it is apparent in all the studies that these traditional forms of social organization are being dissolved. Then, too, as the Africans migrate to the new industrialized cities, despite their effort to maintain the traditional forms of social organization or create new forms of associations based upon the traditional culture, they are unable to do so. What is happening to the urbanized African is very similar to what happened and continues to happen to the southern Negro who with his background of folk culture migrates to the industrial cities of the United States. Of course, the African's culture may be more resistant to change because the folk culture of the American Negro is essentially a subculture, since even the folk Negro lives in the twilight of American civilization. But the disintegration of the American Negro's traditional folk culture and the reorganization of his social life in the urban environment is very similar to what is occurring in the urban areas of Africa. . . .

. . . One of the most important phases of the reorganization of life among urbanized Africans is the development of new forms of associations. As the traditional African society dissolves or disintegrates, the fabric of a new social life is coming into existence in the urban environment. These new forms of social life . . . represent adjustments to new situations for which the traditional culture does not provide solutions. There are, for example, new types of economic associations which approximate in form and purpose the labor unions of the Europeans and perhaps even more important the new political organizations with nationalistic aims. Then as the traditional religions disintegrate, there are all sorts of cults formed to meet the new conditions of city living. Although the situation of the American Negro in the city is not exactly the same, there are many parallels.[45]

A. L. Epstein, discussing recent scholarly work on urbanization in Africa, makes a somewhat different point in distinguishing be-

[45]   E. Franklin Frazier, "The Negro Family in Chicago," in Burgess and Bogue, eds., *Contributions to Urban Sociology*, pp. 415–17.

tween *urbanization* and *urbanism*.[46] Urbanization is seen "as involving a process of movement and change; its essence is that it creates the possibility of discontinuity with some preexisting set of conditions," while urbanism is "the way of life" in urban areas. Many fundamental questions on urbanization remain to be answered, but the relevant literature is growing rapidly, in quantity and in quality.[47]

SOCIAL ORGANIZATION   The study of social organization was in some respects the least explicitly developed of the three basic perspectives of the Chicago School. Organization as such was neglected—perhaps *assumed* would be more accurate—in the focus on social process, change, and social disorganization. Social organization was recognized as a basic division of the discipline, but its study tended to be viewed as auxiliary to other interests, as, for example, the delineation of "natural areas" of the city, the nature of social control, the nature and effects of processes associated with urbanization, or of other social changes.

It was in the work of Everett C. Hughes that the study of social organization, as such, received its most sophisticated treatment and made the greatest impact on the discipline. Hughes's focus on institutional analysis anticipates much of the later work in this area by sociologists and presaged other developments in what we now know as the sociology of occupations and professions, as well as important aspects of the study of large-scale formal organizations and political sociology.[48] This area is here represented by excerpts from Hughes's doctoral dissertation.

[46]   A. L. Epstein, "Urbanization and Social Change in Africa," *Current Anthropology* 8, no. 4 (1967): 275–96; reprinted in Gerald Breese, ed., *The City in Newly Developing Countries* (New York: Prentice-Hall, 1969), pp. 246–63.

[47]   See, e.g., "Comments" on Epstein and his "Reply," in ibid., pp. 263–84. See also the discussions and bibliographies in Paul K. Hatt and Albert J. Reiss, Jr., eds., *Cities and Society: The Revised Reader in Urban Sociology* (Glencoe, Ill.: The Free Press, 1957); and relevant articles in the *International Encyclopedia of the Social Sciences*, in Breese, ed., *The City*, and in Hauser and Schnore, eds., *The Study of Urbanization*.

[48]   See also E. C. Hughes, *Men and Their Work* (New York: The

In his preface to this work Hughes acknowledged that his interest in the subject matter and his point of view were greatly influenced by the lectures of Robert E. Park. "The constant theme of those lectures was the transformation of unique events into social facts which gather themselves into wholes changing and moving according to rules of their own." Hughes's interest was in the development of the Chicago Real Estate Board, "presented with attention to those of its features which illuminate the processes by which institutions in general seem to grow." Institutions, he concludes, "are just those social forms which grow up where men collectively face problems which are never completely settled. In various times and places, men have voluntarily met to solve problems. It seems likely that when they do so, and continue to do so for long enough, they produce relationships and ideas which succeeding generations accept somewhat involuntarily. The Real Estate Agents set out to solve immediate questions; they are creating an institution."[49]

Hughes's elegant prose, the care with which he approaches his task, and his fine sense of the significance of his inquiry speak to many aspects of social life in the city.

SOCIAL PSYCHOLOGY OF CITY LIFE   Provocative and useful theoretical perspectives concerning the social psychology of city life abound, but the efficacy of most is at least open to question on empirical grounds.[50] Perhaps the greatest empirical contribution of

---

Free Press at Glencoe, 1968) ; Morris Janowitz, *The Professional Soldier* (Glencoe, Ill.: The Free Press, 1960) ; Howard S. Becker, Blanche Geer, E. C. Hughes, and Anselm S. Strauss, *Boys in White* (Chicago: University of Chicago Press, 1961) ; Peter M. Blau, *The Dynamics of Bureaucracy* (Chicago: University of Chicago Press, 1955) ; Amitai Etzioni, *A Comparative Analysis of Complex Organizations* (New York: The Free Press of Glencoe, 1961).
49   Everett C. Hughes, *The Growth of an Institution: The Chicago Real Estate Board* (The Society for Social Research of the University of Chicago, series 2, monograph 1, 1931).
50   See, e.g., David Reisman, Nathan Glazer, and Reuel Denney, *The Lonely Crowd: A Study of the Changing American Character* (New Haven: Yale University Press, 1950) ; Anselm L. Strauss, ed., *The American City: A Sourcebook of Urban Imagery* (Chicago: Aldine, 1968).

the early Chicago sociologists in this area lay in the many studies of ethnic groups and particular social situations that they conducted in that city, establishing a tradition which persists to this day. This topic is covered in part 4.

An outgrowth of these studies, and of the basic ecological perspective on city life, was Louis Wirth's article "Urbanism as a Way of Life." Here Wirth discussed the social organizational and social psychological concomitants of his definition of a city "as a relatively large, dense, and permanent settlement of socially heterogeneous individuals."[51] Among these, Wirth stressed the "superficiality, the anomymity, and the transitory character of urban social relations," the weakening of traditional bonds of kinship and friendships, and the ascendency of secondary relations between persons based on utilitarian considerations. The consequences were seen as disorganizing, both for traditional forms of social organization and for human personality. The fact that anthropologists failed to find these in some instances of urbanized primitive peoples led to serious challenges of Wirth's position. However, much of this debate has been irrelevant, for Wirth, like others at Chicago during this period, clearly was referring to cities which were experiencing rapid and large scale influx of heterogeneous immigrant peoples, and under conditions of industrialization. He was not referring to all cities in all times.

Another and more serious problem arose with respect to Wirth's analysis and the general stress of the Chicago School on social disorganization. This had to do with the failure to conceptualize adequately the simultaneous existence within the city of diversity in behavior and in forms of social organization, and of intensely meaningful interpersonal relationships. The existence of both was recognized, but not effectively dealt with theoretically. Matza has suggested that "the Chicagoans conceived disorganization [but] they described diversity."[52]

[51]   *American Journal of Sociology* 44 (July 1938): 1–24, repr. in Reiss, ed., *Wirth on the City*, p. 66.
[52]   And in so doing, they provided the major impetus for the "naturalistic" study of social life. See David Matza, *Becoming Deviant* (New York: Prentice-Hall, 1969), p. 48. From the Chicago School, see especially, Norman S. Hayner, *Hotel Life* (Chapel Hill: University of North Carolina Press, 1936).

Mitchell suggests that the theoretical problem lies in the failure to "specify the causal linkage between the general conditions of urban life and the behavior of individuals within them." This linkage was never made explicit; it was assumed rather than investigated. That is, the general determinants of the urban situation— economic, demographic, ecological, and administrative factors— limit and condition human behavior, but do not create it.[53] Wirth's own research on the ghetto and much else in the work of the Chicago School demonstrated the great diversity of social forms and interpersonal relationships which develop in the metropolis, in large part in adaptation to these conditions, and in fact related these types of behavior to variations in the ecology and social organization of the city.[54] Conceptually, role and reference group theory and the notion of social networks make it possible to reconcile contradictions in the findings and interpretations of the social psychology of city life. The number, content, and intensity of relationships among persons occupying different roles, and the interests and values upon which these relations are based, vary enormously from one person to another, and among groups located variously in the social order. There is some variation even in the simplest of societies. In the metropolis of the Chicagoans it sometimes seemed overwhelming. The studies in depth of groups, communities, mechanisms of communication, and processes of change which were begun at Chicago provided the basis for later theoretical understanding.

With respect to the broader field of social psychological theory an argument can be made that modern exchange theory and refer-

[53]   See J. C. Mitchell, "The Concept and Use of Social Networks," in J. C. Mitchell, ed., *Social Networks in Urban Situations* (Manchester: Manchester University Press, 1969).

[54]   Everett Hughes's comment (in personal correspondence) is both informative and amusing: "Although I had not thought of it much until now, it is no doubt important that Park was retired at the end of the 1920s. He traveled around the world looking at multiracial regions. . . . He really did nothing more on the study of cities except to visit them. Louis Wirth then put on the mantle of the student of cities. I always have thought that he did not go on in Park's imaginative way, but rather became a bit too much a disciple on the theory side. Louis used to say all those things about how the city is impersonal—while living with a whole clan of kin and friends on a very personal basis."

ence group theory owe much to the early studies of Shaw and McKay, and particularly of Whyte, all represented in part 5. Another perspective of social psychology is its concern with human nature, here represented by Ellsworth Faris's classic statement. Faris sets forth in beautiful prose the fundamentally social nature of man, recognizing that he is also basically a biological being. For a time it appeared that sociologists had forgotten the latter fact—at least they very much neglected it. Today, interest in the emerging field of sociobiology promises to rectify this imbalance.[55]

STRUCTURE, PROCESS, AND CHANGE   Part 3 begins with Earl S. Johnson's classic discussion of the function of the central business district. Essentially ecological in its approach, the paper demonstrates a deep appreciation for the interrelationships of various parts of the metropolis and the governing processes which determine the character of the central business district. It is also a call for more research on the population characteristics of the central business district.[56]

Cecil C. North's brief paper "The City as a Community" proposes research on "the communal process" with the suggestion that this process can be objectively measured by examining the extent to which various special interests undertake cooperative efforts, and the effectiveness of such efforts in behalf of some common good. Later research has demonstrated the importance of this kind of organization to modern social life.[57] Examination of the

[55]   With respect to exchange and reference group theory, see, e.g., George C. Homans, *Social Behavior: Its Elementary Forces* (New York: Harcourt, 1961); Muzafer Sherif and Carolyn W. Sherif, *Reference Groups: Explorations into Conformity and Deviation of Adolescents* (New York: Harper and Row, 1964). With respect to sociobiology, see *Biology in the Behavioral Sciences*, Proceedings of the National Institute of Mental Health Program Directors Meeting, November 4–5, 1966, The University of Chicago, ed. Lloyd J. Roth, Maurice S. Goldstein, and Albert S. Moraczewski; David C. Glass, "Genetics and Social Behavior," in Social Science Research Council, *Items*, 21, no. 1 (March 1967): 1–5.

[56]   See e.g., Gerald W. Breese, *The Daytime Population of the Central Business District of Chicago* (Chicago: University of Chicago Press, 1949).

[57]   See, e.g., Herbert Goldhamer, "Voluntary Associations in the United States," and Morris Axelrod, "Urban Structure and Social Par-

nature of relationships among various classes of group life—for example, voluntary associations, the institutions of government, and various networks of families—remains of great importance in behavioral science research.[58]

CULTURAL HERITAGES OF THE METROPOLIS Among processes influencing the character of social life, whether in city or countryside, few are more important than those associated with religion, nationality, and other aspects of cultural heritage. Two papers reflecting somewhat different theoretical and methodological traditions inform the nature of these processes.

Paul F. Cressey's examination of population succession in Chicago is an excellent example of a type of ecological study with which the Chicago School became identified. It typifies, also, the concern of these scholars with process and change as dynamic features of urban life. Methods of indexing such matters have been improved, but the conceptual apparatus with which such problems are approached is little changed from Cressey's day. The position of the specific ethnic groups discussed has changed, as some older groups have become almost completely assimilated into the life of the city. Ethnicity, however, continues to be an important variable in the life of the modern metropolis.[59]

---

ticipation," in Hatt and Reiss, eds., *Cities and Society*; Nicholas Babchuck and C. Wayne Gordon, *The Voluntary Association in the Slum*, University of Nebraska Studies, no. 27 (Lincoln: University of Nebraska, 1962); and Gans, *The Urban Villagers*.
[58]   See, e.g., Homans, *Social Behavior*; Scott Greer, *The Emerging City: Myth and Reality* (New York: The Free Press of Glencoe, 1962); Peter M. Blau, *The Dynamics of Bureaucracy* (Chicago: University of Chicago Press, 1955); Blau, *Exchange and Power in Social Life* (New York: John Wiley and Sons, 1964); Herbert Gans, *The Levittowners: How People Live and Politic in Suburbia* (New York: Pantheon Books, 1967).
[59]   See, e.g., Suttles, *The Social Order of the Slum*; Harold Finestone, "Reformation and Recidivism among Italian and Polish Criminal Offenders," *American Journal of Sociology* 72 (May 1967): pp. 575–88; *Report of the National Advisory Commission on Civil Disorders*, Washington, D.C.: USGPO, 1968; Angus Campbell and Howard Schuman, "Racial Attitudes in Fifteen American Cities," and Peter H. Rossi, et al., "Between

"The Immigrant Community," by W. I. Thomas enriches these processes by means of personal documents. Thomas's data suggest the very nature of the process by which ethnic groups are formed, and show that ethnic identity represents in part an attempt to transfer the primary relationships of peasant communities to the more secular and impersonal society which immigrants have found upon arriving in this country. Poles and Italians, for example, did not think of themselves as such when they first reached these shores. Thomas notes that Italian immigrants to New York City tended first to locate in patterns similar to their old world associations, with families and individuals from the same provinces and towns in Italy settling together. Personal documents confirm the strength of such early locality identifications. After a time, however, common experiences in a sometimes alien society drew them together, *as Italians.* Most importantly, they were defined by non-Italians, not as Sicilians or residents of Palermo, etc., but *as Italians.* Frazier and others find that Negroes in the United States experienced much these same problems and processes of identity, greatly exacerbated by their status as slaves and by policies designed to prevent development among Negroes of the types of ethnic, political, religious, and economic organizations which were so important to groups which emmigrated voluntarily to America.[60] Thus, while the "traumas of the immigration experience" continue to be of importance to an understanding of the experience of all immigrant peoples,[61] the experience of the Negro in America is not typical of other groups in this country, nor indeed of Negroes in Africa, as noted above.[62] The "Black Power" movement, its emphasis on indigenous economic

White and Black: The Faces of American Institutions in the Ghetto," published as *Supplemental Studies for the National Advisory Commission on Civil Disorders,* Washington, D.C.: USGPO, 1968.

[60]   E. Franklin Frazier, *The Negro Family in Chicago* (Chicago: University of Chicago Press, 1932).

[61]   See, e.g., Andrew M. Greeley, "Religion and Academic Career Plans: A Note on Progress," *American Journal of Sociology* 72 (May 1967): 668–72.

[62]   See also J. Clyde Mitchell, *The Kalela Dance,* Rhodes-Livingstone Paper no. 27, 1957; and "American Cities and African: A Comparison," Monro Lectures, Edinburgh University, 1967 (Forthcoming).

and political institutions, the identification of black "brothers" and "sisters" with one another, and the theme that "Black is Beautiful," represent efforts to create conditions among Negroes similar to those which occurred much earlier among immigrant groups. The intensity of the rhetoric of this movement and of relations between blacks and whites in this country must be seen in the light of a combination of many years of repression, coupled with repeated promises of advancement and equality and the failure to deliver on these promises.[63] But neither the rhetoric nor the strained and often violent quality of relations between the races should be seen as unique historically. Similar feelings and activities have characterized virtually every immigrant group in the United States, as well as groups which for one reason or another have found themselves in the position either of defending the status quo or fighting for rights lost or desired.[64]

Contemporary problems thus are placed in historical and comparative perspective and in the context of processes to some degree generalizable from that experience. The establishment of indigenous institutions and the achievement of political and economic power and social identity have been stabilizing influences for a variety of ethnic and other special-interest groups. The development of mechanisms by which these interests may be recognized and met or mediated has had the effect of legitimating these interests both for those who may be centrally involved in the conflict and for others who react and with whom ultimate power often resides. Examples in this country are plentiful: the continued appearance of politicians at ethnic festivals and other special occasions, the evolution of labor-management relations, the emergence of associations serving many special interests, from internal promotion to lobbying in the halls of Congress and in state legislatures, public relations, or what have you.

[63]   Much of the literature relevant to this point is reviewed in Jerome Skolnick, *The Politics of Protest*, National Commission on the Causes and Prevention of Violence (Washington, D.C.: USGPO, 1969).
[64]   For historical documentation see the papers published in Hugh Davis Graham and Ted Robert Gurr, eds., *Violence in America: Historical and Comparative Perspectives*, National Commission on the Causes and Prevention of Violence (Washington, D.C.: USGPO, 1969).

COMMUNICATION   The importance to social life in modern society of the inventions of mass communication and transportation, wrote William F. Ogburn, "justifies the statement that they constitute the second phase of the industrial revolution."[65] Three papers in this section treat different aspects of mass communication, an area in which Chicago sociologists pioneered.[66] Herbert Blumer's discussion of the influence on mass behavior of motion pictures is imaginative and frankly speculative. Several of his observations have been the focus of more recent research concerning the influence of television and other media on youngsters. Helen MacGill Hughes discusses the transition of newspapers from purveyors almost entirely of political news to emphasis on items of human interest. She examines questions which continue to be at issue: What constitutes news and to what extent does its reporting influence the course of events, to what extent do advertisers and pressure groups influence the policies and political preferences of newspapers, how objective are news reports, etc. Frederick G. Detweiler describes the Negro press as of the 1930s. Again the focus is on change: "The Negro paper began as an extended editorial, but it has been gradually justifying itself as a newspaper." Detweiler's commentary on some of the major issues with which the black press was concerned, their policies with respect to these issues and their influence are somewhat dated, yet relevant to contemporary issues. That press is more affluent and varied now, and tends to be less in the vanguard and more a reporter of—and at times a reactor to—the more vigorous and variegated civil rights and black militant movements of the latter half of the twentieth century. The role of mass media, especially of television, in the struggle of minority groups to bring about change—no less than the fundamental transformation of institutions—is a much debated topic on which solid knowledge still is lacking.[67]

65   William F. Ogburn, "Man and His Institutions," *Publications of the American Sociological Society* 29 (August 1935): p. 38.
66   For examples of concern with other aspects of communication, see, in addition to papers reprinted in this volume, E. W. Burgess, "Communication," *American Journal of Sociology* 34:117–29, 1072–80, and 35:991–1001; Robert E. Park, "Reflections on Communications and Culture," *American Journal of Sociology* 44:187–205.
67   See the investigations in this regard in *Report of the National Ad-*

THE IMPACT OF CHANGE   Some would hold that study of social change is *the* fundamental concern of sociology, so much so that it cannot be isolated as a single topic but must be regarded as integral to all aspects of social life.

So great are the changes in our time—and so elusive and impersonal is their threat—that their impact on people and on institutions often is neglected, or celebrated chiefly by novelists or popular journalists. Careful, systematic studies of the "natural history" of institutional attempts to cope with change are rare. Part 3 concludes, appropriately, with one of these—S. C. Kincheloe's insightful analysis of the impact of social change on a particular institution —a "dying" church on Chicago's West Side.

SOCIAL WORLDS   The term "social world" is descriptive of the attempt to portray life *as it is experienced by participants* in a particular group, community, or institution. It is not as "objective" or systematic as are certain other descriptive devices of the social scientist, but it adds a human quality which the social scientist often is accused of lacking. Some sociologists of the Chicago School found the device effective and complementary to other methods of investigation. It was from this combination of techniques of investigation and presentation that some of the most attractive and "classic" sociological works of this period emerged.

In "The Taxi-Dance Hall as a Social World," Paul G. Cressey describes some of the meaning of the hall for the girls and their patrons, the special language and the values which pervade this social world, and its structure. While he does not use the term, he has sketched for us the *subculture* of the taxi-dance hall. The study was carried out while Cressey was a caseworker and special investigator for the Juvenile Protective Association of Chicago, beginning in 1925. Having very soon discovered that proprietors and their associates were unwilling to cooperate in the study, Cressey sent observers into the halls in effect as participant observers. The naive and moralistic tone of the first investigator cited in this chapter

visory Commission on Civil Disorders; and Robert K. Baker and Sandra J. Ball, *Violence and the Media* National Commission on the Causes and Prevention of Violence (Washington, D.C., USGPO, 1969).

did not prevent Cressey and his observers from securing an intimate picture of this social world and many other aspects of the taxi-dance hall—its personnel and clientele, ecological setting and organizational processes. Cressey, and Burgess in his Introduction to the book, also treat the factors which created taxi-dance halls and their social worlds, e.g., commercial exploitation of "the demands for feminine society of homeless and lonesome men crowded into the rooming-house districts of our larger cities."[68]

In their discussion of "the world of the lower class," Drake and Cayton indicate that "most of the time during the depression years the masses of the lower class (Negroes) could not afford to pay for admission to commercial dance halls except on special occasions. When they wanted to dance they simply 'pitched a boogie-woogie' at home, using the radio or a Victrola for music; or they congregated at a buffet-flat or tavern where the more affluent would feed nickels into a juke-box."[69]

Lower-class people will *publicly* drink and play cards in places where people of higher status would lose their "reputations"—in the rear of poolrooms, in the backrooms of taverns, in "buffet-flats," and sometimes on street corners and in alleys. They will "dance on the dime" and "grind" around the juke-box in taverns and joints, or "cut a rug" at the larger public dance halls. They will "clown" on a street corner or in public parks. . . These centers of lower-class congregation and festivity often become points of contact between the purveyors of pleasure "on the illegit" and their clientele—casual prostitutes, bootleggers, reefer peddlers, "pimps," and "freaks." Some of these places are merely "fronts" and "blinds" for the organized underworld.

Whyte, in his classic study of an Italian slum, documents the existence in that community of a "complex and well-established" social order. Street corner groups, the racket (largely numbers and other forms of gambling), the police, politics, the church, and "old country" ties all were found to be structured according to "a hier-

---

[68]   Ernest W. Burgess, "Introduction" to Paul G. Cressey, *The Taxi-Dance Hall* (Chicago: University of Chicago Press, 1932), p. xii.
[69]   St. Clair Drake and Horace R. Cayton, *Black Metropolis: A Study of Negro Life in a Northern City* (New York: Harcourt, Brace, 1945), pp. 609–10. (Rev., and enl. ed., Harper and Row, 1962.)

archy of personal relations based upon a system of reciprocal obligations."[70] The nature of these relationships is similar to those described by Drake and Cayton in Chicago's "black belt" in the sense that their impact on behavior was based less upon formal institutional norms than upon informal rules and understandings and situational factors. Both communities produced behavior defined by the larger society as deviant—crime and delinquency, vice, political corruption.

Major differences in the social worlds described by Drake and Cayton and by Whyte relate to the more severe economic circumstances of the black community and much less political "clout," to the fact of less institutional stability and tradition, as in the case of family life, religion, and "old world ties," and to the nature of other relations of the two ethnic groups with the larger society. It may or may not be the case that the norm of reciprocity which Whyte finds to be so basic in Cornerville is less the basis of social life in the lower class world of black metropolis. If so, the reason for the difference is likely to be found in the greater instability of both interpersonal and institutional relationships in the urban black lower class, and in the greater incidence of social disabilities located there.[71]

[70]   William Foote Whyte, *Street Corner Society: The social Structure of an Italian Slum*, rev. ed. (Chicago: University of Chicago Press, 1955), p. 272.

[71]   Cf., discussions in Elliot Liebow, *Tally's Corner: A Study of Negro Streetcorner Men* (Boston: Little, Brown, 1967); and James F. Short, Jr. and Fred L. Strodtbeck, *Group Process and Gang Delinquency* (Chicago: University of Chicago Press, 1965). Hylan Lewis, in his "Foreword" to *Tally's Corner*, writes that "carry-out shops, laundromats, and record shops have recently come to the ghetto in numbers. They join taverns, pool halls, liquor stores, corner groceries, rooming houses, secondhand stores, credit houses, pawn shops, industrial insurance companies, and storefront churches as parts of a distinctive complex of urban institutions that have undergone changes in adapting to the effective wants, limited choices, and mixed tastes of inner-city residents. Inner-city carry-out shops serve many functions other than selling prepared food. Among other things they may serve as informal communication centers, forums, places to display and assess talents, and staging areas for a wide range of activities, legal, illegal, and extra-legal" (pp. vii–viii).

Drake and Cayton capture the tenuous nature of relationships involved in a type of common-law marriage. If social exchange is based on elemental facts related to opportunities and needs, among the "unstable poor," life is crisis-ridden, "constantly trying to 'make do' with string where rope is needed. Anything can break the string"—and often does.[72]

By way of contrast, Cornerville is remarkable for the stability of personal, group, and institutional relationships. Poverty and other problems existed in Cornerville, as in black metropolis, but poverty was not so severe, and the stability of relationships on the corner, in the family, in religion, politics, business, and the rackets —in short, in ways of life which had become traditional in this ethnic community—offered protection from at least some of the adversity experienced by the residents of black metropolis.

Many in lower-class communities suffer social disabilities which severely handicap their chances for success in the larger society, and few of their residents have access to positions of real power. But the people in the Cornervilles of America have achieved a large degree of autonomy in the conduct of affairs in their own communities and they have access to considerable power in this respect, power which black communities only recently have begun to mobilize.

The Whyte and the Drake and Cayton pieces bridge the gap between the Chicago "generations" of the 1920s and '30s and those of the '40s and '50s. More than a difference in student generations is thereby bridged. Whyte was a product as much of Harvard, where he was a junior fellow while conducting his study, as of Chicago, where he received his degree and later taught. Drake received his degree as a student of the Department of Anthropology, and his work with Cayton was based upon a combination of sociological and anthropological research methods developed particularly by

[72]   S. M. Miller, "The American Lower Class: A Typological Approach," *Social Research* (Spring 1964). Republished in the Syracuse University Youth Development Reprint Series, pp. 1–22. See, also, Liebow's discussion of Negro streetmen and their women as fathers and mothers, husbands and wives, friends, lovers, and exploiters, in *Tally's Corner*.

W. Lloyd Warner, who held appointments in both departments.[73] This fertile combination typified the close and productive relationships between various social science disciplines at Chicago during this period.

SOCIAL PROBLEMS AND SOCIAL CONTROL   If the central problem of sociology is social control—a view attributed to Robert E. Park—its study has most often involved description and analysis of specific aspects of deviant or otherwise socially defined problem behavior; and among no group of scholars was this endeavor pursued with more vigor or profit than by students of the old Chicago School. Indeed, articles and volumes treating such behavior rate well in quantity and in quality among "modern sociological classics." The selections presented here represent basic contributions in the constant search for systematic knowledge concerning recurring human frailties—juvenile delinquency, vice, poverty, family life, and mental disorder.

"The Distribution of Commercialized Vice in the City," by Walter C. Reckless, examines this fascinating topic in the context of the "natural areas" of the city and the processes which create them. Its slightly moralistic tone was not uncommon among many of the early Chicago sociology students and some of their mentors, but it became less common under the guidance of Thomas, Park, and others as the goal of scientific sociology gained ascendancy. That change in emphasis was perhaps a first step in correcting a tendency in much sociological work to neglect the importance of social control activities by powerful elements in "respectable" society in creating "social problems." Later generations of sociologists, including many trained at Chicago, have done much to redress this imbalance.[74]

Probably no single book has influenced the course of thought

[73]   See W. Lloyd Warner, "A Methodological Note," in Drake and Cayton, *Black Metropolis*.
[74]   See, e.g., Erving Goffman, *Asylums* (New York: Doubleday, 1961); Howard S. Becker, *Outsiders* (New York: Free Press of Glencoe, 1963); Kai T. Erikson, *Wayward Puritans* (New York: John Wiley and Sons, 1966); Anthony M. Platt, *The Child Savers: The Invention of Delinquency* (Chicago: University of Chicago, 1969).

and social action concerning juvenile delinquency so much as *Social Factors in Juvenile Delinquency*,[75] from which selections are reproduced in this volume. The series of volumes which preceded and succeeded it did much to establish the major conclusions and the traditions of sociological research and theory concerning delinquency, and particularly of group delinquency.[76] So great was the impact of these studies that, nearly twenty years after them, the group nature of juvenile delinquency was more taken for granted than studied. Only recently have empirical efforts been joined with theoretical formulations stimulated by Shaw and McKay and others to produce new thinking and evidence concerning delinquency.

The family, its traditional functions changed and beset by disorganizing forces, has been the subject of much attention by social scientists.[77] Among these forces was the depression of the 1930s.

[75]   Clifford R. Shaw and Henry D. McKay, *Social Factors in Juvenile Delinquency*, vol. 2 of *Report on the Causes of Crime*, National Commission on Law Observance and Enforcement (Washington, D.C.: USGPO, 1931).

[76]   Clifford R. Shaw, et al., *Delinquency Areas* (Chicago: University of Chicago Press, 1929); Shaw, *The Jack-Roller: A Delinquent Boy's Own Story* (ibid., 1930); Shaw, *Brothers in Crime* (ibid., 1936); Shaw, *The Natural History of a Delinquent Career* (ibid., 1931); Shaw, and Henry D. McKay, *Juvenile Delinquency and Urban Areas* (ibid., 1942; rev. 1969). See also, Frederic M. Thrasher, *The Gang: A Study of 1,313 Gangs in Chicago* (Chicago: University of Chicago Press, 1927; abr. 1963). More recently, see Albert K. Cohen, *Delinquent Boys* (Glencoe, Ill.: Free Press, 1955); Richard A. Cloward and Lloyd E. Ohlin, *Delinquency and Opportunity: A Theory of Delinquent Gangs* (Glencoe, Ill.: Free Press, 1960); Walter B. Miller, "Lower Class Culture as a Generating Milieu of Gang Delinquency," *Journal of Social Issues* 24, no. 3 (1958): 5–19; Short and Strodtbeck, *Group Process and Gang Delinquency*. Muzafer Sherif and Carolyn W. Sherif, *Reference Groups: Exploration into Conformity and Deviation of Adolescents* (New York: Harper and Row, 1964); Irving Spergel, *Street Gang Work: Theory and Practice* (Reading, Mass.: Addison-Wesley, 1966).

[77]   For an early discussion of these forces and related trends, see William F. Ogburn and Clark Tibbits, "The Family and Its Functions," chapter 13 in *Recent Social Trends in the United States*, Report of the President's Research Committee on Social Trends (New York: Whittlesey House, 1934), pp. 661–708.

Among studies of effects of the depression, *The Family and the Depression* by Ruth Shonle Cavan and Katherine Howland Ranck, a chapter of which is reprinted here, is outstanding. "Historians of science," wrote Leonard S. Cottrell, Jr., in a review of the book, "will record that most of the things sociologists said about the depression were in the nature of speculation or suggestions as to what might be or might have been studied in the depression. *The Family and the Depression* is one of the few fragments of actual sociological research material to be salvaged from this era of lost opportunities."[78]

In their study of the distribution of mental disorders in urban areas, Robert E. L. Faris and H. Warren Dunham contributed to delineation of the classic ecological patterns of social ills in Chicago:

> Cases of mental disorders, as plotted by residences of patients previous to admission to public and private hospitals, show a regular decrease from the center to the periphery of the city, a pattern of distribution previously shown for such other kinds of social and economic phenomena as poverty, unemployment, juvenile delinquency, adult crime, suicide, family desertion, infant mortality, communicable disease, and general mortality.[79]

Faris and Dunham went on to examine—and to reject, on the basis of their data—the "drift hypothesis," that is, that the mentally ill become economic failures and, as a consequence, drift to the slum. Contrary to this notion, they found that many individuals diagnosed as schizophrenics were born in deteriorated areas and had spent their lives in such areas.[80] Faris and Dunham also found that rates of mental illness among Negroes and the foreign-born varied by type of community area, as did those of whites and the

[78]   Leonard S. Cottrell, Jr., in *American Journal of Sociology* 44 (January, 1939) : 590.

[79]   *Mental Disorders in Urban Areas: An Ecological Study of Schizophrenia and Other Psychoses* (Chicago: University of Chicago Press, 1939).

[80]   Caplow, Bahr, and their associates discount the "drift" hypothesis, also for occupants of skid row. See, e.g., Theodore Caplow, Howard M. Bahr, and David Sternberg, "Homelessness," *International Encyclopedia of the Social Sciences*, pp. 494–99.

native-born. As with other social problems, the pattern of distribution could not be accounted for by race or place of birth.

In the final paper in this volume Faris discusses various social characteristics of the mentally ill, with special reference to schizophrenia, and speculates on the process of social and cultural isolation as a causal factor.[81]

Assessment

Assessment of so complex a phenomenon as has been here discussed is hazardous indeed. Much has been said in the foregoing pages of the richness and the abundance of the Chicago School, of its empirical thrust and emphasis on process and change. Assessment is made both easier and more difficult by limitations of scope in the present volume; easier because focus on urban sociology relieves us of responsibility to cover the enormous range of interests of the Chicago sociologists; more difficult because that entire range influenced what those sociologists did and what they had to say about the metropolis.

There has, of course, been convergence, as well as specialization, in theory and substance both within and between disciplines of the behavioral sciences. Some instances of this convergence were anticipated by the Chicago School, if less than adequately conceptualized.

I refer here not only to interdisciplinary research and organization, or to the emergence of "political sociology," "behavioral political science," varieties of social psychology and "sociobiology," or to the even more recently emerging "geosociology."[82]

81   For further discussion of these relationships see Melvin L. Kohn and John A. Clausen, "Social Isolation and Schizophrenia," *American Sociological Review* 20, no. 3 (June 1955): 265–73. Recent studies of delinquency question some aspects of Faris's interpretation of social isolation as a factor distinguishing gang and nongang members in slum areas, however. Members of delinquent gangs are found *not* to be socially skilled —in fact they are likely to be socially disabled in ways which relate to the character of gang interaction and behavior.

82   See, e.g., *The Annals of the American Academy of Political and Social Science* (May 1970), a special issue, edited by Samuel Z. Klausner, "Society and Its Physical Environment."

Distinctions within sociology which have been responsible for intense research specialization likewise are challenged. Specialized studies of deviant behavior, collective behavior, political, economic, and organizational behavior are inadequate to the understanding of ghetto riots, mass demonstration and protest, delinquent gangs' involvement in corporate enterprise, and so forth. They never were adequate, of course, but specialization served the purpose—and doubtless will continue to do so—of generating highly specific bodies of knowledge and sophisticated methodologies. The growth of such special knowledge has, in turn, led to fuller understanding of the complexity of social life. But social life transcends specialization, and critical problems often are left unattended.[83] There is evidence that sociology is being transformed in this respect, not alone from the prodding of our younger colleagues. It could be argued that the early Chicago sociologists were more "relevant" to the problems faced by the society they studied than has been the case since.

Robert E. Park, in his introduction to *The Strike*, noted that "war, revolution, and the strike are, fundamentally considered, elementary forms of political action. They are, in other words, forms in which issues are raised, forced upon a sometimes reluctant public, and eventually, in some fashion, settled. . . . the public has, in the long run . . . made the rules of the game and decided the issues."[84] And Hiller, in the same volume, concluded that conflicts such as he had analyzed "tend to produce changes in the notions concerning property; for the control of large-scale industry ceases to be the exclusive prerogative of the employer and the investors in the enterprise. The nature of management is modified by the concession of 'rights' which are exacted by the employees and the consumers."[85] Forty years later, sociological analysts have suggested that ghetto riots represent a similar challenge to "dominant

---

[83]   As recognized in the Report of the Special Commission on the Social Sciences of the National Science Board, Orville G. Brim, Jr., Chairman, *Knowledge into Action: Improving the Nation's Use of the Social Sciences* (Washington, D.C.: USGPO, 1969).

[84]   E. T. Hiller, *The Strike: A Study in Collective Action* (Chicago: University of Chicago Press, 1928), pp. vii–viii.

[85]   Ibid., p. 11.

conceptions of property rights," and a variety of social movements became politicized in·protest and confrontation.[86]

The concerns of sociology and the activities of sociologists in the face of such massive problems are much influenced by a characteristic style, as well as the substance, associated with the Chicago School. Indeed, it might be argued that the legacy of Chicago to mid-twentieth century sociology—now that all "schools" are agreed on the necessity for and interdependence of theory and observation—is style. Of the several sociological styles emerging during this period, the merits of which have been subject to continuous and fruitful debate, the Chicago School, more than any other, developed a sensitivity to *process*.[87] It was, and is, interested in what is happening and why. This style, though less elaborate and elegant than that of Parsonian derivation, and less precise than that based on the Lundbergian tradition or on carefully controlled experimental work, is more closely tied to efforts to understand phenomena on the basis of intimate and detailed knowledge.

The Chicago School has been productive of statements of relationships, some of a very abstract theoretical order (as in the case of George Herbert Mead[88]), others of a more empirical nature. The distinctiveness of this Chicago style is based on continuous observation or monitoring of unfolding events in their natural setting, in contrast both to discrete samplings of opinion or other relevant data by means of surveys, or to the study of contrived situations in a laboratory setting. The full impact on sociology of the Chicago contribution in this respect has not yet been realized. Immersion in the social scene on a continuous basis sensitized the Chicago sociologists to process and produced much of our sociological theory dealing with mechanisms of change, whether of personalities, occupations, families, social groups, institutions, communities, cities,

[86]   See Russell Dynes and E. L. Quarantelli, "What Looting in Civil Disturbances Really Means," in *Law and Order: Modern Criminals*, ed. James F. Short, Jr., Trans-action Books (Chicago: Aldine, 1970).
[87]   I am indebted to Albert Cohen for suggestions relating to this discussion of sociological style.
[88]   See, e.g., Anselm Strauss, ed., *George Herbert Mead on Social Psychology* (Chicago: University of Chicago Press, 1964).

or populations. Aside from the Chicago school, American sociology has had remarkably little to say about this.

Conclusion

The personal and social, as well as intellectual, relationships of the Chicago School were complex. In this volume are represented a father and son (Ellsworth and R. E. L. Faris) and a husband and wife (Everett and Helen MacGill Hughes). The two Cresseys (Paul F. and Paul G.) were cousins (though neither was related to Donald .R., himself a Chicago product by way of his mentor, Edwin H. Sutherland). The list of family relationships might easily be extended. The point is not so much that family ties came to exist, but that such relationships symbolize a deep and sincere identification of many who were touched by Chicago School students and faculty, united in their enthusiasm for the sociological enterprise as it was practiced and preached at Chicago. Sociologists from other institutions often remark on this school identity—some admiringly, some no doubt disparagingly, and some in awe of the attraction that annually brings a large number of sleepy-eyed Chicagoans together at the "Chicago Breakfast" held in conjunction with the meetings of the American Sociological Association.

Indeed, the Chicago School evinces some of the characteristics of a social movement, as does at least one of the social action programs that was its intellectual child, the Chicago Area Project.[89] Certainly in those early days there was social unrest among sociologists who believed that their discipline should be more concerned with the totality of contemporary society. But this motivation was felt elsewhere as well as at Chicago. So why did it prosper there? The answer may lie in the fortunes which brought together the unusually broad, but contemporary, scholarly interests and the charismatic nature of some of those who became leaders of the Chicago School—Thomas, the classicist–social psychologist, Park, the newspaperman-scholar, and Burgess, their student and, later, collaborator.

[89] See my discussion of this point in "Introduction to the Revised Edition" of Shaw and McKay, *Juvenile Delinquency and Urban Areas.*

Attempts have been made to "institutionalize" the movement, with only moderate success. Too often, those who claim the mantle of the Chicago School have engaged in uninspired imitations. Perhaps this failure results from the fact that some have sought to imitate rather than emulate, confusing the spirit with *a* method or *an* approach. Few departments of sociology offer the *combined* interests which characterized the Chicago School, as Robert Faris so clearly demonstrates in his history. And in few universities have the disciplines so successfully cross-fertilized one another.

I hope that this volume may contribute to an appreciation of the vitality, freedom from dogmatism, and essential integrity of the Chicago School.

I. Chicago

1

Harvey W. Zorbaugh

THE SHADOW OF THE SKYSCRAPER

It is a veritable Babel, in which some thirty or more tongues are spoken. . . . Gunmen haunt its streets, and a murder is committed in them nearly every day in the year. It is smoke-ridden and disfigured by factories and railway yards, and many of its streets are ill-paved. Moreover, the people who throng them are more carelessly dressed than those in Fifth Avenue, and their voices not so well modulated as those of the inhabitants of Boston. Their manners, too, are of the kind the New Yorker defines as western.—CHATFIELD-TAYLOR, *Chicago*

The Chicago River, its waters stained by industry, flows back upon itself, branching to divide the city into the South Side, the North Side, and "the great West Side." In the river's southward bend lies the Loop, its skyline looming toward Lake Michigan. The Loop is the heart of Chicago, the knot in the steel arteries of elevated structure which pump in a ceaseless stream the three millions of population of the city into and out of its central business district. The canyon-like streets of the Loop rumble with the traffic of commerce. On its sidewalks throng people of every nation, pushing unseeingly past one another, into and out of office buildings, shops, theaters, hotels, and ultimately back to the north, south, and west "sides" from which they came. For miles over what once was prairie now sprawls in endless blocks the city.

The city's conquest of the prairie has proceeded stride for stride with the development of transportation. The outskirts of the city

From *The Gold Coast and the Slum*, by Harvey W. Zorbaugh (Chicago: University of Chicago Press, 1929), pp. 1–16. Reprinted by permission of Mrs. Harvey W. Zorbaugh.

have always been about forty-five minutes from the heart of the Loop. In the days of the horse-drawn car they were not beyond Twenty-second Street on the South Side. With the coming of the cable car they were extended to the vicinity of Thirty-sixth Street. The electric car—surface and elevated—again extended the city's outskirts, this time well past Seventieth Street. How far "rapid transit" will take them, no one can predict.

Apace with the expansion of the city has gone the ascendancy of the Loop. Every development in transportation, drawing increasing throngs of people into the central business district, has tended to centralize there not only commerce and finance, but all the vital activities of the city's life. The development of communication has further tightened the Loop's grip on the life of the city. The telephone has at once enormously increased the area over which the central business district can exert control and centralized that control. The newspaper, through the medium of advertising, has firmly established the supremacy of the Loop and, through the news, focused the attention of the city upon the Loop. The skyscraper is the visible symbol of the Loop's domination of the city's life. The central business district of the old city—like that of modern London—with its six- and eight-story buildings, sprawled over an unwieldy area. But the skyscraper, thrusting the Loop skyward thirty, forty, fifty stories, has made possible an extraordinary centralization and articulation of the central business district of the modern city. Drawing thousands daily into the heart of the city, where the old type of building drew hundreds, the cluster of skyscrapers within the Loop has become the city's vortex.

As the Loop expands it literally submerges the areas about it with the traffic of its commerce. Business and industry encroach upon residential neighborhoods. As the roar of traffic swells, and the smoke of industry begrimes buildings, land values rise. The old population moves slowly out, to be replaced by a mobile, shifting, anonymous population bringing with it transitional forms of social life. Within the looming shadow of the skyscraper, in Chicago as in every great city, is found a zone of instability and change—the tidelands of city life.

A part of these tidelands, within ten minutes' walk of the Loop

and the central business district, within five minutes by street ca·
or bus, just across the Chicago River, lies the Near North Side,
sometimes called "North Town." Within this area, a mile and a half
long and scarcely a mile wide, bounded by Lake Michigan on the
east and by the Chicago River on the south and west, under the
shadow of the Tribune Tower, a part of the inner city, live ninety
thousand people, a population representing all the types and contrasts that lend to the great city its glamor and romance.

The first settlers of Chicago built upon the north bank of the
Chicago River, and Chicago's first business house and first railroad
were on Kinzie street. But early in Chicago's history destiny took
its great commercial and industrial development southward, and
for several decades the North Side was a residential district, well-
to-do and fashionable. The story of early Chicago society centers
about homes on Ohio, Erie, Cass, and Rush streets; and street after
street of old stone fronts, curious streets some of them, still breathe
an air of respectability reminiscent of earlier and better days and
belying the slow conquest of the slum.

Here change has followed fast upon change. With the growth
of the city commerce has encroached upon residential property,
relentlessly pushing it northward or crowding it along the lake
shore, until now the Near North Side is chequered with business
streets. Into this area, where commerce is completing the conquest
of the community, has crept the slum. Meantime great industries
have sprung up along the river, and peoples speaking foreign
tongues have come to labor in them. The slum has offered these
alien peoples a place to live cheaply and to themselves; and wave
upon wave of immigrants has swept over the area—Irish, Swedish,
German, Italian, Persian, Greek, and Negro—forming colonies,
staying for a while, then giving way to others. But each has left its
impress and its stragglers, and today there live on the Near North
Side twenty-nine or more nationalities, many of them with their
Old World tongues and customs.

The city's streets can be read as can the geological record in
the rock. The old stone fronts of the houses on the side streets;
old residences along lower Rush and State, crowded between new
business blocks, or with shops built along the street in front of them;

a garage with "Riding Academy" in faded letters above its doors; the many old churches along La Salle and Dearborn streets; an office building growing out of a block of rooming-houses; "Deutsche Apotheke" on the window of a store in a neighborhood long since Italian—these are signs that record the changes brought about by the passing decades, changes still taking place today.

The Near North Side is an area of high light and shadow, of vivid contrasts—contrasts not only between the old and the new, between the native and the foreign, but between wealth and poverty, vice and respectability, the conventional and the bohemian, luxury and toil.

At the corner of Division Street and the Lake Shore Drive stands a tall apartment building in which seventeen-room apartments rent at one thousand dollars a month. One mile west, near Division Street and the river, Italian families are living in squalid basement rooms for which they pay six dollars a month. The greatest wealth in Chicago is concentrated along the Lake Shore Drive, in what is called the "Gold Coast." Almost at its back door, in "Little Hell," is the greatest concentration of poverty in Chicago. Respectability, it would seem, is measured by rentals and land values![1]

The Near North Side is not merely an area of contrasts; it is an area of extremes. All the phenomena characteristic of the city are clearly segregated and appear in exaggerated form. Not only are there extremes of wealth and poverty. The Near North Side has the highest residential land values in the city, and among the lowest; it has more professional men, more politicians, more suicides, more persons in *Who's Who*, than any other "community" in Chicago.[2]

The turgid stream of the Chicago River, which bounds the Near North Side on the south and the west, has played a prominent part in its history. A great deal of shipping once went up the river, and tugs, coal barges, tramp freighters, and occasional ore boats still

[1]   United Charities of Chicago, *Sixty Years of Service*. In 1920–21 there were 90 contributors to the United Charities in less than a square mile on the Gold Coast, and 460 poverty cases in the square mile behind it.
[2]   Taking figures for five widely differing "communities" in Chicago,

whistle at its bridges and steam slowly around its bends. This shipping caused commerce and industry to locate along the river, and today wharves, lumber and coal yards, iron works, gas works, sheet metal works, light manufacturing plants and storage plants, wholesale houses for spices, furs, groceries, butter, and imported oils line both sides of the river for miles, and with the noise and smoke of the railroads make a great barrier that half encircles the Near North Side, renders the part of it along the river undesirable to live in, and slowly encroaches northward and eastward.

"North Town" is divided into east and west by State Street. East of State Street lies the Gold Coast, Chicago's most exclusive residential district, turning its face to the lake and its back upon what may lie west toward the river. West of State Street lies a nondescript area of furnished rooms: Clark Street, the Rialto of the half-world; "Little Sicily," the slum.

The Lake Shore Drive is the Mayfair of the Gold Coast. It runs north and south along Lake Michigan, with a wide parkway, bridle path, and promenade. On its western side rise the imposing stone mansions, with their green lawns and wrought-iron-grilled doorways, of Chicago's wealthy aristocracy and her industrial and financial kings. South of these is Streeterville, a "restricted" district of tall apartments and hotels. Here are the Drake Hotel and the Lake Shore Drive hotel, Chicago's most exclusive. And here apartments rent for from three hundred fifty to a thousand dollars a month.

this fact is clearly brought out:

Community	Popula-tion	*Who's Who*	Physi-cians	Poli-ticians	Poverty Cases	Suicides
Back of the Yards*	39,908	1	28	4	185	8
Bridgeport†	64,875	0	44	12	180	3
Lawndale‡	105,819	1	212	14	251	6
Woodlawn§	69,594	31	185	14	48	8
Near North	83,819	151	212	30	555	28

* Immigrant community back of the Stockyards.

† Polish "area of first settlement" on the Southwest Side.

‡ Jewish "area of second settlement" on the West Side.

§ South Side residential community, surrounding the University of Chicago, containing many professional men and women.

Indeed, the Lake Shore Drive is a street more of wealth than of aristocracy; for in this midwest metropolis money counts for more than does family, and the aristocracy is largely that of the financially successful.

South of Oak Street the Lake Shore Drive, as it turns, becomes North Michigan Avenue, an avenue of fashionable hotels and restaurants, of smart clubs and shops. North Michigan Avenue is the Fifth Avenue of the Middle West; and already it looks forward to the day when Fifth Avenue will be the North Michigan Avenue of the East.

On a warm spring Sunday "Vanity Fair" glides along "the Drive" in motor cars of expensive mark, makes colorful the bridle-paths, or saunters up the promenade between "the Drake" and Lincoln Park. The tops of the tan motor busses are crowded with those who live farther out, going home from church—those of a different world who look at "Vanity Fair" with curious or envious eyes. Even here the element of contrast is not lacking, for a mother from back west, with a shawl over her head, waits for a pause in the stream of motors to lead her eager child across to the beach, while beside her stand a collarless man in a brown derby and his girl in Sunday gingham, from some rooming-house back on La Salle Street.

For a few blocks back of "the Drive"—on Belleview Place, East Division Street, Stone, Astor, Banks, and North State Parkway, streets less pretentious but equally aristocratic—live more than a third of the people in Chicago's social register, "of good family and not employed." Here are the families that lived on the once fashionable Prairie Avenue, and later Ashland Boulevard, on the South and West sides. These streets, with the Lake Shore Drive, constitute Chicago's much vaunted Gold Coast, a little world to itself, which the city, failing to dislodge, has grown around and passed by.

At the back door of the Gold Coast, on Dearborn, Clark, and La Salle streets, and on the side streets extending south to the business and industrial area, is a strange world, painfully plain by contrast, a world that lives in houses with neatly lettered cards in the window: "Furnished Rooms." In these houses, from midnight to dawn, sleep some twenty-five thousand people. But by day houses and streets are practically deserted. For early in the morning this population hurries from its houses and down its streets, boarding cars and busses, to work in the Loop. It is a childless area, an area of young men and young women, most of whom are single, though some are married, and others are living together unmarried. It is a world of constant comings and goings, of dull routine and little romance, a world of unsatisfied longings.

The Near North Side shades from light to shadow, and from shadow to dark. The Gold Coast gives way to the world of furnished rooms; and the rooming-house area, to the west again, imperceptibly becomes the slum. The common denominator of the slum is its submerged aspect and its detachment from the city as a whole. The slum is a bleak area of segregation of the sediment of society; an area of extreme poverty, tenements, ramshackle buildings, of evictions and evaded rents; an area of working mothers and children, of high rates of birth, infant mortality, illegitimacy, and death; an area of pawnshops and second-hand stores, of gangs, of "flops" where every bed is a vote. As distinguished from the vice area, the disintegrating neighborhood, the slum is an area which has reached the limit of decay and is on the verge of reorganization as missions, settlements, playparks, and business come in.

The Near North Side, west of Clark Street from North Avenue to the river, and east of Clark Street from Chicago Avenue to the river, we may describe as a slum, without fear of contradiction. For this area, cut off by the barrier of river and industry, and for years without adequate transportation, has long been a backwater in the life of the city. This slum district is drab and mean. In ten months the United Charities here had 460 relief cases. Poverty is extreme. Many families are living in one or two basement rooms for which they pay less than ten dollars a month. These rooms are stove heated, and wood is sold on the streets in bundles, and coal in small sacks. The majority of houses, back toward the river, are of wood, and not a few have windows broken out. Smoke, the odor from the gas works, and the smell of dirty alleys is in the air. Both

rooms and lots are overcrowded. Back tenements, especially north
of Division Street, are common.[3]

Life in the slum is strenuous and precarious. One reads in the
paper of a mother on North Avenue giving away her baby that the
rest of her children may live. Frequently babies are found in alley-
ways. A nurse at the Passavant Hospital on North La Salle tells of
a dirty little gamin, brought in from Wells Street, whose toe had
been bitten off by a rat while he slept. Many women from this
neighborhood are in the maternity ward four times in three years.
A girl, a waitress, living at the Albany Hotel on lower Rush Street,
recently committed suicide leaving the brief note, "I am tired of
everything. I have seen too much. That is all."[4]

Clark Street is the Rialto of the slum. Deteriorated store buildings, cheap dance halls and movies, cabarets and doubtful hotels,
missions, "flops," pawnshops and second-hand stores, innumerable
restaurants, soft-drink parlors and "fellowship" saloons, where men
sit about and talk, and which are hangouts for criminal gangs that
live back in the slum, fence at the pawnshops, and consort with the
transient prostitutes so characteristic of the North Side—such is
"the Street." It is an all-night street, a street upon which one meets
all the varied types that go to make up the slum.

[3]   A five-room house on Hill Street, the rooms in which are 9 × 12 ×
10 feet high, has thirty occupants. Another nurse told the writer of being
called on a case on Sedgewick Street and finding two couples living in one
room. One couple worked days, the other nights; one couple went to bed
when the other couple got up. Mrs. Louise De Kowen Bowen (*Growing Up
with a City*), reminiscing of her United Charities experiences, tells of a
woman who for three years existed on the food she procured from garbage
cans and from the samples of department store demonstration counters.
She adds:
    "Sometimes fate seems to be relentless to the point of absurdity, as in
one case I remember of an Italian family. . . . The man was riding on a
street car and was suddenly assaulted by an irate passenger. . . . His nose
was broken and he was badly disfigured. . . . A few days later, on his way
home from a dispensary where he had gone to have his wound dressed, he
fell off a sidewalk and broke his leg. The mother gave birth to a child the
same day. Another child died the following day, and the eldest girl, only
fourteen years old, who had been sent out to look for work, was foully assaulted on the street." Such is the life of the slum!
[4]   *Chicago Evening American*, December 21, 1923.

The slum harbors many sorts of people: the criminal, the radical, the bohemian, the migratory worker, the immigrant, the unsuccessful, the queer and unadjusted. The migratory worker is attracted by the cheap hotels on State, Clark, Wells, and the streets along the river. The criminal and underworld find anonymity in the transient life of the cheaper rooming-houses such as exist on North La Salle Street. The bohemian and the unsuccessful are attracted by cheap attic or basement rooms. The radical is sure of a sympathetic audience in Washington Square. The foreign colony, on the other hand, is found in the slum, not because the immigrant seeks the slum, nor because he makes a slum of the area in which he settles, but merely because he finds there cheap quarters in which to live, and relatively little opposition to his coming. From Sedgwick Street west to the river is a colony of some fifteen thousand Italians, familiarly known as "Little Hell." Here the immigrant has settled blocks by villages, bringing with him his language, his customs, and his traditions, many of which persist.

Other foreign groups have come into this area. North of "Little Sicily," between Wells and Milton streets, there is a large admixture of Poles with Americans, Irish, and Slavs. The Negro, too, is moving into this area and pushing on into "Little Hell." There is a small colony of Greeks grouped about West Chicago Avenue, with its picturesque coffee houses on Clark Street. Finally, there has come in within the past few years a considerable colony of Persians, which has also settled in the vicinity of Chicago Avenue. The slum on the Near North Side is truly cosmopolitan.

In the slum, but not of it, is "Towertown," or "the village." South of Chicago Avenue, along east Erie, Ohio, Huron, and Superior streets, is a considerable colony of artists and of would-be artists. The artists have located here because old buildings can be cheaply converted into studios. The would-be artists have followed the artists. And the hangers-on of bohemia have come for atmosphere, and because the old residences in the district have stables. "The village" is full of picturesque people and resorts—tearooms with such names as the Wind Blew Inn, the Blue Mouse, and the Green Mask. And many interesting art stores, antique shops, and stalls with rare books are tucked away among the old buildings. All in all, the picturesque and unconventional life of "the village" is again in striking contrast to the formal and conventional life of the Gold Coast, a few short blocks to the north.

One has but to walk the streets of the Near North Side to sense the cultural isolation beneath these contrasts. Indeed, the color and picturesqueness of the city exists in the intimations of what lies behind the superficial contrasts of its life. How various are the thoughts of the individuals who throng up Michigan Avenue from the Loop at the close of the day—artists, shop girls, immigrants, inventors, men of affairs, women of fashion, waitresses, clerks, entertainers. How many are their vocational interests; how different are their ambitions. How vastly multiplied are the chances of life in a great city, as compared with those of the American towns and European peasant villages from which most of these individuals have come. What plans, plots, conspiracies, and dreams for taking advantage of these chances different individuals must harbor under their hats. Yet they have little in common beyond the fact that they jostle one another on the same street. Experience has taught them different languages. How far they are from understanding one another, or from being able to communicate save upon the most obvious material matters!

As one walks from the Drake Hotel and the Lake Shore Drive west along Oak Street, through the world of rooming-houses, into the slum and the streets of the Italian Colony one has a sense of distance as between the Gold Coast and Little Hell—distance that is not geographical but social. There are distances of language and custom. There are distances represented by wealth and the luster it adds to human existence. There are distances of horizon—the Gold Coast living throughout the world while Little Hell is still only slowly emerging out of its old Sicilian villages. There are distances represented by the Gold Coast's absorbing professional interests. It is one world that revolves about the Lake Shore Drive, with its mansions, clubs, and motors, its benefits and assemblies. It is another world that revolves about the Dill Pickle Club, the soap boxes of Washington Square, or the shop of Romano the Barber. And each little world is absorbed in its own affairs.

For the great majority of the people on the Gold Coast—excepting those few individuals who remember, or whose parents remember, the immigrant communities out of which they have succeeded in climbing—the district west of State Street exists only in the newspapers. And from the newspapers they learn nothing reassuring. The metropolitan press pictures this district as a bizarre world of gang wars, of exploding stills, of radical plots, of "lost" girls, of suicides, of bombings, of murder. . . .

Beyond . . . newspaper reports, little is known of the world west of State Street by the people of the Gold Coast. Their affairs rarely take them into the river district. The reports of social agencies are little read. It is a region remote.

But to the people who live west of State Street the Gold Coast is immediate and real. It is one of the sights of the town. They throng its streets in going down to the lake on hot summer days. From the beach they gaze up at the magnificent hotels and apartments of Streeterville, and at the luxurious and forbidding mansions of the Lake Shore Drive. They watch the streams of costly automobiles and fashionably dressed men and women. The front pages of the newspapers they read as they hang to straps on the street cars in the evening are filled with pictures of the inhabitants of the Gold Coast, and with accounts of their comings and goings. It all enlists the imagination. Consequently the people from "back west" enormously idealize the Gold Coast's life. They imitate its styles and manners. The imagination of the shop girl, of the immigrant, of the hobo plays with these externals of its life. In the movie they see realistic pictures of "high society." These they take to be the inner, intimate life of which they see the externals along the Lake Shore Drive. As a result the social distance from Death Corner to the Drake Hotel is no less than the distance from the Casino Club to Bughouse Square.

The isolation of the populations crowded together within these few hundred blocks, the superficiality and externality of their contacts, the social distances that separate them, their absorption in the affairs of their own little worlds—these, and not mere size and numbers, constitute the social problem of the inner city. The community, represented by the town or peasant village where everyone knows everyone else clear down to the ground, is gone. Over large areas of the city "community" is little more than a geographical expression. Yet the old tradition of control persists despite changed conditions of life. The inevitable result is cultural disorganization.

II Basic Perspectives

THE CITY IS . . . the natural habitat of civilized man.

* * *

There are forces at work within the limits of the urban community—within the limits of any natural area of human habitation, in fact—which tend to bring about an orderly and typical grouping of its population and institutions. The science which seeks to isolate these factors and to describe the typical constellations of persons and institutions which the co-operation of these forces produce is what we call human, as distinguished from plant and animal, ecology.

* * *

The same patient methods of observation which anthropologists like Boas and Lowie have expended on the study of the life and manners of the North American Indian might be even more fruitfully employed in the investigation of the customs, beliefs, social practices, and general conceptions of life prevalent in Little Italy on the lower North Side in Chicago, or in recording the more sophisticated folkways of the inhabitants of Greenwich Village and the neighborhood of Washington Square, New York.

* * *

The multiplication of occupations and professions within the limits of the urban population is one of the most striking and least understood aspects of modern city life. From this point of view, we may, if we choose, think of the city, that is to say, the place and the people, with all the machinery and administrative devices that go with them, as organically related; a kind of psychophysical mechanism in and through which private and political interests find not merely a collective but a corporate expression.

15

In the city every vocation, even that of a beggar, tends to assume the character of a profession and the discipline which success in any vocation imposes, together with the associations that it enforces, emphasizes this tendency—the tendency, namely, not merely to specialize, but to rationalize one's occupation and to develop a specific and conscious technique for carrying it on.

*   *   *

The city, . . . is something more than a congeries of individual men and of social conveniences—streets, buildings, electric lights, tramways, and telephones, etc.; something more, also, than a mere constellation of institutions and administrative devices—courts, hospitals, schools, police, and civil functionaries of various sorts. The city is, rather, a state of mind, a body of customs and traditions, and of the organized attitudes and sentiments that inhere in these customs and are transmitted with this tradition. The city is not, in other words, merely a physical mechanism and an artificial construction. It is involved in the vital processes of the people who compose it; it is a product of nature, and particularly of human nature.

ROBERT E. PARK

2

Roderick D. McKenzie

THE ECOLOGICAL APPROACH
TO THE STUDY
OF THE HUMAN COMMUNITY

THE YOUNG sciences of plant and animal ecology have become fairly well established. Their respective fields are apparently quite well defined, and a set of concepts for analysis is becoming rather generally accepted. The subject of human ecology, however, is still practically an unsurveyed field, that is, so far as a systematic and scientific approach is concerned. To be sure, hosts of studies have been made which touch the field of human ecology in one or another of its varied aspects, but there has developed no science of human ecology which is comparable in precision of observation or in method of analysis with the recent sciences of plant and animal ecology.

I. *The Relation of Human Ecology to Plant and Animal Ecology*

Ecology has been defined as "that phase of biology that considers plants and animals as they exist in nature, and studies their interdependence, and the relation of each kind and individual to its environment."[1] This definition is not sufficiently comprehensive to include all the elements that logically fall within the range of human ecology. In the absence of any precedent let us tenta-

Reprinted from *The American Journal of Sociology*, vol. 30, no. 3, November, 1924.

[1] *Encyclopedia Americana*, New York (1923), p. 555.

18 RODERICK D. MC KENZIE

tively define human ecology as a study of the spatial and temporal[2] relations of human beings as affected by the selective, distributive, and accommodative forces of the environment. Human ecology is fundamentally interested in the effect of *position*,[3] in both time and space, upon human institutions and human behavior. "Society is made up of individuals spatially separated, territorially distributed, and capable of independent locomotion."[4] These spatial relationships of human beings are the products of competition and selection, and are continuously in process of change as new factors enter to disturb the competitive relations or to facilitate mobility. Human institutions and human nature itself become accommodated to certain spatial relationships of human beings. As these spatial relationships change, the physical basis of social relations is altered, thereby producing social and political problems.

A great deal has been written about the biological, economic, and social aspects of competition and selection, but little attention has been given to the distributive and spatial aspects of these processes. The plant ecologist is aware of the effect of the struggle for space, food, and light upon the nature of a plant formation, but the sociologist has failed to recognize that the same processes of competition and accommodation are at work determining the size and ecological organization of the human community.

The essential difference between the plant and animal organism is that the animal has the power of locomotion which enables it to gather nutriment from a wider environment, but, in addition to the power to move in space, the human animal has the ability to contrive and adapt the environment to his needs. In a word, the human community differs from the plant community in the two

2   As indicated later on in this paper, ecological formations tend to develop in cyclic fashion. A period of time within which a given ecological formation develops and culminates is the time period for that particular formation. The length of these time periods may be ultimately measured and predicted, hence the inclusion of the temporal element in the definition.
3   The word "position" is used to describe the place relation of a given community to other communities, also the location of the individual or institution within the community itself.
4   R. E. Park and E. W. Burgess, *Introduction to the Science of Sociology*, p. 509.

dominant characteristics of mobility and purpose, that is, in the power to select a habitat and in the ability to control or modify the conditions of the habitat. On first consideration this might seem to indicate that human ecology could have nothing in common with plant ecology, where the processes of association and adjustment result from natural unmodifiable reactions; but closer examination and investigation make it obvious that human communities are not so much the products of artifact or design as many hero-worshippers suppose.[5]

The human community has its inception in the traits of human nature and the needs of human beings. Man is a gregarious animal: he cannot live alone; he is relatively weak and needs not only the company of other human associates but shelter and protection from the elements as well. Brunhes says there are three essentials to the inception of the human community: the house, the road, and water.[6] Food may be transported more easily than shelter or water; the latter two therefore constitute, even under the most nomadic conditions, the essential elements in giving a location and a spatial fixity to human relations.[7] This is exemplified under our present regime of automobile tourist life, where water and shelter become the determining factors in the location of the camp.

The size and stability of the human community is, however, a function of the food supply and of the role played in the wider ecological process of production and distribution of commodities. When man makes his living from hunting or fishing, the community is small and of but temporary duration; when agriculture becomes the chief source of sustenance, the community is still small but assumes a more permanent character; when trade and commerce develop, larger communities arise at points of break in conveyance, that is, at the mouths of rivers, junctions of streams,

[5]   Although the actions of individuals may be designed and controlled, the total effect of individual action is neither designed nor anticipated.

[6]   *Human Geography*, p. 52.

[7]   Brunhes points out by a series of maps the very intimate relation between the distribution of human habitations and the water systems of different countries. He also demonstrates the relation of the modern industrial community to the regions of coal deposits.

at waterfalls, and shallows where streams are forded. As new forms of transportation arise, new points of concentration occur and old points become accentuated or reduced. Again, as goods for trade are made in communities, still other points of concentration come into existence, determined largely by sources of power and raw material.[8]

II. *Ecological Classification of Communities*

From the standpoint of ecology, communities may be divided into four general types: first, the primary service community, such as the agricultural town, the fishing, mining, or lumbering community, which serves as the first step in the distributive process of the outgoing basic commodity and as the last stage in the distributive process of the product finished for consumption. The size of such communities depends entirely upon the nature and form of utilization of the extractive industry concerned, together with the extent of the surrounding trade area. The community responds in size to any element that affects the productivity of the economic base or the extent of the area from which it draws its sustenance. But, in any event, so long as such a community does not assume any other function in the larger ecological process, it cannot grow in population beyond a few thousand inhabitants.

The next type of community is the one that fufills the secondary function in the distributive process of commodities. It collects the basic materials from the surrounding primary communities and distributes them in the wider markets of the world. On the other hand, it redistributes the products coming from other parts of the world to the primary service communities for final consumption. This is commonly called the commercial community; it may, however, combine other functions as well. The size of this type of com-

[8]   The close relation existing between the coal and iron areas and the location of modern industrial communities has frequently been pointed out. L. C. A. Knowles says: "Apart from special and exceptional circumstances industry in Europe and the United States tends to grow up within easy railway access to the great coal areas and on these areas the population is massed in towns" (*The Industrial and Commercial Revolutions in Great Britain during the Nineteenth Century*, p. 24).

munity depends upon the extent of its distributive functions. It may vary from a small wholesale town in the center of an agricultural plain to that of a great port city whose hinterland extends halfway across the continent. Growth depends upon the comparative advantages of the site location.

The third type of community is the industrial town. It serves as the locus for the manufacturing of commodities. In addition it may combine the functions of the primary service and the commercial types. It may have its local trade area and it may also be the distributing center for the surrounding hinterland. The type is characterized merely by the relative dominance of industry over the other forms of service. There is practically no limit to the size to which an industrial community may develop. Growth is dependent upon the scope and market organization of the particular industries which happen to be located within its boundaries. Industrial communities are of two general types: first, those that have diversified and multiple industries organized on a local sale of products, and, second, those that are dominated by one or two highly developed industries organized on a national or world-sale of products.

The fourth type of community is one which is lacking in a specific economic base. It draws its economic sustenance from other parts of the world, and may serve no function in the production or distribution of commodities. Such communities are exemplified in our recreational resorts, political and educational centers, communities of defense, penal or charitable colonies. From the standpoint of growth or decline such communities are not subject to the same laws that govern the development of towns that play a part in the larger productive and distributive processes.[9] They are much more subject to the vicissitudes of human fancies and decrees than are the basic types of human communities. Of course, any community may and usually does have accretions added to its population as a result of such service. It

[9]   To be sure, if the interests in question are commercialized, the growth of the community is subject to the same laws of competition as the other types of communities, with the exception that change is likely to be more rapid and fanciful.

may, for instance, be the seat of a university, of a state prison, or it may be a recreational resort for at least certain seasons of the year.

III. *Determining Ecological Factors in the Growth or Decline of Community*

The human community tends to develop in cyclic fashion. Under a given state of natural resources and in a given condition of the arts the community tends to increase in size and structure until it reaches the point of population adjustment to the economic base. In an agricultural community, under present conditions of production and transportation, the point of maximum population seldom exceeds 5,000.[10] The point of maximum development may be termed the point of culmination or climax, to use the term of the plant ecologist.[11] The community tends to remain in this condition of balance between population and resources until some new element enters to disturb the *status quo*, such as the introduction of a new system of communication, a new type of industry, or a different form of utilization of the existing economic base. Whatever the innovation may be that disturbs the equilibrium of the community, there is a tendency toward a new cycle of adjustment. This may act in either a positive or negative manner. It may serve as a *release* to the community, making for another cycle of growth and differentiation, or it may have a retractive influence, necessitating emigration and readjustment to a more circumscribed base.

In earlier conditions of life, population was kept down to the community balance by variations in the death rate, or, as in the case of Greek cities, the surplus population emigrated in groups to establish new colonies—offshoots of the mother-city. Under modern conditions of communication and transportation, population adjustment is maintained by a ceaseless process of individual migrations. As a result of the dynamic conditions prevailing

10   See H. P. Douglass, *The Little Town*, p. 44.
11   F. E. Clements, *Plant Succession*, p. 3. Carr-Saunders refers to the point of population adjustment to resources as the "optimum."

throughout the civilized world during the last fifty years, many communities have passed through swift successive cycles of growth or decline, the determining factors being changes in forms and routes of transportation and communication and the rise of new industries.

Some advantage in transportation is the most fundamental and most important of the causes determining the location of a distributing center. It may almost be said to be the only cause for the formation of such centers. For some reason or reasons a particular place is more conveniently and cheaply reached by many people than any surrounding point; and, as a result, they naturally exchange commodities there. The country store is located at the crossing of roads. There also is the village. In a mountain country the market town is at the junction of two, or, still better, of three valleys. Another favorite location is the end of a mountain pass, or a gap that is a thoroughfare between two valleys. If rivers are difficult to cross, settlements will spring up at the safest ferries or fords. In a level plain, a town will be near its center, and a focus of roads or railroads in such a plain, fertile and populous, will almost surely make a city.[12]

It is the railroad and the steamship that determine where a new business shall be developed, quite as often as the government policy. The grant of special rates and privileges to shippers is nowadays the most efficient kind of protection.

It is this quickening and cheapening of transportation that has given such stimulus in the present day to the growth of large cities. It enables them to draw cheap food from a far larger territory and it causes business to locate where the widest business connection is to be had, rather than where the goods or raw materials are most easily produced. And the perfection of the means of communication, the post-office and the telegraph, intensifies the same result.[13]

The entire net increase of the population of 1870 to 1890 in Illinois, Wisconsin, Iowa, and Minnesota was in cities and towns possessing competitive rates, while those having non-competitive rates decreased in population, and in Iowa it is the general belief that the

[12]   J. Russell Smith, *Industrial and Commercial Geography* (1913), p. 841.
[13]   A. T. Hadley, "Economic Results of Improvement in Means of Transportation," quoted in Marshall, *Business Administration*, p. 35.

absence of large cities is due to the earlier policy of the railways giving Chicago discriminating rates.[14]

The advent of the trolley line and more recently of the automobile has produced still further disturbing elements in the growth of human communities. Their effect has been chiefly to modify the life of the small town or village, causing the decline of some and the sudden growth of others. The introduction of these two forms of transportation, more particularly of the automobile, has been the most potent force in our recent American history in affecting redistribution of our population and in the disorganization of our rural and small-town institutions, which grew up on the basis of a horse-and-vehicle type of mobility.[15]

The evolution of new types of industry is another feature that becomes a determining factor in the redistribution of the country's population. As we review our census reports we see the emergence each decade of one or more important industries; first, the textile industry causing concentrations of population in the eastern states, then the development of the iron and steel industry with its center of operations gradually shifting farther and farther west, and more recently the advent of the automobile and oil industries making for enormous concentration of population in certain states of the Union, also the motion-picture industry with its concentrated center in southern California. The emergence of a new industry has a far-reaching effect in disturbing the *status quo* of communal life. Competition soon forces the new industry to concentrate its productive enterprises in one or two communities; these communities then serve as great magnets drawing to themselves the appropriate population elements from communities far and near.

IV. *The Effect of Ecological Changes on the Social Organization of Community*

Population migrations resulting from such sudden pulls as are the outcomes of unusual forms of release in community

[14]   L. C. A. Knowles, *The Industrial and Commercial Revolutions in Great Britain during the Nineteenth Century* (1921), p. 216.
[15]   See Gillette, *Rural Sociology* (1922), pp. 472–73.

growth may cause an expansion in the community's development far beyond the natural culmination point of its cyclic development, resulting in a crisis situation, a sudden relapse, disorganization, or even panic. So-called "boom towns" are towns that have experienced herd movements of population beyond the natural point of culmination.

On the other hand, a community which has reached the point of culmination and which has experienced no form of release is likely to settle into a condition of stagnation. Its natural surplus of population is forced to emigrate. This type of emigration tends to occasion folk-depletion in the parent community. The younger and more enterprising population elements respond most sensitively to the absence of opportunities in their home town. This is particularly true when the community has but a single economic base, such as agriculture, lumbering, mining. Reformers try in vain to induce the young people to remain on the farms or in their native villages, little realizing that they are working in opposition to the general principles of the ecological order.

Again, when a community starts to decline in population due to a weakening of the economic base, disorganization and social unrest follow.[16] Competition becomes keener within the community, and the weaker elements either are forced into a lower economic level or are compelled to withdraw from the community entirely. There are, of course, periodic and temporary fluctuations in the economic balance, due either to circumstances which affect the entire economic order or to the vicissitudes of the particular industry from which the community draws its sustenance. These temporary fluctuations, however, while important from the standpoint of social well-being, do not comprise the basic determinants of community development.

The introduction of an innovating element into the adjustment of a community may be designated as the initial stage of an invasion which may make for a complete change in the structure and organization of the community. The introduction of a new mode of transportation, for instance, may transform the economic organiza-

[16]   For a good statistical summary of the decline in village population in the United States from 1900 to 1920, see Gillette, *Rural Sociology*, p. 465.

tion of a community and make for a change in population type.

Thus the Harlem Railroad transformed Quaker Hill from a community of diversified farming, producing, manufacturing, selling, consuming, sufficient unto itself, into a locality of specialized farming. Its market had been Poughkeepsie, twenty-eight miles away, over high hills and indifferent roads. Its metropolis became New York, sixty-two miles away by rail and four to eight miles by wagon-road.

With the railroad's coming, the isolated homogeneous community scattered. The sons of the Quakers emigrated. Laborers from Ireland and other European lands, even negroes from Virginia, took their places. New Yorkers became residents on the Hill, which became the farthest terminus of suburban travel.[17]

The establishment of a new industry, especially if it displaces the previous economic base, may also make for a more or less complete change of population without greatly modifying the size of the community. This condition is exemplified in many of the small towns of the state of Washington which have changed from lumbering to agriculture or from one type of agriculture to another. In many cases few of the previous inhabitants remained after the invasion of the new economic base.

As a community increases in size, however, it becomes better able to accommodate itself to invasions and to sudden changes in number of inhabitants. The city tends to become the reservoir into which the surplus population drains from the smaller communities round about.

V. *Ecological Processes Determining the Internal Structure of Community*

In the process of community growth there is a development from the simple to the complex, from the general to the specialized; first to increasing centralization and later to a decentralization process. In the small town or village the primary universal needs are satisfied by a few general stores and a few simple institutions

[17]   Warren H. Wilson, "Quaker Hill," quoted in Sims, *Rural Community*, p. 214.

such as church, school, and home. As the community increases in
size specialization takes place both in the type of service provided
and in the location of the place of service. The sequence of development may be somewhat as follows: first the grocery store,
sometimes carrying a few of the more staple dry goods, then the
restaurant, poolroom, barber shop, drug store, dry-goods store,
and later bank, haberdashery, millinery, and other specialized
lines of service.[18]

The axial or skeletal structure of a community is determined
by the course of the first routes of travel and traffic.[19] Houses and
shops are constructed near the road, usually parallel with it. The
road may be a trail, public highway, railroad, river, or ocean harbor, but, in any case, the community usually starts in parallel relation to the first main highway. With the accumulation of population and utilities the community takes form, first along one side
of the highway and later on both sides. The point of junction or
crossing of two main highways, as a rule, serves as the initial center of the community.

As the community grows there is not merely a multiplication of
houses and roads but a process of differentiation and segregation
takes place as well. Residences and institutions spread out in cen-
trifugal fashion from the central point of the community, while
business concentrates more and more around the spot of highest
land values. Each cyclic increase of population is accompanied by
greater differentiation in both service and location. There is a
struggle among utilities for the vantage-points of position. This
makes for increasing value of land and increasing height of buildings at the geographic center of the community. As competition
for advantageous sites becomes keener with the growth of population, the first and economically weaker types of utilities are
forced out to less accessible and lower-priced areas. By the time

---

[18]   In actual count of some thirty-odd communities in and around
Seattle this was about the sequence of development.
[19]   The axial or skeletal structure of civilization, Mediterranean, Atlantic, Pacific, is the ocean around which it grows up. See Ramsay Traquair,
"The Commonwealth of the Atlantic," *Atlantic Monthly*, May, 1924.

the community has reached a population of about ten or twelve thousand, a fairly well-differentiated structure is attained. The drugstore, the department store, and the hotel holding the sites of central part is a clearly defined business area with the bank, the highest land value. Industries and factories usually comprise independent formations within the city, grouping around railroad tracks and routes of water traffic. Residence sections become established, segregated into two or more types, depending upon the economic and racial composition of the population.

The structural growth of community takes place in successional sequence not unlike the successional stages in the development of the plant formation. Certain specialized forms of utilities and uses do not appear in the human community until a certain stage of development has been attained, just as the beech or pine forest is preceded by successional dominance of other plant species. And just as, in plant communities, successions are the products of invasion, so also in the human community the formation, segregations, and associations that appear constitute the outcome of a series of invasions.[20]

There are many kinds of intra-community invasions, but in general they may be grouped into two main classes: those resulting in change in use of land, and those which introduce merely change in type of occupant. By the former is meant change from one general use to another, such as of a residential area into a business area or of a business into an industrial district. The latter embraces all changes of type within a particular use area, such as the changes which constantly take place in the racial and economic complexion of residence neighborhoods, or of the type of service utility within a business section. Invasions produce successional stages of different qualitative significance, that is, the economic character of the district may rise or fall as the result of certain types of invasion. This qualitative aspect is reflected in the fluctuations of land or rental values.

The conditions which initiate invasions are legion. The following are some of the more important: (1) changes in forms and

[20]   Compare F. E. Clements, *Plants Succession*, p. 6.

routes of transportation;[21] (2) obsolescence resulting from physical deterioration or from changes in use or fashion; (3) the erection of important public or private structures, buildings, bridges, institutions, which have either attractive or repellent significance; (4) the introduction of new types of industry, or even a change in the organization of existing industries; (5) changes in the economic base which make for redistribution of income, thus necessitating change of residence; (6) real estate promotion creating sudden demands for special location sites, etc.

Invasions may be classified according to stage of development into (a) initial stage, (b) secondary or developmental stage, (c) climax. The initial stage of an invasion has to do with the point of entry, the resistance or inducement offered the invader by the prior inhabitants of the area, the effect upon land values and rentals. The invasion, of course, may be into an unoccupied territory or into territory with various degrees of occupancy. The resistance to invasion depends upon the type of the invader together with the degree of solidarity of the present occupants. The undesirable invader, whether in population type or in use form, usually makes entry (that is, within an area already completely occupied) at the point of greatest mobility. It is a common observation that foreign races and other undesirable invaders, with few exceptions, take up residence near the business center of the community or at other points of high mobility and low resistance. Once established they gradually push their way out along business or transportation thoroughfares to the periphery of the community.

The commencement of an invasion tends to be reflected in changes in land value. If the invasion is one of change in use, the value of the land generally advances and the value of the building declines. This condition furnishes the basis for disorganization. The normal improvements and repairs are, as a rule, omitted, and the owner is placed under the economic urge of renting his prop-

---

[21]   For good discussion of the effect of new forms of transportation upon communal structure see McMichael and Bingham, *City Growth and Values* (1923), chap. 4; also Grupp, *Economics of Motor Transportation* (1924), chap. 2.

erty to parasitic and transitory services which may be economically
strong but socially disreputable, and is therefore able and obliged
to pay higher rentals than the legitimate utilities can afford. It is
a well-known fact that the vices under the surveillance of the police
usually segregate in such transitional areas.[22]

During the course of development of an invasion into a new
area, either of use or type, there takes place a process of displace-
ment and selection determined by the character of the invader and
of the area invaded. The early stages are usually marked by keen-
ness of competition, which frequently manifests itself in outward
clashes. Business failures are common in such areas and the rules
of competition are violated. As the process continues, competition
forces associational groupings. Utilities making similar or complementary demands of the area tend to group in close proximity to
one another, giving rise to subformations with definite service
functions. Such associations as amusement areas, retail districts,
market sections, financial sections, and automobile rows are examples of this tendency.

The climax stage is reached in the invasion process once the
dominant type of ecological organization emerges which is able
to withstand the intrusions of other forms of invasion. For example, in the development of a residential district, when it is not
controlled in advance by building restrictions, the early stages of
growth are usually marked by wide variations in the type and
value of buildings constructed. But, in the process of development,
a uniform cost type of structure tends to dominate, gradually
eliminating all other types that vary widely from the norm, so that
it is customary to find a considerable degree of economic homoge-
neity in all established residential districts. The same process operates in areas devoted to business uses, competition segregates
utilities of similar economic strength into areas of corresponding
land values, and at the same time forces into close proximity those
particular forms of service which profit from mutual association

[22]   By actual count in the city of Seattle over 80 per cent of the disorderly houses recorded in police records are obsolete buildings located
near the downtown business section where land values are high and new
uses are in process of establishment.

such as financial establishments or automobile display-rooms. Once a dominant use becomes established within an area, competition becomes less ruthless among the associational units, rules of control emerge, and invasion of a different use is for a time obstructed.

The general effect of the continuous processes of invasions and accommodations is to give to the developed community well-defined areas, each having its own peculiar selective and cultural characteristics. Such units of communal life may be termed "natural areas,"[23] or formations, to use the term of the plant ecologist. In any case, these areas of selection and function may comprise many subformations or associations which become part of the organic structure of the district or of the community as a whole. It has been suggested that these natural areas or formations may be defined in terms of land values,[24] the point of highest land value representing the center or head of the formation (not necessarily the geographic center but the economic or cultural center), while the points of lowest land value represent the periphery of the formation or boundary line between two adjacent formations.

Each formation or ecological organization within a community serves as a selective or magnetic force attracting to itself appropriate population elements and repelling incongruous units, thus making for biological and cultural subdivisions of a city's population. Everyone knows how racial and linguistic colonies develop in all of our large cities, but the age and sex segregations which take place are not quite so obvious to common perception. In the city of Seattle, which has in general a sex composition of 113 males to 100 females, the downtown district, comprising an area inscribed by a radius of half a mile or so, has from 300 to 500 males to every 100 females. But in the outlying districts of the city, except in one or two industrial sections, these ratios are reversed. Females predominate in numbers over males in all the residential neighborhoods and in the suburbs of the city. This same condition is true with regard to the age distribution of population. The school census shows an absolute decline in the number of children of

[23]   A term used by members of the Department of Sociology in the University of Chicago.
[24]   This has also been suggested by the Chicago group.

school age in the central districts of the city although the total population for this area has shown an increase for each decade. It is obvious, then, that the settler type of population, the married couples with children, withdraw from the center of the city while the more mobile and less responsible adults herd together in the hotel and apartment regions near the heart of the community.

This process of population-sifting produces not only increasing mobility with approach from the periphery to the center of the formation, but also different cultural areas representing different mores, attitudes, and degrees of civic interest. The neighborhoods in which the settler type of population resides, with their preponderance of women and children, serve as the custodians of the stabilizing and repressive mores. It is in the Seattle neighborhoods, especially those on the hill-tops, that the conservative, law-abiding, civic-minded population elements dwell. The downtown section and the valleys, which are usually industrial sites, are populated by a class of people who are not only more mobile but whose mores and attitudes, as tested by voting habits, are more vagrant and radical.

3

Everett Cherrington Hughes

THE GROWTH OF AN INSTITUTION:

THE CHICAGO

REAL ESTATE BOARD

The Earmarks of an Institution

IN THESE PAGES we do not observe a dinosaur's bones, for
which we must imagine the flesh, but the struggling flesh itself of a
living and yet young institution in the city of Chicago. Our thesis is
that the ways of the past may be illuminated by those of the present
as well as the reverse. While our knowledge of present institutions
has been given depth by reconstructions of things ancient, it has
too often been the practice to attribute ancient social forms to oc-
cult forces which we cannot quite understand, and which, like
giants, are now extinct.

The Chicago Real Estate Board, began its career within the
memory of men now living. Yet its influence has spread until it
deals directly with all who live in houses or do business in them.
Only the hoboes escape it. The leases which we so seldom read, but
so frequently sign, are its handiwork. The janitor who heats our
flats seeks his increase in wages from this ever-watchful body, not
from the irresponsible tenant or the anonymous landlord. It has
had its say about the very materials of which our houses are built
and about the width of the streets we live on. We utter a new slogan
"City Beautiful," and discuss "zoning," not knowing that the words
came from this omnipresent urban institution.

From Everett C. Hughes, *The Growth of an Institution: The Chicago
Real Estate Board* (Chicago: The Society for Social Research of the
University of Chicago: Series 2, Monograph 1, 1931), chapters 1, 2, 3,
and 13. Adapted by permission of Everett C. Hughes, this material was
originally written in 1927 and 1928.

Yet it is a frank and open thing. The newspapers mention its affairs almost daily. Few public bodies take so many pains to be known and felt. It is characteristic of city life that people in general live in the midst of powerful institutions of whose existence they are scarcely aware. At forty the individual man may be an enthusiastic inside supporter of one which his schoolbooks did not mention. Our occupations take us into unknown worlds. Such considerations make it both interesting and important to study such a thing as the Chicago Real Estate Board.

Few members of this body know the names of its founders. Harper Leech once said that business quickly forgets its heroes and its victories. Resting on past glory is a pastime of nations and sects. Yet this business institution does not have a past, which lives in precedent, rules of practice and a hard-won place among the forces which control the complex life of a modern city. Those who deal with it know what to expect of it in times of crisis. It is not capricious.

Nor is such an institution overconscious of its future. Socialists dream of a new Jerusalem which may or may not be realized on earth. Our institution is concerned with this world. It grew out of the day-by-day facing of emergencies. No one foresaw just what it would become. In that it is like Lloyd's.

At no time, so far as we are aware, did any group of men say to each other: "Go to; let us make the greatest centre of insurance in the world." Even association waited for well over a century, and incorporation for nearly two centuries. Certain men took their seats at a coffeehouse table, and pledged themselves individually, for a consideration, to take upon themselves the perils of the sea, men-of-war, fire, enemies, pirates, thieves, etc., with all other perils which might come to the hurt or detriment of the subject-matter of insurance. The coffee-house was frequented by all sundry, and the merchants of that day found reliable men at some of the tables who would give them good assurance. Amid all the changes of the centuries, with the growth of banks and limited liability companies, the two great principles of individual trading (each for himself and not one for another), and unlimited liability have been maintained. It is a striking example of evolution as distinguished from creation. Conditions have been made, rules instituted not in preparation for new factors and developments, but to systematize a practice which had already been adopted to meet the requirements of commerce as they arose.[1]

The Chicago Real Estate Board began more consciously and with a definite purpose. Programs of legislation have been projected and pursued assiduously for years on end; but they have had to do with pressing problems rather than with eternal principles. No group of men deliberately planned the present character and policy of the institution on the basis of given premises. Its character developed as a by-product of its activity.

The excellence of America as a social laboratory inheres not only in the variety of social groups which have grown up on her soil, but also in the fact that things move quickly enough for significant changes to be recorded within the life span of a generation. Europeans say that America is disorderly. So it is, but in her disorder institutions have been born and died. Some are adaptations of old forms; others are new. Sects have flourished by the hundred only to be outdone by others. New types of business institutions have come into being, have struggled against their predecessors, and have given way to still newer upstarts.

In spite of constant change, it may be that the many new associations of men in the new world may teach us something of the nature of human institutions in general. There has been much talk of a genetic approach to the study of society, but only occasionally has anyone adopted the method of studying the rise of some particular institution which has begun under our very eyes. Such an account should have, like a motion picture of a plant growing, the scientific merit of illuminating the processes by which other things of the same general sort have arisen and may be expected to grow.

I. THE CONCEPT "INSTITUTION"   The conceptions of what an institution is have run the gamut from some vague essence mysteriously inherited from untold generations of the dead to so specific and probably fleeting a thing as yesterday's meeting of housewives to protest the price of eggs. Most definitions of the term strike a middle ground by including both the notion of some-

[1]   Wright and Fayle, *A History of Lloyd's*, 2.

thing not too new or passing and that of people engaged together in some sort of activity.

Few people will allow that the institution is a material thing, such as a building of brick and mortar. In America, the building might be a church today and a garage tomorrow. An old cathedral, however, is a symbol as well as the seat of an institution. Its aroma of age seems to guarantee that those who enter it in the future will do the same sort of thing there as was done by those who entered it in the past and are buried there. One cannot imagine the priest and his flock starting a curb market in the cathedral of a Sunday morning, but it is not unthinkable that the same people, including the priest, should visit a duly appointed curb market on Monday and engage in hectic speculation. Institutions may be conceived as the social structures within which men take their various places to do collectively the things that are right and proper with respect to some particular aspect of life. In our democratic society at least, it does not shock us to think that a given man has a place in several such structures, and that he consequently comports himself in several divergent manners. But that very fact makes it the more puzzling to find wherein lies the unity and the continuity of the institution itself, and leads some people to insist that it really has neither. . . .

The thing which Baldwin calls the "principal role" of the institution is the perennial organizing principle of its moment-to-moment activity. It is the interpretation given by the present individuals to the conceptions inherited from their predecessors. Our thesis is that the institution, as a thing both past and present, can be best defined and certainly best studied through the roles which it has played and does now play. These roles exist in the minds of the people within and also of the people outside the institution. The something we call social sanction is a set of demands upon and expectations of a present group carrying the banner of its forebears.

II. THE LIFE CYCLE OF AN INSTITUTION   Even if one wishes to study that most tenuous feature of an institution, its spirit or function, one cannot do so significantly without observing men in action. The meeting to protest the price of eggs is not an institution; it has no past and probably no future. But it might become an institution.

In the study which follows we see a group of men gather for a purpose almost as specific as the lowering of the price of eggs. The very specificity of purpose required that they leave their wives and individual troubles at home; they assembled as real estate agents. In the brief period of forty-five years at least two business generations have come and gone. The group is acquiring a past, and with it, a role which transcends the lives of individual members. The very overtness of its beginning makes this group easy to study. It has kept a diary. Lloyd's of London had been growing and doing business for a century before it suddenly realized that it was an organized group. Tradition was first, and organization second. That story is harder to unearth, but the process had a time, place, and people just as truly as the Chicago Real Estate Board's beginnings.

Any institution may be studied as something which had a beginning, and which may grow old. In that it is like any of the behaving units which are known to us in the world of living things. "A family is a structure which has its own beginning and its own end. The beginning of a family as a phenomenon of social life . . . is set by a "Stammvater." But by which one? Has not every father in turn a father?"

. . . We hope in this study to give a point of view from which any institution at all may be understood, although the facts presented have a locus and a date. To achieve this purpose of presenting an institution in its typical rather than its unique aspects, we may conceive its beginning not as an event, but as the starting point of a process. Age becomes a matter, not of years, but of a cycle of change which is certain to occur if some external contingency does not intervene to bring it to an untimely end. A strange story is told of a boy who died of senile decay at the age of seven. Senility ordinarily occurs after the passage of a great and somewhat fixed number of years, but that should not divert our attention from the fact that old age is a matter of the changes within a man rather than of a number of annual journeys of the earth around the sun.

It is commonplace to say that an old institution is different from a newly initiated group, but it is less common to add that the difference between the two is inevitable. A new group cannot create tradition by fiat. An old one, no matter what its purpose, cannot avoid it. Tradition and stability are by-products of continued collective activity and of the turnover of generations. Old age overtakes institutions, as it does men, by stealth while they are engaged in pursuing their private ends. Once it arrives, both may be proud of it, although it is never the end and aim of life.

These inevitable changes which occur in the course of an institution's life constitute its life cycle. The most important of these changes is the building up of a body of tradition and precedent. This serves as spectacles through which living adherents of the institution see the present and pressing world. It gives them a sense of what things matter and how crises are to be met. If long isolation allows "the cake of custom" to become too thick, the institution may lose its capacity to act with reference to the world that is. It may become, as Bagehot said in his "Physics and Politics," incapable of discussion, and will resort to that device of the damned, impassioned oratory.

R. E. Park has stated two ideas fundamental to the consideration of the life cycle of an institution. The first is that the community is a constellation of institutions. The second says that an institution arises in a social movement. The simplest social movement is a spatial one, as suggested in the pithy phrase, "Die Familie beginnt mit dem Einwanderer."

The specific suggestion we have to make for the study of institutions follows from these two notions. It has to do with the role assumed by an institution and its counter confirmation or rejection by the community. The continuity of life of an institution, its life cycle, may be described in terms of its role from the moment it begins in a social movement until its demise. It is through its role or roles that an institution socializes successive generations of individuals to the point of acting through it and as part of it. Cooley comments on the "character and function" which enable the institution to live on. We might even call it entelechy or destiny.

This intimate and distinctive character of an institution might be compared to the theme of a symphony, continually recurring, and of which the whole organism of the music is a various unfolding. Like that it is a pattern through the web which this particular loom turns out. To ascertain this and set it forth may call for as much imagination and insight as to distinguish and describe the ego of a person. And like that it becomes, when we have grasped it, the focus of our study.[2]

One of the characteristics of a social movement is what W. I. Thomas calls "the redefinition of a situation." The redefinition begins in some sort of collective behavior, in which individuals are realigned in relation to each other and eventually to some object of action. In collective action a group is born. The temperance movement bore the Women's Christian Temperance Union, the Anti-Saloon League, and the Prohibition Party. These groups set out to create a new conception of "liquor" and the "liquor interests." Under their earnest and skillful hands the genial and florid spirit of German beer was transformed into a hideously leering John Barleycorn. To their eyes prohibition was the paramount issue before America. Their role was that of defining the attitude of the public and controlling the action of the body politic toward that issue. With that end gained, the situation is again redefined. The Prohibition party died of success. It scarcely became an institution before it played out. Votes are no longer needed. The parent group, the Anti-Saloon League, lives on, but its mission is slightly changed. It is now the enforcer of prohibition, a role which demands another type of action. The proper administrators must be appointed and kept in line. Success has raised the Anti-Saloon League to the estate of "vested interest." It has passed through more "institution years" than has the Socialist party in America, which latter is yet an insurgent and a reformer, although older in solar years. The Anti-Saloon League is repeating in a major key and masterful rhythm the theme it began in a pleading minor.

When, in the course of its life, the role of a group changes too violently, the problem arises whether it has retained its identity. "Is this the party of Thomas Jefferson?" On the other hand, certain changes are the natural result of the very action of the group. One

[2]   Cooley, "The Case Study of Small Institutions as a Method of Research," *Proceedings of the American Sociological Society*, XXII (1928), 150.

of these is the accumulation of tradition itself. Institutions develop
through certain characteristic phases, meeting crises each of which
presents alternatives. The most useful classification of institutions
would be in terms of these processes and the changing policy by
which it preserves some still more fundamental role to which its
identity hangs. The role assumed with its effects upon the community and countereffects upon the institution furnish a significant approach to the study of any institution considered as a going concern
and not as a logical abstraction. There lie the continuity and identity
of the institution.

III. TYPES OF INSTITUTIONS   At least two types of institutions may be distinguished on the basis of marked difference in the
social movements which give them life. One begins in a sect, as for
example the Methodist Episcopal Church. It began in "revivals."
Its motif was personal religion, originating in violent, thorough-
going, and regenerating conversion. The experience was presumed
to bring about equally violent revolutions in conduct. The presump-
tion was verified by fact in thousands of cases.

The Methodist movement was also a revolt against the Church.
Whatever new doctrine it had was incidental and has long been lost.
The articles of religion adopted by the Methodist Episcopal Church
a century and a half ago are those of the Church of England, slightly
expurgated. There are bishops, rituals, and legislative bodies. Yet
one would never mistake the Church of America for the Church of
England. The significant thing about the newer one is the role it
assumed as saver of souls and reformer of morals. Wesley was a de-
nouncer of questionable practices. The Methodist Episcopal Church
has a Bureau of Temperance and Public Morals with a bishop at its
head. The Anti-Saloon League was born and nursed, and grew to
a precocious maturity, in the bosom of this virile church. These are
developments in machinery necessary to the very role of the movement as it has come from its inception. The technique must change
as the movement becomes a firm institution.

Such changes are often assumed to represent fundamental
changes in the role of the institution. The sect, bitter and denuncia-
tory, possessed of the exclusive secrets and blessings of God, takes

itself apart to pray. It is an eccentric organization; perhaps it is insane, for its notion of itself is so absurd that the world may laugh at it when it does not persecute it otherwise. Grown to maturity, the sect is transformed into the powerful denomination, administered by men skilled in propaganda and political action, a force to be compromised with, not persecuted. The difference may not be in the fundamental role which governs its action. To be sure, the role is modified, just as is one's personality, by rebuffs and successes. The modifications are precisely what we should study; they constitute the life cycle.

A type of institution whose beginnings are less stormy and whose career appears less colorful arises from the conscious cooperation of competitors in a given occupation. Leadership in the sect is at first inspired. The group is spontaneous and expressive. In this second kind of group, indulgence in demonstrations is more likely to indicate approaching demise. It may reflect the inability of the competing persons to gain the consensus necessary to collective action. The medieval guilds became sectarian on their deathbeds. They were born in cool sanity and died in feverish delirium. The sect is born in delirium and becomes cool and canny in maturity.[3]

The particular institution which is the object of this study is of the cooler sort. A group of renting agents was organized for action with reference to certain immediate interests. The definition of these interests has changed with experience, and with the growth and the technique of the real estate business. If the interests of real estate owners and dealers have changed, or if they have been given broader and longer definition, usually it has been the Real Estate Board which has foreseen the change and has given the new definition.

If this institution turns evangelist and reformer, it does so in the interest of the real estate market and the agent's place in it. The Chicago Real Estate Board, in other words, is a distinctly secular organization, unromantic in its aims and practical in its methods.

Institutions based on occupation are no new thing under the sun. In a very simple agricultural society, the family may include

[3]   Kramer, *The Progress and Decline of the English Craft Guilds.*

the function of control with which such institutions are concerned.[4]
The rigid castes of India have had as one of their functions the
preservation of an occupational place for each. Rome had its guilds.
The members called each other "brother," feasted, worshiped, and
died together. Institutions of a similar sort grew up in the towns of
medieval Europe. They too had their celebrations, and also codes
of behavior which eventually became controlling moral obligations.

The established professions of today have each a tradition, a
role and a tenuous sort of organization. Each has its own history in
which it has come from the mere practice of a craft or a branch of
magic to a high estate. The dentists have scarcely got up the ladder.
The surgeons some generations ago parted company with their
fellow wielders of the edged tool, the guild of barbers. There are life
cycles of occupations. A profession represents a point in the cycle;
it is old, controlled, and highbrow.

Of recent years numerous new occupations have seen the light,
although some start in the dark. Real estate dealing is but one. Its
life cycle appears in the following account.

The Natural History of Land as a Commodity

Although human society has always and everywhere had its
feet on the ground, land has not always been for sale. Herein lies the
story of whole societies and their relation to the land on which they
rest. The dependence of a plant upon the soil in which its roots are
imbedded is complete, direct and not to be trifled with on pain of
death. The deeper its roots and the higher its limbs, the more unal-
terable is its position. A man is equally dependent upon the land,
but never quite so mortally fixed to a spot. He has legs, not roots.
Yet his legs and his power-driven seven-league boots have not made
the individual man equally at home in all places and all climes.

Modern men have spied out and possessed new lands in the
name of the cross, the king, and the home market. Trade stretches
to remote corners and multiplies more than apace. The individual
man gets his wants satisfied by a bit of this from one continent, a bit

---

[4]   Durkheim, *De la division du travail social*, Preface à la deuxième
édition, "Quelques remarques sur les groupements professionels."

of that from some island, and himself uses the earth for little except a sidewalk. Wages and prices are his seismographs, delicately set to record a drought in the Cuban sugar country or tightness in Lombard Street. The plant is mortally sensitive to its root soil. The ultimate man may be lightly sensitive to the fertility of all parts of the earth.

The above refers to economic dependence; there is also a sentimental attachment to places. The relation between the two involves the whole history of man. Perhaps the man does not live whose body and soul synchronize in their wanderings; nor is there one so indifferent to all places as was Kipling's proud cat. The European immigrant is accused of filling his stomach in America, while his spirit hovers with congenial kin about his native church tower. From the dispersion until now the Jew has prayed that his bones might rest in Palestine with the holy dust of the patriarchs. Meanwhile he has pursued earthly fortune in strange lands. His Palestine has naught to do with the bargain counter. Mecca and Zion are not for sale.

Where man nourishes both body and soul from one soil, there is the true homeland. In such a place sentimental and economic value meet. It is thus that Reymont pictures the Polish peasant on his land, Zola, the French peasant; and thus is the Chinese villager described.[5]

As the attachment of men to the soil varies, so varies the scheme of value put upon it and the method of transfer. In Romania, it takes a revolution to change ownership; in England, perhaps a death. In the hotel, one writes his name in the book, and rests for a night.

Strictly speaking, there is never transfer of land, for it is immovable. But men move or are moved from one place to another. In the measure that they move, land becomes a commodity.[6]

LAND WITH A PRICE: THE CITY   The large city is at once the place of least personal attachment to and the greatest scarcity

[5]   Reymont, *The Peasants*; Zola, *La Terre*.
[6]   Ely and Morehouse, *Elements of Land Economics*, "The Physical Characteristics of Land."

of land. The struggle for "standing room" is manifest in the crowding of the sidewalks and the height of buildings. The latter varies, roughly speaking, directly as the number of people who frequent different parts of the city's area.[7]

Within the city every individual is in constant need of a place to sleep, and every shop must have a place of business. For each class of person and for each type of enterprise, there is a natural habitat where he may thrive best. For it, he must pay. The wolf at the city widow's door is a rent collector. The first charge against the gross income of a business is likewise the rent. Real estate men have classified businesses precisely on the basis of the percentage of income which they can afford to turn to this paramount item.

This gives a paradoxical turn to our statement that there is less personal attachment to land in the city than elsewhere. The answer is that the value of land in the city is secular and always capable of being expressed in terms of money. Individuals and even businesses move about restlessly from one location to another.

Freedom of movement inheres in the very manner in which an urban population grows. The large city has drawn its population from the country and from smaller towns. This may not be so obvious in Europe, but it is true even of old cities.[8] The newest city is the one which has drawn most of its population from elsewhere. Chicago has grown from naught to three millions in less than a century. Many of its inhabitants are here only after a series of moves. Some have made a revolutionary journey from their ancestral villages in Europe. If these mobilized persons have any sentimental tie to the land, it is not to that where they now live.

Their wanderings do not cease when they enter the city. Two hundred thousand people were expected to move on or about the first of May 1927. The color of the walls or the height of the kitchen sink may send the flatwife hunting for a new cage. Many of the moves are aimless, as those of the hobo who wanders by day and sleeps in a "flophouse" at night. Others are for social advantage, to escape from one's own nationality, or to "keep up with the Joneses."

7   Ely and Morehouse, 19.
8   See Redford, *Labour Migration in England, 1800–1850*, for a description of the cityward trek and its social repercussions.

Others reflect mere increase or decrease in income. The apartment-house dweller is a tenant who owes his landlord nothing but the rent.

An apparent exception to this emancipation from the land is the land-hungry peasant who finds in America his first opportunity to realize his dream. The Chicago Tribune of 1883 tells us of Bohemian Building and Loan Associations. The Pole also is notoriously bent on acquiring a stake in the land, but he finds one parcel of real estate as good as another, provided there is the prospect of selling at a profit. A residence in the basement may be good enough for one of these land misers if only he may collect the rents from the other tenants.

The mobility of persons and institutions within the city has another expression in the change of uses to which land is put. As the city grows, as its various districts increase in area, and displace others, any given piece of land will change in use. It may even have a succession of buildings upon it; if not, the old one will be remodeled for successive types of tenants. This is one of the corollaries of the process described by E. W. Burgess in his article, "The Growth of the City."[9]

Each change of residence of a family involves a transfer of land, or at least a transfer of the right to use floor space in a building. Change of type of use involves a more fundamental transfer, such as a long-time lease or a sale. When such a transfer is to be made, the value of the land comes to articulation in a price. Strictly speaking, there is no price excerpt there be the possibility of sale. In the process which we have been describing, every parcel of land in or near an urban center tends to be priced for actual sale, not only once, but frequently. When the new use finds the scarcity of land acute enough, it will pay the price for the surrounding area and will get it.

Some areas of the city resist such encroachment, by putting other values ahead of price. Property owners banded together to present a solid wall of resistance to the invasion of Negroes on the south side. Eventually price broke the line; once broken, it crumbled. Suburban communities have attempted to keep "undesirables"

[9]   Park and Burgess, *The City*, 50. Also Ely and Morehouse, chap. 3, "The Classification of Land."

out of their sacred precincts. Berwyn and Riverside, to the west of Chicago, have succumbed to flank attacks from Twenty-Second Street, one of the city's avenues for advancement of the foreign born. There is a limit even to the stiffness of village pride.

Churches in or about the "Loop" are potential garages. Residences of the first families furnish quarters of appropriately faded elegance for the roomer and the Bohemian. A few shrines and landmarks resist the desecrating money changers, as does Trinity burial ground at the head of Wall Street. On the whole, however, land in a large American city has lost all value except that of impersonal and secular price in dollars. Space is leased by the cubic foot, and "sky leases" are drawn to secure profit from the space over railway tracks.

Students of the family are now contending that the divorce rate does not correlate so nicely with race, religion, or income as with mobility. Where people move most frequently, the family is in most danger. Some sections of the city, indeed, have not families but footloose and transient individuals. Such social atoms are apt to be politically and socially disfranchised, as Zorbaugh has indicated in "The Gold Coast and the Slum." People who merely tarry in a neighborhood neither know it nor take pride in it. The apartment-house dweller, according to what evidence can be got, goes to the church which is closest, if to any. He gets his religion, as well as his groceries, delicatessen style. In short, the mobility of the city dweller is reflected in the secularization not only of land, but of political life, social organization, and once sacred institutions. Movement always tends to dissolve an existing social order. This is no less true of cityward migration and urban flux than of a barbarian invasion of the Imperial City.[10]

To make a commodity is first of all to make an article movable at will. Man is the article which must move to make land a commodity. He does so in the city. In the maze of real estate transactions which results, flourishes the real estate man. His trade is urban and secular. Land is as near a perfect commodity as the nature of the city and his own efforts can make it. The more nomadic

[10]   Mowrer, *Family Disorganization*; Anderson, *The Hobo*; Zorbaugh, *The Gold Coast and the Slum*; Hayner, *A Study of Hotel Life* (Ms).

the city dweller, the more the real estate agent flourishes. His success is commensurate with the degree to which he can remove from land the halo of sacred sentiment and put into its place the secular value of money.

The Chicago Real Estate Board in Its Cradle

"The oldest, largest, and most influential Real Estate Board in the world." This inscription on its literature, states tersely, if not too humbly, the claim of the Real Estate Board to prestige. Leaving aside the matter of size, age does seem to lend a measure of both stability and adaptability to human associations. The very specific purpose of a new occupational group, or the uncompromising tenets of a new sect may be its undoing. The mortality of associations is perhaps greatest in their early days. The old institution may be so altered that its founders would not recognize it. Part of our purpose is to show how some of these alterations grow naturally out of the very process of engaging collectively in some activity for a long time.

The natural place to begin is with the general situation in which the Real Estate Board began, with the specific purposes which they had in mind, and with the way in which they defined and met their first problems.

I. THE CHICAGO OF THE EIGHTIES   The Chicago of the eighties had just emerged from the "boom town" stage, to that phase in which increase of population seems to proceed by addition rather than by multiplication, but in which the annual numerical increase is greater than ever before. In the forties the population had been multiplied by seven; in the fifties, by four; in the sixties, by a little less than three; in the seventies, by two; and in the eighties, again by two. In 1890, there were 1,099,850 people in Chicago. To compress a million people into some square miles of prairie and swamp within fifty years required activity. When the central part of the young city was burned and a new start made, the activity became a scramble. Chicago real estate men built their shacks in the ashes, and tried to put in order the chaos prevailing in both building and in land titles. They never have denied their intention to make money from the enterprise.

In spite of its "boom" spirit, there were things which seemed impossible to the Chicago of that day. In 1881, George M. Pullman built his model manufacturing town on Lake Calumet; far enough away, he thought, never to be absorbed by the city. A more than enterprising firm opened a subdivision in Hyde Park, and was laughed at. Twelfth Street was too remote a residence for one who hoped to be in the social swim. The idea of building an opera house on East Washington Street was ridiculed on the ground that no one would go so far east to attend a concert. The "Loop" was just turning itself about to face Lake Michigan instead of the main and south branches of the Chicago River.[11]

Although individual enterprise had unbounded optimism in those days, the interests already vested in the center of the city were jealous lest some suburb outstrip the city. The plan for the Belt Line railway to facilitate freight transfer, was condemned lest it take business from downtown.[12] Even many years later, the Chicago Real Estate Board desired the removal of a government engineer who recommended development of the Calumet Harbor, which was still considered a rival to the Chicago River harbor. The World's Fair of 1893 gave Chicago a burst of expansion to the south; a spurt that is still remembered as the bane of many a real estate business in the years which followed.[13] In spite of the city's rapid growth, the men who organized the Real Estate Board in 1883 meant the present "Loop" and its immediate vicinity when they said "Chicago." The center of the city was something to be nursed, and even to be protected from its own suburban offspring.

II. THE CHICAGO REAL ESTATE AND RENTING AGENTS' ASSOCIATION   Two organizations of real estate brokers had failed in Chicago before the present one got under way in 1883. A charter

[11]   *The Chicago Real Estate Board Bulletin, Historical Sketches,* 1910. This bulletin will be abbreviated as *CREBB.*
[12]   Ibid., XIX, 134.
[13]   H. M. Bodfish. "Real Estate Activity in Chicago Accompanying the World's Fair of 1893," *Journal of Land and Public Utility Economics,* LV (1928), 405–16.

member of the present Board attributed these failures to a too narrow conception of the ends which the real estate men might collectively pursue.

Anxiety as to the ultimate success of the organization was felt by many of those present (at the first meeting) on account of the two previous attempts along similar lines, which had resulted in failure. The men, however, who were present at this meeting were of the "I will" order and had large views as to the position which such an organization should fill in our community. This is evidenced by the fact that while early records show action taken on commission rates, forcible entry and detainer suits, legal forms, leases and such matters relating to an agency office, the predominant questions are of a broad character, relating to the future of the city and improvement of its physical and governmental conditions. It was through these latter lines that the Board has grown to be a power in the community. For illustration, I find that the question of tax reform and assessment of property has been a recurring subject, beginning within a year after the Board's organization, and the improved system now in vogue, although far from being ideal, is the result of continued agitation and legislative action, secured by our Board. In this way the *taxpayer* and the *tax-eater* were forced to recognize the Chicago Real Estate Board![14]

We have here the notion that the new organization was to have a hand in those political affairs which concerned real estate interests. The agents had already begun to separate the community into tax-paying sheep, and tax-devouring wolves. The real estate agents were to be the protecting watchdog of the innocent, productive flock.

The words of the resolution to form the organization emphasized the narrower interests of the agents. "Resolved, that it is the sense of the meeting that an organization of REAL ESTATE RENTING AGENTS be formed for mutual protection, and to advance the interests of property in their charge."[15] The Articles of Incorporation of the Chicago Real Estate and Renting Agent's Association stated the purpose even more pointedly: "The object for which it is formed is to secure more system and uniformity in the renting, care

[14]   Wyllys W. Baird, *CREBB*, XIX, 281. Also *Call Board Bulletin* (*CBB*), IX, 7; *CREBB*, XXIII, 1819.
[15]   *Historical Sketch, CBB*, 1892.

and management of real estate in the City of Chicago; to better protect and promote the interests of those entrusting propery to their
care; to protect themselves and their clients against dishonest and
immoral tenants, and to generally correct existing abuses and prevent their future occurrence."[16]

A year later, the organization gave itself a more dignified name
and removed the unveiled insult to the tenant. "The name of such
corporation is 'The Chicago Real Estate Board,' and the object for
which this Association is formed is to enable its members to transact
their buisness, connected with the buying, selling, renting and
caring for real estate, and the loaning of money upon the same to
better advantage than heretofore by the adoption of such rules and
regulations as they may deem proper, and by enabling them to take
united action upon such matters as may be deemed for the common
good."[17]

Under its new name, the organization was not the less concerned
with the essential, but wayward, tenant. One of its first acts was to
develop a system of rating tenants according to their paying habits
and care of premises. The scheme failed, but was soon revived and
has been kept in force ever since.[18]

The press of the day recognized at once that the new guild stood
on the grinding landlord's side of the fence. The Chicago Tribune
of March 18, 1883, under the heading, "The New Brass-Bound and
Iron-Clad Lease," commented that in the uniform lease drawn up
by the Board, "the tenant promises to do everything, and that all the
landlord agrees to do is to receive the rent in advance." The same
paper, a week later, commented on the eagerness of landlords to
build flimsy flats to be rented at high prices to the rapidly increasing population of Chicago, and suggested that it was the tenant who
really needed a champion.

Another press account refers to a lawsuit over renting commissions, with the comment, "It should be a warning to agents and
others trying to steal commissions." A broker tells in the same
paper of being maligned for refusing to break a lease which he
had unwittingly made to a young harlot. In March of that year the

[16]   By-laws, The Chicago Real Estate Board (1910), 3.
[17]   Ibid., 9.
[18]   Historical Sketch, CBB, 1892.

city council passed a revenue ordinance requiring an annual license fee of $50 from each real estate broker. The Board agreed to fight the measure as individuals. A week later the ordinance was reconsidered, in spite of a man of the people who rose to protest intimidation of the city council by the "interests."[19] The theme of *demos* against the "interests" runs through the entire history of this organization; it is a major theme of modern life.

In 1888, the Chicago Real Estate Board established its official publication, the *Call Board Bulletin*, containing minutes of meetings, advertisements of members' businesses, and notices of real estate sales. The first issue of the Bulletin protested against cable cars being allowed on Jackson Street bridge, which had hitherto been reserved for carriages. It suggested that since property owners had paid for the bridge, Mr. Yerkes should build a tunnel at his own expense for his streetcars. The Board had commenced its concern with public improvements in relation to land values and tax rates.[20]

In 1887, the Board offered its rooms as the place for the judicial sales of land by the county. The offer was accepted, and such sales are still held in its headquarters. In addition, a real estate market was held there once a week. Thus began a simple exchange of information as to "offerings and wants" between the member firms.[21]

The Chicago Title and Trust Company was even then advertising its possession of "the one complete record of titles to real estate in Cook County from the U.S. Government down to date."[22] Since this company had titles to sell, and since the real estate man was in daily need of them, the Board was concerned with the affairs of this company from the start.

The first issue of the bulletin also contained news of a Revenue Reform League, consisting of real estate men and property owners, which was seeking equalization of assessments and reduction of the expenses of tax collection.[23]

An early president of the Board summarized the recurrent troubles of the real estate man as follows:

[19]   Chicago Tribune, March 6, 13, and 25, and April 15, 1883.
[20]   *CBB*, I, 13.
[21]   *CREBB*, XIX, 282; *CBB*, I, 75.
[22]   *CBB*, II, 2.
[23]   *CBB*, I, 8.

There are a multitude of questions which may profitably and properly find discussion in the pages of the bulletin. The subject of exclusive agency in its relation to both the agent and the owner. The abuses of legal prerogative in title examinations. Upon what principles of determining prices should we make our valuations? Rapid transit with its correlatives of damage and betterments. To what extent is a purchaser justified in requiring evidences and assurances as to the flawlessness of titles? Are we not possibly drifting into too great technicality and encouraging unwarranted exactions on the part of the buyer of realty? Can real estate in general be made a successful auction commodity? Is the rapid rise of real estate in western cities based on solid reasons —Is it safe and is it desirable? [24]

A resume of the same problems is contained in verses written for the Board's fifth birthday.

> In 1909
> Then Cummings the revenue bill will reform,
> And Yerkes will then keep the streetcars all warm;
> Percy Palmer's long leases will take a new form.
>
> Then brokers for buyers will not have to hunt;
> The Illinois Central won't have the lake front;
> Then twenty-six stories will not be thought high,
> And Kerfoot to build them still higher will try.
>
> To "split a commission" will then be a sin.
> Then all the "For Sale" signs will be taken down,
> Bob Givens will auction away the whole town.
> The census compiler will then write us down,
> Nineteen Hundred Thousand and Nine.
>
> All real estate men will belong to the Board,
> To pay for a license they all will afford.
> And the Bogue and Hoyt "Hyde Park" will have sold.
> A broker's "I.O.U." will be good as gold. . . .
>
> All real estate sharks will get left in the lurch
> The buzzard of peace on our banner will perch
> And Lumly Ingledew
> Will sell the First Methodist Church
> In 1909. [25]

24   *CBB*, I, 3.
25   *CBB*, I, 49.

These lines—as do others written in a humorous and celebrating vein,—give us the central issues which these men conceived as the basis of their cooperative activity. The fact that they were sung at a convivial gathering indicated that the members of the Chicago Real Estate Board had achieved some degree of esprit de corps. They had not, to be sure, and have not yet, that sense of corporate solidarity which expresses itself in hymns of exultation, calling each other "brother," and burying their dead with solemn festivity in a common cemetery.

Given some sense of integration through continuing common interests, and an incipient sentiment of common pride in their organization, these men had begot something which would naturally grow into permanent institutional form. They were businessmen, and as such were inclined to conceive their relationships in the free terms of individual enterprise and cash. But even businessmen may, under certain circumstances, socialize and institutionalize their purposes and interests, thus limiting their individual initiative and freedom of action. Where there is an institution, the individual is held in control in the aspect of life with which the institution deals. The general lines which that control was to take in the Chicago Real Estate Board are to be seen in these early expressions.

Crises and the Life Cycle

I. THE CRISIS   There are practical limitations to the proposition that if one were to know all about one thing he would know all about everything. Yet even the modest proceed by the method of formulating hypotheses for a class of things after having observed one specimen rather closely. All science consists in the application of what we know rather well about some things to other things which we do not know so well. With this apologia we dare make some suggestions about institutions.

In our introduction it was suggested that the natural history of an institution might best be conceived by tracing a series of situations through which it passes and to each of which it acts. The more acute of these situations are crises. The institution, through its functionaries and by use of its previously acquired precedents and ideas, attempts to define the unprecedented situation and to line up its adherents and its appropriate sectors of the public for action. Insofar as the institution be secular and objective, it will tend to accommodate itself to the situation. Such an institution, like Napoleon, lives outside itself. Insofar as it be sectarian, it will enter into conflict. It may retire from the world, as did the Mormons when persecution beset them, and become a community to itself. It may split, and two sects will grow where one grew before.[26]

An institution will not ordinarily be amenable to a flat classification as either secular or sectarian. It is probably better to say that each has its own complex of secular objects and their corresponding defined situations, and also its sacred objects for which it will fight and bleed. As time goes on, these may change. What was sacred may become secular; what was secular may gather a halo of tradition. Thus any classification of institutions will involve behavior in the face of certain typical crises. The traits by which we distinguish institutions from other social forms correspond to and are elucidated by these typical situations.

(a) *Membership and Functionary Crises.* Many groups trace their origin to some crises. Many, likewise, die with the solution of that initial situation. Such a crisis may find its expression in a leader, about whom a group of disciples gathers for emotional expression or action. Often the group ends with the death of the leader. Indeed, the first change of leaders is often a Thermopylae to the institution in process. The sect with inspired leadership has great difficulty in selecting a second apostle.[27] The dictator,

[26]   In the early days of the Methodist Episcopal Church a number of lesser sects split from the main branch. They were protests against the very tendency of the sect to become more secular. The Methodist Protestants would have no bishops, for they considered that Methodism was an escape from bishops. The Free Methodists, the primitive Methodists, the United Brethren, and the Evangelical Church all split off to remain true to the spirit of the movement. No such splits have occurred for a long time. From the mature but still vigorous institution defection is more likely to be individual. It will consist of individual rebels and the emancipated.

[27]   The Zion City sect had Alexander Dowie as its "First Apostle." The members of the sect were under oath, as he said, "to God, to myself as Elijah the Restorer, foretold by Malachi, by St. Peter, and by the Christ himself" (Harlan, *Alexander Dowie*, 4). Such a leader can be displaced only by death or by revolt. Dowie was displaced by the latter, and his

unique and without predecessor, seldom has a genuine successor.

As the sect is transformed into an institution, it develops a mechanism, perhaps by ordeal, for transfer of leadership to a new personnel. The pope still rules by appointment of God, but the appointment is confirmed by a college of cardinals, which is almost invariably inspired to elect an Italian. To insure smooth succession, the group must develop somewhat distinct criteria of prestige whereby the next set of leaders may be recognized and elevated to office.

In the group which we have studied there was never any notion of divine leadership. A strong tendency appears for the effective choice of leaders to be made by those who are themselves already leaders. The membership at large usually ratifies the choice. Occasionally the introduction of a large number of members of slightly different stamp results in a mild leadership crisis, which breaks the continuity but slightly. The inner circle carries on; the others object occasionally.

It proved that the Subscribers, convened at General Meetings, have on various occasions, exercised a supreme authority. . . . These occasional interferences, however, appear to have been the impulse of the moment, and have led to no regular system of Rules and Regulations for the future government of the House Committee, who have been again left to a discretionary exercise of power, till some of the Subscribers, thinking they had exceeded its just limits, again restrained or

---

place taken by Voliva, who controlled the group in much the same way, but did not call himself Apostle. In the Mormon society, the Prophet Joseph Smith was succeeded by Brigham Young who held himself responsible only to God and the deceased Prophet. (Werner, *Brigham Young*, 266). He thereby created a new place for himself, as the earthly representative of the unique original leader of the sect. The Amana sect chose its leader by "inspiration" but it had also a group of "temporal" leaders who were elected annually (Nordhoff, *Communistic Societies*, 37). Zion City has founded a college in which future leaders are to be trained. Mormonism ceased to be a simon-pure sect when its first generation of leaders died and born Mormons took the place of those violently converted from the "world." It will be interesting to see what Soviet Russia will be like when it has leaders who were born and educated under the Soviet regime.

controlled them in the particular instance, by taking the Sense of a General Meeting; and then left them to go on, as before.[28]

Such is the pattern of activity and leadership in a secular institution. Finally, certain activities are carried on by professional functionaries whose term of office is not coincident with that of amateur officers and influential members. The professional functionaries add continuity to activity.[29]

The mustering out of an army produced the Grand Army of the Republic at the close of the Civil War, and the American Legion at the close of the Great War. The former is hanging to dear life, but will soon bid farewell to this earth. The latter persists for the present, and has acquired the chief characteristics of an institution—functionaries, adherents, and a none too modest but well-defined role. It lacks only the potentiality of reproducing the spirit of the returned hero in succeeding generations. Its final crisis will involve that failing.

The permanence of any institution depends upon just this reproduction of successive generations of persons with the interests, sentiments and notions of prestige which will cause them, first, to become identified with the institution, and, second, to conform to the type of behavior necessary to the preservation of the institution's role. The production of these generations of adherents roots in the culture and the economy of the community.

What is begun in the underlying conceptions and economy of the community is brought to completion within the institution itself. The candidate is initiated and educated into the social attitudes which preserve the institution. The process reaches its final goal in the production of professional functionaries whose interest

[28]   From a report of a Special Committee appointed to suggest a set of rules for the operation of Lloyd's, in the year 1811. Quoted in Wright and Fayle, *A History of Lloyd's*, 268.

[29]   The whole study of leadership would receive an impetus if students would take their eyes off so-called general characteristics of leaders, and turn to these two items: (1) the criteria of prestige in particular behaving groups, and (2) the nature of the interaction between the functionary whose interest is consecutive and the amateur adherent whose interest tends to be personal and episodic.

in the institution is continuous and expert. We suggest as one of the characteristics of a mature institution its capacity to produce a continuous stream of persons of the sorts necessary for its continued existence.

The maturity of the institution lies further in the elaboration and definition of types of persons, each with distinctive functions within the group and with equally definite relationships to each other and the rest of the world. This is social sanction in the fullest sense: to produce carriers of the code and policy which represent the function of the institution. England produces no boy who wants to be President. French Quebec is said to produce the nuns for all of Canada and many for the United States. The slums of the city produce politicians, but few clergymen. New England produces scientists and other scholars beyond its fair share; Virginia produces military men. Governments are aware of the principle behind these facts, and make their educational policies to fit. Sometimes it even becomes a problem to produce mothers.

Every moment of the life of an institution is a potential crisis in this connection. If, for howsoever brief a time, the stream dries up, the institution is at an end. The crisis of personnel is also a code crisis, for the code lives in the persons who make up the institution at a given moment. The effectiveness of the code is always conditioned by the new people who come into the group. This is true of the number as well as types of persons. This aspect of the Chicago Real Estate Board has been considered under the membership policy and with reference to types of real estate men.

Conversely, the institution resolves crises in the lives of the individuals who are attached to it. A ceremony celebrates in some conventional way the event which the individual could not meet alone. It may avenge a wrong done to the person, as does the family in some societies. It may try his case at law, as does the real estate board or the medical fraternity. The church has a funeral ceremony which takes our attention from our individual loss. The shock of change from single life is softened under the excitement of the nuptials. There is even a ceremony for absolution from sin; our sin is not our own, but that of mankind. It is washed away in one grand sacrifice, shared by all the elect. One need only present himself periodically to have forgiveness renewed in due form; he need not face each sin alone.

(b) *The Policy Crisis.* If a group arise in a crisis, and fail to redefine its role after its first failure or success, it will automatically die. For instance, when rents are high and dwellings scarce, Tenants' Protective Associations swarm up like Green Bay flies. Like the flies, they are gone when the sun rises. We call the type of crisis in question a policy crisis rather than a crisis in the role of the group because generally it arises in connection with some specific action. The people in an institution do not often say to themselves, "Shall we change the fundamental role of our group?" They do question the particular action thus, "Is this or not in accordance with the role of our group?"

The group becomes an institution by making its role perennial rather than episodic. It concerns itself with situations which are recurrent. It is the functionary above all who serves to sort out the recurrent from the occasional problem, and to put the policy into relatively permanent terms. As the group grows older, its function-aries gain vision and a feeling for what is ultimately important. They put every occurrence into a setting of its future consequences. Thus the policy becomes well established and precedents are care-fully watched.

A crisis is forced from without when some other force upsets the balance of power among the institutions of the community. A labor group may challenge the Real Estate Board's role as representative of the landlord. A change in the technique of financing land transfer may cause it to struggle and face about in its policy in regard to real estate corporations. The too rapid change of use of property may lead it to invade the sacred property rights which it is pre-sumed to defend.

It is just at this point that the institution brings sacred objects out of their shrines and puts them on the dissenting table. In such cases the final, irreducible essence of the institution's role is re-vealed. When there arises a crisis which it can not or will not solve by the collective secularization of the elements involved, then the very existence of the institution is jeopardized. In their prime, the guilds compromised with each other. In their old age, new types of manufacture and foreign goods threatened them. They could no longer compromise. The very interests of the individual members became divergent; each saved his hide as best he could. The guilds could no longer exist. The community intervened and put them out of their misery. Adherents, function, and sanction disappeared in a lump.

Thus far, the Chicago Real Estate Board has met no such crisis. Should the very fact of real estate agency be threatened, the institution could not conceivably compromise the situation without changing itself beyond recognition. The individual members might escape into other businesses. The function, the actuality of their group would be gone.

Some group might then make a ritual of the usual procedure of the meetings of the Board, and found a lodge of ancient free and accepted real estate agents. It would then become an esoteric society whose behavior would be expressive. Perhaps they would present dramatic conceptions of selling real estate to gullible buyers, and give high-sounding names to the parts of the players as in a communion service or in the ceremonies of a secret society. In this reincarnation the institution would assume the role of the elect. Conflicts might arise as to which possessed the true ritual, and which was the real successor to the original group. Sects might even arise, revivals could be held, and an apostolic succession developed. There are historical precedents for events as fanciful as these.

(c) *The Position Crisis.* An institution has its roots in a community. It has position. In the modern world the removal of its adherents often forces the institution to be transplanted. In every city of considerable size one finds institutions which have moved and others which have been left behind in changed communities where they strive in vain to exist. The church furnishes a tangible example because it has a sacred building which remains as a forlorn monument when its people depart. The abandoned church, the downtown church, the institutional church, and the mission are types whose present nature is a result of the movement of people in the city.[30] The growth of the city may also bring rivals which threaten the place of existing institutions.

Migrations of its adherents may result in that peculiar triangle

[30]   Kincheloe, "Major Reactions of City Churches," *Religious Education*, XXIII, 868–74.

of functionary, patron, and clientele which one finds in the institutional church. Such an institution gives full play to the functionary, who secures financial support from absentee patrons by the use of sentimental appeals, and ministers to suppliant clients who may curse the hand that feeds them.[31] Such an institution must have three policies; one for the patrons, another for the frequenters, and a third for the functionaries themselves.

In America we have a group of institutions whose presence is due to the immigration of European peoples. The Russian church established branches here. It seems not to have adopted itself to the changes which took place in its transplanted communicants. Revolts have flared up against the very type of church governments which the Russians accepted in docile silence at home.[32] The writer attended a series of meetings at which Lithuanian Catholics demanded that their priest allow an audit of the parish accounts. In New England there is bitter conflict between Irish clergy and French Canadian laymen. At home the French Canadian is unspeakably loyal to his church; in New England a number of them have refused to obey even on threat of excommunication.[33]

The foreign-language newspaper is a result of migration, but it is usually a brand new institution developed to meet the cultural crisis of the immigrant people. The high mortality of such newspapers, as shown by Park in *The Immigrant Press*, indicates that the normal life cycle of such ends as the crisis is dissolved by the Americanization of its readers. In other cases differences of a sectarian sort bring them to violent ends even before the readers are assimilated.

Probably no institution remains unaltered when removed to a new community. Some are immovable by nature. The castes of India are rooted to the spot; removal would destroy their sacred character. Others can be moved, but show modification. The village

---

31   In such cases one might better say that the patron is the client for it is he whom the functionary must satisfy and keep. Those who receive the service are casual customers, who come and go according to their need or liking one's brand of goods.
32   Davis, *The Russian Immigrant*, 34.
33   *La Presse* (Montreal), April 10, 1928, et passim.

church changes its character in a city apartment house area; it may have to advertise and hire a paid staff to do what the village elders and wives did for the love of it.

The very modifications resulting from the slipping of a community from under the institution or from the removal of institution itself but emphasize the importance of a deep-rooting of the institution in a cultural base. The immigrant institutions of America are only quasi or marginal institutions. Time will tell which of them will persist with permanent roles in the new world.

Not all institutions require so firm a rooting in a cultural base as do those mentioned above. As a general proposition it is probably true that the more sacred an institution is and the more it depends upon personal loyalty, the greater its dependence upon a cultural base. The more secular institutions, and especially such a thing as a stock market, seem to get their spatial location with reference to factors much more complicated than the mere place of residence of some group of people.

The Chicago Real Estate Board has its office near the places of business of its members. Since the institution does not concern itself with their private lives, it need not know the home addresses of the Realtors. The places of business, in turn, find their places in relation to each other. Thus we have the tendency of this and other institutions like it to find a place in the specialized central districts of large cities. They find position not with reference to the home, which is the ultimate base of culture and loyalty, but with reference to professional and commercial movements and activities. Hence such institutions face a crisis not when their people move, but when these specialized movements are dislocated. This is one of the problems with which human ecology is concerned.

(d) *The Distribution of Institutions.* Under the name of Human Ecology, interest has lately been turned to the distribution of people and institutions over the surface of the earth. The problem is not simply the relation of man and his communities to the earth itself; the primary interest is in those processes whereby men, and their institutions, move about in relation to each other, and what happens to them in the moving.

It is apparent that among the factors in the distribution of communities are the complex movements of goods. One may visualize an inclusive process of movement and location in which men and goods participate. In this process have grown up centers which perform specialized services to other parts or perhaps all of the world. London, for example, is called the "world ledger." R. D. McKenzie has developed the notion of "dominance" to express the relationship of centers of communities to their peripheries.[34]

In one of its aspects such a center is the place where exists a set of specialized institutions. London is the place where the functionaries of credit, insurance, and trade intelligence operate with a technique and a universe of discourse all their own. London also either produces or attracts the men who are possessed of the genius to continue its primacy in worldwide transactions. It is the center of credit institutions.

Likewise it has been noticed that, within a city, institutions find spatial relationship to each other. Each has its "natural habitat." The mission, the settlement house, the labor hall: each finds its proper place. The downtown district presents a concentration of those institutions which spread their influence over the community but are dependent for their location upon the distribution of other institutions about them and, finally, upon the distribution of the population. It is a mutual dependence, for once the community is established, the very distribution of population is conditioned by what already exists at the center. In London, the center is significantly called "the City."

The human ecologists have also put new emphasis upon the frontier. The frontier is the periphery of an expanding community. It may be an open expanse, where further extension of the community finds no barrier except nature, and no inducement except pressure from within combined with the lure of Eldorado. The frontier may also be another community, as the Orient. In either case, the community extends itself by taking with it its own institutions. But they must be adapted to new conditions. Even new institutions may arise to meet the emergencies of the case. When the frontier is extended at the expense of existing communities, as in

[34]   McKenzie, "The Ecological Approach to the Study of the Human Community," *American Journal of Sociology*, XXX, 287.

the Orient, the resulting institutions may bear the marks of both communities. The protectorate is an example. In any case the frontier is a place of change, an important aspect of which is the disorganization and reorganization of institutions.

Even the city may be considered a frontier in one respect. It is a place where new occupations and interests are continually being developed, and where immigrating peoples are being initiated into an economic and social life which is strange to them.[35] The institutions of the city present an adaptation in the wake of these processes.

If one could present every conceivable type of crisis which might have to be faced by an institution, he would have thereby a pattern into which the life cycle of any institution might be cast. In terms of adaptations to such we classify an institution as sectarian or secular; as young, mature, or old. Tradition is but a deposit of action in the face of crises. Indeed, it is with reference to these typical crises and their consequences that we see the traits in terms of which we distinguish the social institutions.

II. INSTITUTIONS AS SOCIAL FORCES   A good deal of the controversy as to the nature of the units of which society is made could be avoided if the purpose of the analysis were made clear. One may descend from the Great Society to some social atom. Each unit on which he fixes attention may be equally real. All will be essentially hypothetical. It may be true that each person involved in a political landslide may be reduced to electrons, neurons, and glands. But to study the landslide or a zoning movement in terms of electrons or of glands illuminates the nature of neither the electron nor the movement. Behind what he sees in a laboratory the observer's imagination pictures the nerve response and the conditioned reflex. Behind human experience, he sees persons, institutions, or even a Great Society, according to the focus of his attention.

The student of crime fixes on the person as the unit which offers

35   Sombart has discussed this process of the accommodation of people to new economic and social systems in a very comprehensive manner. Cf. *Hochkapitalismus.*

the best insight to his problem. The person exists and is defined in terms of his own organization of impulses and also in terms of his relationships to social groups. For certain purposes, the institution itself is the most fruitful unit of investigation. In studying it one must recognize the persons in whom it exists. We have already noticed that successive generations of persons are initiated into an institution, live in it, and then die or leave it. Some associations of men, on the contrary, are brief. They flare up and die; yet for the moment they act as units and impress themselves upon our experience. The institution has an existence of its own for the observer who is trying to describe the continuity and organization of society. When we say that a community is a constellation of institutions, we are not thereby ruling out other orders of units.[36]

(a) *The Institution and the City.* Maunier has defined the city as a contraction of a community or of part of a community, both population and social activity are compressed. James tells us that in a city traffic on the streets increases in geometric ratio as the population grows. Crime, divorce, wealth, poverty, news, business, and other phenomena occur out of proportion to the mere number of people. So also do specialization and the division of labor and, finally, social organization itself.

The city, as we have said, is a complex local group. But the simpler groups of which it is composed are themselves either *local groups*, or on the contrary *personal associations* without distinctive geographical localization. In the former case the city is made up of juxtaposed groups, each of which has its distinct location in the city territory. In the latter case the secondary groups which constitute the city are confounded geographically and occupy the urban territory without dividing it. The districts (quartiers), the trades (metiers), of the Middle Ages, occupying each its own street, are divisions of the former class. Families or the professions of the present, whose members are scattered throughout the city, are examples of the second.[37]

In a village common sentiments, traditions, and personal relationships are more intimate and perhaps even more complex than

36   Park, *The City*, p. 115.
37   Maunier, "The Definition of the City," *American Journal of Sociology*, XV, 546.

in the city. Such relationships are present in the city, but they tend to be hidden under the complexities of structure and of associations which overtly serve some specific purpose.[38] The territorial and personal associations of the urban community are in constant flux. That is the theme of studies on social and personal disorganization. Our attention has, on the other hand, been directed toward these overt and somewhat formal groups which are so important a part of the city's life. Our account has touched but a small corner of this life; yet we have seen a great number of such units involved. There are hundreds of other groups, playing their parts, meeting their crises and setting the world in order according to their own lights.

The very opposite of this complexity may be seen in a Mennonite community or the early Mormon settlements. These communities had each but one institution. A virile sect united in one set of functionaries all of the interests and activities of the Great Salt Lake community. When its splendid isolation was shattered by the advancing frontier of the "world," the community became more complex and differentiated in its organization. The Latter-day Saints had to compete with a secular world; the very competition destroyed the inclusiveness of the institution which had until then been coterminous with the community.

The manor likewise was at once an institution and a community. Competition with an outside world destroyed it also and put in its place a wider world with a more elaborate and less localized organization.[39] Durkheim suggests that the modern world has been

[38]   MacIver, *Community*, p. 129. "We must note that communal life is not confined within those associational moulds which answer to specific types of common interest. The life of community encompasses those forms and as it were clothes with living flesh and blood that associational skeleton."

[39]   The town of Pullman, was, in its early days, essentially a community of one institution. The Pullman Company was employer, landlord, banker, city government, schoolmaster, librarian, publisher, and moral preceptor to its people. When it tried to be priest also, it failed. Pullman was started as model town; but as time went on the essential unity of the community was dissipated from within. Little by little the people developed their own institutions. The first revolt was in religion; fifteen churches were founded in the first year of the town's existence, and Mr. Pullman's handsome Greenstone edifice stood empty.

produced by the supplanting of isolated "social segments" by more intimately connected "social organs."[40] The city represents the acme of this transformation. Social organization, as represented in institutions, reaches its greatest point of elaboration there. Even very queer people can have institutions of their own in the city. It is an elaboration expressed not only in number but also in the variety and in the manifold relationships of these units to each other.

(b) *Institutional Politics.* In this study we have been led into a peculiar sort of politics, apparently without loyalties or grudges. In this sort of politics it appears more clearly than ever that the institution is a comprehensible and important unit in the urban community. Especially it shows that public opinion is no misty emanation from some undifferentiated mass. It has sources and it has mechanisms. At least in the cases with which we have dealt, it has proceeded from a technical, somewhat complicated idea in the minds of a few vitally and continually interested men toward a simple, somewhat sentimental notion, framed in a stereotype, for a larger group whose interest is episodic and emotional.[41] Eventually all issues must be put into terms suitable for treatment by the governing body which has the last word. The institution, moreover, is not only a source of public opinion, but it is an enforcer, a fountain of that motive power which the general public supplies only in crises.

Under our system of government the citizen goes to the polls as an individual supposedly possessed of his right mind and resident in a particular precinct. His vote is one unit, commensurate with that of any other individual. In the formulation of issues and opinion, and in the enforcement of legislation once passed, the real unit is more often the institution or "interests." The vote is but an incident in the political process. Even decisive defeat at the polls does not decide an issue behind which lie such interests. It comes up again in new clothing and presses its case.

In their day, the guilds exerted an influence which reached to

40   Durkheim, see 4 above.
41   See Lippmann, *Public Opinion*; Also, *The Phantom Public.*

the throne. To have the freedom of a city one had to belong to a guild, an interest group. The Russian Soviet frankly recognizes the trade as a political unit. With us, it operates on its own recognizance and adapts itself to a system in which the final result is determined by the counting of unclassified noses.

Not all of the institutional units involved in politics are of the same sort of origin as the one we have studied. The Prohibition movement originated sentimentally, but now even it has a group of institutions whose functionaries think in terms of technique and political bargains. These professionals are interested as continuously and expertly in their reforms as is the real estate agent in his market. Even moral issues are likely to be fought out in terms of institutional units.

The political party may be conceived as one of the institutional units of the community. Its place may be peculiar in that it seeks primarily to maintain itself, while it uses the "issue" as a technical device for that purpose. The process is essentially the same.

(c) *Commodities and Institutions.* The city is also the place where new commodities are made. The process of transforming a sacred thing into a commodity is much the same whether it be land or something else. The end is always to rob the thing of strictly personal or local value. We have noted how long is the chain between client and customer in selling real estate. The agent has a technique for bringing anonymous buyers into contact with anonymous sellers. It is that impersonal contact of competition which does not involve touch or the communication of feelings and sentiments. It seems likely that when an exchange of services involves people at a distance from each other, the deal assumes the form of a transaction and the service becomes a commodity. Even the older professions are hard put to it to prevent their services from being commercialized where the social distances are great.

When anything is dealt in as a pure commodity, the persons who come to market do so as strangers. Thomas relates how the Polish peasants, who cannot talk money matters when they meet as neighbors, go to the annual fair and, pretending that they have never met before, haggle over the price of a cow. Weber upholds the theory that the first trader was a wanderer, a stranger to his customers.[42] It is said that Jews sometimes used to deal through a Gentile to avoid becoming worked to a pitch of passion in their bargaining. They knew each other too well. In the true market, one need not feign this strangeness. The problem, indeed, lies in the other direction. The professional man and the politician try to create personal relationships. Even the church tries in vain to know its people, but in its very attempt is forced to catalogue them into types rather than to meet them as individuals.

The significance of all this lies in the type of order which arises in relation to a commodity, as in distinction from something personal or something sacred. There is order in the exchange of products in a Polish village. There is an order in the personal standards of the older professions. But in both cases the order involves the person with all his accompanying status, sentiments, allegiances, and inhibitions. The order in relation to the commodity grows out of competition. A new group of institutions arises to exert control and establish order without respect of persons.

Here appears an interesting paradox. The very organization which is bent on making land a commodity is also bent on introducing into the dealings of real estate men something approaching the control which the elder professions have attempted to establish over their practice. It is likely that there is a constant tendency in any group for objects and ideas to become sacred. The purpose behind it may be forgotten, and the object may stand on its own. The Chicago Real Estate Board has brought sacred matters into the open air of the forum. It may eventually try to put them or other matters back into the sanctuary of tradition. Social change is, in part, the process of secularizing objects and values and then crystallizing them solidly in their new forms.

We have here just the story of how a group of men engaged in an occupation acted together to gain control over their occupation and its commodity. The control they wished to develop had as its aim the development of a true market. The conceptions which they had to start with were simple. Implicit in their actions, and expressed in their conflicts, one finds an isolation of those matters

42   Weber, *Gesammelte Aufsätze*.

upon which they could act collectively from those on which they could not do so. Control emanates from their collective action. Their expressed conceptions may not have kept exact pact with their action, but they have not been far behind. We may fairly assume that control will go much further, become more definite as well as broader, and tend meanwhile to transcend the individuals who operate under it. It may be that some other group will start with the conceptions of this one as a point of departure. Even so, the study of the growth of occupation of professional control will best prceed from such definite groups.

4

Ellsworth Faris

THE NATURE OF HUMAN NATURE

HUMAN NATURE, as English vernacular speech uses it, is a
very paradoxical term. On the one hand it is the culprit explaining,
if not justifying, acts that are wicked and lapses that are weak.
When our priests and pastors are disappointed in us, human nature
is our alibi. It nullifies the work of pacifists and prohibitionists, and
might almost be defined as that with which fanatical reformers fail
to reckon. On the other hand, human nature is sometimes a beautiful discovery and a pleasant surprise. When queer, fierce, and
savage folk act in a comprehensible fashion we call them human
as an honorific ascription. When human nature was discovered in
the slaves it led ineluctably to their emancipation. Seen in the un-
touchables of India, it is at this moment in process of raising their
status. To find them human is good and leads men to praise and
draw near.

In the attempt to sharpen the denotation of the term, which is
the object of this paper, it is proposed to consider: how the experience of human nature arises; some obstacles to its realization; the
relation of heredity to heritage; with a briefer mention of the mutability of human nature and the problem of individuality.

I

There is, then, first of all, this question: How did you and I
get to be human, and how do others come to seem to be human?

Reprinted from *The Urban Community*, ed. Ernest W. Burgess (Chicago:
University of Chicago Press, 1926), pp. 21–37.

Every careful reader of Cooley and Mead has long been familiar with a clear answer to the first part of the question. One's consciousness of one's self arises within a social situation as a result of the way in which one's actions and gestures are defined by the actions and gestures of others. We not only judge ourselves by others, but we literally judge that we are selves as the result of what others do and say. We become human, to ourselves, when we are met and answered, opposed and blamed, praised and encouraged. The process is mediate, not immediate. It is the result of the activity of the constructive imagination, which is still the best term by which to denote the redintegrative behavior in which there is a present symbol with a past reference and a future consequence.

The process results in a more or less consistent picture of how we appear, the specific content of which is found in the previously experienced social gestures. Not that all men treat us alike. It is trite to say that we have many selves, but it is profoundly true, and these are as many as the persons with whom we have social relations. If Babbit be husband, father, vestryman, school trustee, rotarian, and clandestine lover he obviously plays several different rôles. These rôles, or personalities, or phases of his personality are built up into a more or less consistent picture of how one appears in the eyes of others. We are conscious of ourselves if, when, and only when, we are conscious that we are acting like another. These rôles are differently evaluated. Some have a high, others a low, rating, and one's comparative estimation of the worth of his membership in his several groups has a social explanation, in spite of the fact that many would seek a physiological explanation.

As a banker or realtor Babbit may stand high, though as a golfer he may be a dub; his church status may be low and his club self high, and so through the list. The movements, vocabulary, habits, and emotions he employs in these different rôles are all accessible to careful study and accurate record, but the point can hardly be obvious since it is so widely neglected that the explanation of these habits and phrases and gestures that accompany the several rôles is to be sought chiefly in the study of the group traditions and social expectations of the several institutions where he belongs. No accessible inventory of his infantile impulses would enable the prediction of the various behavior complexes concerned in the several personal rôles. Moreover, whatever the list of personalities or rôles may be, there is always room for one more and, indeed, for many more. When war comes Babbit will probably be a member of the committee of public defense. He may become executive officer of a law enforcement league yet to be formed. He may divorce his wife or elope with his stenographer or misuse the mails and become a federal prisoner in Leavenworth. Each experience will mean a new rôle with new personal attitudes and a new axiological conception of himself.

One's conception of one's self is, therefore, the result of an imagined construct of a rôle in a social group depending upon the defining gestures of others and involving in the most diverse types of personality the same physiological mechanisms and organs. Both convict and pillar of society, churchman and patron of bootleggers, employ receptors such as eyes, ears, and nose, and effectors including arms, legs, and tongue. The way in which these are organized is, however, only to be investigated by studying the collective aspects of behavior. Your personality, as you conceive it, results from the defining movements of others.

And if this be true it is *a fortiori* certain that our conception of other selves is likewise a social resultant. The meaning of the other's acts and gestures is put together into an imagined unity of organization which is our experience or conception of what the other one is. In Cooley's phrase, the solid facts of social life are the imaginations we construct of persons. It is not the blood and bones of my friend that I think of when I recall him as such. It is rather the imagined responses which I can summon as the result of my experience with him. Should misunderstandings arise and friendship be shattered, his nervous organization and blood count would probably remain unaltered, though to me he would be an utterly different person. Whether he be my friend or my enemy depends axiologically upon my imagination concerning him. In order to deal with this material we must imagine imaginations.

The ability to conceive of human nature thus always involves the ability to take the rôle of another in imagination and to discover in this manner qualities that we recognize in ourselves. We regard as inhuman or non-human all conduct which is so strange that we cannot readily imagine ourselves engaging in it. We speak of inhuman cruelty when atrocities are so hard-heartedly cruel that we cannot conceive of ourselves as inflicting them. We speak of inhuman stupidity if the action is so far remote from intelligent behavior that we feel entirely foreign to it. And conversely, in the behavior of non-human animals and, in extreme cases, with regard to plants and even inanimate objects, there is a tendency to attribute unreflectively human motives and feelings. This accounts for the voluminous literature of the "nature fakers." To sympathize with the appealing eyes of a pet dog, or the dying look of a sick cat, or to view the last gasps of a slain deer is to have just this experience. Wheeler, a foremost authority on the behavior of insects, writes of "awareness" of the difference between her eggs on the part of a mother wasp, and of the "interest" that other insects take in the welfare of their progeny. The fables and animal stories of primitive and of civilized peoples could not have been spoken but for this tendency of our imagination to attribute human qualities when some behavior gives a clue of similarity to our own inner life. Examples of this process could be indefinitely cited from St. Francis preaching sermons to his "brother wolf" and to the birds, the romantic poets who speak to the dawn and get messages from the waves, the lover whose pathetic fallacy sees impatience in the drooping of the rose when Maud is late to her tryst, all the way to Opal, who loved the fir tree because he had an "understanding soul." The experience is entirely normal. The most unromantic mechanist may, in emotional moments, be carried unreflectively into an unwitting and immediate attribution of human impulses and motives to non-human objects.

Human nature is, therefore, that quality which we attribute to others as the result of introspective behavior. There is involved a certain revival of our own past, with its hopes, fears, loves, angers and other subjective experiences which in an immediate and unreflective way we read into the behavior of another. The German concept *Einfühlung*, while not exactly the same notion, includes the process here denoted. It is more than sympathy; it is "empathy."

Now the process wherein this takes place is primarily emotional. The mechanism is operative in all real art. In our modern life the drama and the novel are largely responsible for the broadening of our sympathies and the enlarging of our axiological fraternities. There is some plausibility to the disturbing remark of a colleague of the writer who declared that one can learn more about human nature today from literature than from science, so called. If federal regulation continues to increase it might be well to pass a law forcing all parents of small children to read *The Way of All Flesh*. Books on criminology are valuable, but so is *The House of the Dead*. Culprits, offenders, and violators of our code are human, but in order that we may realize the fact it is necessary for us to see their behavior presented concretely so that we can understand and, understanding, forgive. "There, but for the grace of God, goes John Wesley." Perhaps you and I might have been murderers.

There is a curious, and at first, puzzling, difference in the attitude of two groups of specialists concerning the nature and the mental capacity of preliterate or so-called "primitive" peoples. The anthropologists and sociologists of the present day are almost unanimous in their opinion that so-called "savages" do not differ in their mental capacity or emotional possibility from modern civilized peoples, taken by and large and as a whole. Contemporary biologists, on the other hand, are in many cases very reluctant to admit this, and many of them categorically and insistently deny it. Now it cannot be the result of logical conclusions from research methods of scientific men in the case of the biologists, for their work is confined chiefly to anatomical structures and the physiology of segments. Their conclusions arise from other than focal interests.

On the face of it the situation is curious. The biologist has long ago demonstrated the surprisingly essential identity of the nervous system in all mammals. The rat or the dog is almost as useful for the vivisectional investigation of the human nervous system as a human subject would be. Element for element, the nervous system of the sheep is the same as in man, the differences being quantitative. *A fortiori*, the nervous system of the Eskimo and the German are not significantly different. The biologist works with identical material, but concludes by assuming great and significant differences between the different races. The anthropologist and sociologist works with strongly contrasted phenomena. He discusses and studies polyandry, witchcraft, and shamanism, socially approved infanticide, and cannibalism, and such divergent practices that one would expect him to posit much greater differences than even his biologist colleague would assert. An investigator from Mars (one may always invoke this disinterested witness) would probably expect the biologist who studies identical forms to be inclined to rate them all alike, and might infer that the anthropologist who studies such divergent customs would place them in a contrasting series.

The explanation seems fairly apparent. The biologist deals objectively, thinking in terms of dissections and physical structures. The anthropologist deals sympathetically and imaginatively. His work takes him into the field where he gets behind the divergencies and finds that the objects of his study have pride, love, fear, curiosity, and the other human qualities which he recognizes in himself, the differences being only in the form and expression. Thus, by an introspective sympathy, he comes to know them as human.

The limitations of introspective psychology need no elaboration in these days when extreme behaviorism has thrown out the infant with the bath. The uncontrolled exaggerations that arose out of the unverifiable imaginings of introspectionists brought about a violent reaction not wholly undeserved. It is not proposed here to make even a disguised plea for introspective methods. The essential point is not the desirability, but the inevitability, of just this type of imagination by which alone we recognize others as human, and which ultimately rests on our ability to identify in others what we know to be true in ourselves.

Imaginative sympathy enables us to recognize human nature when we see it and even to assume it where it is not. Conversely, when the behavior is so different that we lack the introspective clue we find difficulty in calling it human. Such limitation is more true of our emotional moments than of calm and reflective periods. Recent questions on race prejudice reveal the fact that, in the American group which was investigated, the most violent race prejudice,

the greatest social distance, existed in respect of the Turks. It was
further revealed that most of those who felt a strong aversion
against Turks had never seen a Turk, but they had heard and read
and believed stories of their behavior which account for the attitude. One story describes Turkish soldiers stripping a captured
pregnant woman, betting on the sex of the foetus, and disembowel-
ling her to see who should win the money. Such conduct we call
inhuman since we cannot imagine ourselves as engaging in it under
any circumstances. If we are to regard all members of the genus
homo as human it is essential that the traditions of all races and
their mores be sufficiently like our own to enable us to understand
them sympathetically. It is easy to show that Americans who go to
Turkey and understand the Turks not only find them human, but
often praise and admire them. And all because the emphatic imagination enables us to play their part and understand their
motives.

II

The chief limitation to the imaginative sympathy enabling
us to call others human is the phenomenon which Sumner calls
ethnocentrism. By an extension of the term, which is here presented
with a prayer for indulgence, we may distinguish three types of
ethnocentrism which are in effect three degrees of the phenomenon.
Ethnocentrism, as ordinarily used, is the emotional attitude which
places high value on one's own customs and traditions and belittles
all others, putting as least valuable those that differ most. The universality of ethnocentrism is evidenced from the discovery that all
preliterate peoples who have considered the question have worked
out the answer in the same terms. It is obvious to a Nordic that the
African and Mongol are inferior to himself, and hardly less obvious
that the Mediterranean is intermediate between his own highness
and the low-browed tribes of the tropic forests. But for more than
a generation it has been familiar to specialists that Eskimos, Zulus,
and Pueblos have exactly the same feeling toward us. The customs
with which we are familiar are best. Mores which differ most widely
arise from the social life of an inferior people. We are supremely

human; they are only partially so. To Herbert Spencer the high-headed and proud-hearted Kaffirs—who would in their turn have spoken contemptuously of his bald head and his helplessness in the forest—were intermediate between the chimpanzee and the English. They were only partly human. The writer of these lines once made what he felt to be a very good speech to an audience of naked savages, speaking in their own tongue with certain native proverbs and allusions to their folk-tales. The reward for this skill was the frank and surprised admission that at least one white man was intelligent and could make a decent argument like any other human being. The Texas farmers whose province had been invaded by an agricultural colony of Bohemians used to refer to them as hardly human since their women worked in the fields and often the whole family went barefooted. Ethnocentric narrowness includes the group in sympathy-proof tegument which blinds men to the human qualities of differing peoples.

The second form of ethnocentrism is harder to establish, but must be asserted. It is seen in its quintessence in the writings of McDougall and his followers. Human nature consists of instincts and if a list of these be called for they are promptly produced. The instinct of warfare is axiomatic and the proof is found in the military history of our people. But the list of instincts turns out to be merely a renaming and hypostatization of our own social customs. The instincts have been set down in a fixed list because men failed to distinguish between their immediate social heritage and the inborn tendencies of their infants. It is therefore a kind of scientific ethnocentrism, which conceives as native and human that which is acquired and social and leads to the conclusion that those with widely different customs must either have some instinct omitted from their repertory, as McDougall plainly says of some of the interior Borneo tribes, or else (and this comes to the same thing) they have these instincts in a different degree from those which we have received from our forebears; that is to say, the customs of other people, if they are sufficiently different, are due to the fact that their nature is not quite like ours. They are really not quite human, or, to say the least, differently human.

The third variety of ethnocentrism is somewhat more subtle.

It is the limitation due to language. It is the penalty for having to speak in one language without knowledge of the others. The dreary list of sentiments, feelings, and emotions in some books is written as if all the words in the world were English words. We make sharp distinctions between fear, terror, and awe and, forgetting that these are limited to our vocabulary, expect to find the fundamental traits of human nature adequately described thereby. If we read German we may become interested in the distinction between *Mut* and *Tapferkeit*. Not knowing Japanese, we lose the precious insight which their idioms would give us in the inability of their language to make a neuter noun the subject of a transitive verb. A yet unpublished statement by a most eminent psychologist, written three months ago, is concerned with a discussion of "what emotions do" and "what intelligence does," in the behavior of human beings. No Japanese would make such an egregious blunder—not necessarily because of different capacity for analysis, but because his mother-tongue is incapable of such erroneous metaphysical reification. Linguistic ethnocentrism, if we may so name this, would disappear if our minds were competent and our years enough to allow us to know all the languages of the earth; but until utopia comes the handicap can be partly overcome by a conscious recognition of its existence and by an obstinate and repeated attempt to get outside of the limitations of our own etymology into a sympathetic appreciation of the forms of speech of stranger men.

Ethnocentrism, then, is essentially narrowness. It is enthusiasm for our own due to ignorance of others. It is an appreciation of what we have and a depreciation of what differs. It is essentially a lacking of sympathetic dramatization of the point of view of another. It must be transcended if we are really to know what protean varieties human nature may assume.

III

From the question of how human nature is recognized it is a natural transition to the problem of how it is constituted. The current form of most interest is an old problem still exciting lively interest; the relation of inherited tendencies to social organization;

the relation of instincts to institutions; heredity, to environment; nature, to nurture.

This paper is written under the conviction that sociology and social psychology must rely chiefly on facts from the collective life of societies for their material. Two fields of inquiry, among many others, can be cited as providing relevant material. One is the study of preliterate peoples and the other is the consideration of modern isolated religious groups. There is found among primitive people such a protean variety of social and cultural organization, such various forms of religious, political, and family life, that it would seem impossible to account for them on the basis of definite instincts. When one society refuses entirely to produce children, another tribe kills all unbetrothed girls, still another practices infant cannibalism, while yet others manifest tender solicitude for all their children, and when unto these are added accounts of bizarre marriage customs and religious conceptions and tendencies, it is hard to see how the conception can be carried through without assuming different instincts in each tribe.

The isolated religious sects of the eighteenth and nineteenth centuries are even more valuable to the theorist since the complete history of many of the customs is known, an advantage not possessed by the ethnologist as a rule. It is possible to describe in detail a time when there were no Quakers, Dunkards, Mormons, Shakers, or Perfectionists. The rise of polygamy can be traced in Mormonism, and the abandonment of the marriage relation among the Shakers can be dated and described.

McDougall has seen this difficulty and has met it with a certain *naïveté*. He has only to assume that strikingly different customs have been produced by peoples with differing instincts, or with instincts of different degrees of strength or intensity. The Shakers would therefore be adequately explained by assuming a selection of people who had no sex instincts, or very weak ones. The peaceful tribes would be those lacking the instinct of pugnacity, which leads him to the logical conclusion that the French have a different instinct from the English, and to the popular psychology which gives to the Anglo-Saxon the instinct for representative government which the Italians and Orientals are assumed to lack.

Thus the assumption that instincts produce customs turns out to be a mere tautology, and the human race disappears as a biological species. A zoölogist who describes the migrating salmon or the breeding habits of seal or the incubating instincts of penguins is dealing with a single species whose members exhibit a universality of action. But if this formulation of instincts be followed out, every tribe or race must be assumed to have different instincts, and the basic error of the whole instinct psychology stands revealed. Then instinct merely becomes another name for custom.

Were all our knowledge of human nature limited to a single flash of information through a given moment of time it might be impossible to criticize this serious error. Fortunately, there is history. The Mormons began without polygamy, lived through a long period when plural marriage was customary, and then, through the stress of circumstances, abolished the practice. The English colonies have circled the earth, while the French remain at home drinking in the cafés of Paris, but there was a time when the French colonies occupied vast territories in the New World, and there is ample evidence of a considerable settlement of French both in Canada and Louisiana. The warlike Nordics dreamed of a heaven of warfare and slaughter, but when Norway seceded from Sweden something went wrong with their fighting instinct and, obstinately enough, they settled the matter by a peaceable arrangement. If customs change, and they do, and if instincts cause customs, then instincts change as often as the customs. But a changing instinct is no instinct, for instincts by hypothesis are constant.

The problem of social origins is not solved, but the history of many customs and institutions is in our possession and it is quite certain that the whole concatenation of unique and unrepeated circumstances must be invoked to explain the creation of any one of them. And when once the organization appears, the new members of the group who grow up within it or who are initiated into it take on the group attitudes as *representations collectives*, securing all their fundamental satisfactions in ways which the group prescribes. The true order, then, lies in exactly the reverse of the instinct-to-institution formulation. Instead of the insincts of individuals being the cause of our customs and institutions, it is far truer to say

it is the customs and institutions which explain the individual behavior so long called instinctive. Instincts do not create customs.
Customs create instincts, for the putative instincts of human beings
are always learned and never native.

Exactly when human nature begins is a problem. But that it
does, in each individual, have a definite beginning is an axiom. The
newborn has not a developed personality. He has neither wishes,
desires, nor ambitions. He does not dream of angels nor think the
long thoughts of youth. He acquires a personality. He does not
acquire his heredity. He acquires his personality. A quarter of a
century ago this acquisition was shown by Cooley to happen in the
first groups, the primary groups, into which he is received. He becomes a person when, and because, others are emotional toward
him. He can become a person when he reaches that period, not
always exactly datable, when the power of imagination enables him
to reconstruct the past and build an image of himself and others.

IV

An inescapable corollary of the foregoing is the mutability
of human nature. Despite the chauvinists, the cynics, and the abso-
lutists of every sort, human nature can be changed. Indeed, if one
speaks with rigorous exactness, human nature never ceases to be
altered; for the crises in life and nature, the interaction and diffusion of exotic cultures, and the varying temperaments possessed by
the troops of continuously appearing and gradually begotten children force the conclusion that human nature is in a continual state
of flux. We cannot change it by passing a law, nor by a magical act
of the will, nor by ordering and forbidding, nor by day-dreaming
and revery, but human nature can be changed. To defend militarism
on the ground that man is a fighter and the fighting instinct cannot
be changed is merely to misinterpret and to rationalize an important fact; that the custom of warfare is very old and can be abolished
only gradually and with great difficulty. To assume that the drinking habits of a people or their economic structure or even the family organization is immutably founded upon the fixed patterns of
human nature is to confuse nature and custom. What we call the

stable elements of human nature are in truth the social attitudes of individual persons, which in turn are the subjective aspects of long-established group attitudes whose inertia must be reckoned with but whose mutability cannot be denied. Having been established through a long period of time, and appearing to the youth as normal and natural, they seem to be a part of the ordered universe. In reality they are continually being slightly altered and may at any time be profoundly modified by a sufficiently serious crisis in the life of the group.

The history of social movements is but a record of changing human nature. The antislavery movement, the woman's movement, the temperance movement, the interestingly differing youth movements in Germany, China, and America—these are all natural phenomena in the field of sociology, and are perhaps most accurately described as the process of change which human nature undergoes in response to the pressure of unwelcome events giving rise to restlessness and vague discontent. Such movements, when they generate leaders and develop institutions passing on to legal and political changes, create profound alterations of the mores and thoroughly transform not only the habits of a people and their nature as they live together but also the basic conception of what constitutes human nature. The present conception in the West of the nature of woman, including her mental capacity and ability to do independent creative work, is profoundly different from the conception which anybody entertained in the generations before the woman's movement began.

But for the limitations of space the problem of individuality and character should receive extended treatment in this discussion. This being impossible, a brief word must suffice. There is so much of controversy here and so much of confusion that many seem to be hypnotized by mere phrases. It is much too simple to say that the individual and society are one, for it is difficult to know which one. The heretic, the rebel, the martyr, the criminal—these all stand out as individuals surely not at one with society. Nor does it seem adequate merely to say that the person is an individual who has status in a group. For it does not appear that before the acquisition of status the individual has any existence. Certainly if he has he does not know it. The conception which it would be profitable to develop lies in the direction of the assumption that out of multiple social relations which clash and conflict in one's experience the phenomenon of individuality appears. The claims of the various social groups and relations and obligations made on a single person must be umpired and arbitrated, and here appears the phenomenon of conscience and that of will. The arbitrament results in a more or less complete organization and ordering of the differing rôles, and this organization of the subjective social attitudes is perhaps the clearest conception of what we call character. The struggles of the tempted and the strivings of courageous men appear, when viewed from the outside, to be the pull of inconsistent groups, and so indeed they are. But to you and me who fight and hold on, who struggle amid discouragement and difficulties, there is always a feeling that the decision is personal and individual. Someone has been the umpire. When the mother says, "Come into the house," and Romeo whispers, "Come out onto the balcony," it is Romeo who prevails, but it is Juliet who decides.

Individuality may then, from one standpoint, be thought of as character, which is the subjective aspect of the world the individual lives in. The influences are social influences, but they differ in strength and importance. When completely ordered and organized with the conflicting claims of family, friends, clubs, business, patriotism, religion, art and science all ordered, adjudicated, and unified, we have not passed out of the realm of social influence, but we have not remained where the social group, taken separately, can be invoked to explain the behavior. Individuality is a synthesis and ordering of these multitudinous forces.

Here human nature reaches its ultimate development. Henley, lying weak and sick, suffering great pain, called out that he was captain of his soul. To trace back the social antecedents of such a heroic attitude is profitable and germane, but it is never the whole story until we have contemplated this unique soul absolutely unduplicated anywhere in the universe—the result, if you like, of a thousand social influences, but still undubitably individual. It was

Henley who uttered that cry. That you and I so recognize him and appreciate him only means that we also have striven. We know him and understand him because of our own constructive, sympathetic imagination. He who admires a masterpiece has a right to say, I also am an artist.

III Structure, Process,
Communication, and Change

5

Earl S. Johnson

THE FUNCTION OF THE CENTRAL
BUSINESS DISTRICT IN THE
METROPOLITAN COMMUNITY

THE GROWTH OF THE METROPOLITAN REGION has raised
many new problems in the field of social control. Many of these
follow from the nature of the new pattern of land use and population distribution which has developed on the periphery of the central city. Although on its political side the region is characterized by
independence from the central city, social and economic bonds
render them highly interdependent. One of the most significant
criteria of this unity is that which is furnished by the fact that, in
at least its major economic activities, it is organized around a single
market. The central business district of the central city is the market
place of the metropolitan community.

The method of analysis used here to study the nature of this
unity is, primarily, that employed by the human ecologist. In this
approach people and institutions are viewed from an external standpoint and largely in their distributive and competitive aspects. The
human ecologist is not, however, interested in the graphic and distributive treatment of social data for its own sake. He realizes that
in actuality social phenomena are not merely physical things but
have their bases in living beings. For purposes of scientific con-
ceptualization, however, he consciously singles out the physical and
the external aspects of these essentially social data as the objects of
his attention and treats them, as far as possible, as if they operated
in isolation.

Reprinted from *Third Year Course in the Study of Contemporary Society*,
10th ed. Copyright 1942 by The University of Chicago.

The central business district of the metropolis is the area in which are located those highly specialized persons and institutions which exert a directing, co-ordinating, and facilitating influence on the market activities of the entire metropolitan region. Its position marks the ecological, though not necessarily the geographical, center of this region. By metropolitan community is meant a spatial and symbiotic pattern, the parts of which are tributary to a city which has reached the stage in which its predominant economic functions have become those of executive management, administration, and financial control. Considered as a spatial and symbiotic pattern, its population is an aggregate of individuals distributed in a determinate order over an area with more or less definite boundaries. If, from the ecological point of view, these units are considered as men rather than as merely physical things, it is as *economic* men, who according to their characteristics, are not social creatures in the sense of admitting any moral claims on one another but whose relations to one another are purely secular and utilitarian— that is, symbiotic.

The fact that the geographical and ecological centers of a community do not necessarily coincide deserves some further elaboration. The geographical center is that point which is equidistant from every point on the periphery of a community. This could, of course, hold only if the periphery described a perfect circle. In any actual urban community, therefore, any point could be only the approximate geographical center, and even if it were this coincidence would be accidental rather than essential in its significance. But obviously even this coincidence could not exist in the case of a port city whose position, with reference to its hinterland, must be off-center. Topographical factors other than bodies of water would likewise render it impossible for the central business district to occupy this approximate position.

But this district does, invariably, occupy the *ecological* center of the metropolitan community. It does so because the ecological center is that position which, owing to the time-cost transportation relations (rather than linear distance relations) which it bears to all parts of the community, permits a complex of economic institutions and persons located there to discharge their functions with a maximum of efficiency. Stated in another way, it is that area in the central city of the metropolitan community where certain market institutions, which are by their very nature dependent upon an extensive market area, are able to maintain themselves despite exceedingly high land values and rents. The boundaries of the metropolitan region are determined by the number and degree of the relations which exist between the central city and its satellite communities. The greater the distance from the central city, the fewer are the functions, though not necessarily less important, for which the satellites depend on it. The ecological pattern of the region may then be conceived of ideally as having a single center, the market place, and varying but concentric peripheries.[1]

The metropolitan community may now be defined in terms of the functional interrelation between the central business district of the central city and the larger metropolitan area. It is *that total area composed of many discrete areas each of which delimits, spatially, a zone over which the central business district exercises a certain degree of dominance.*

It will be noted that this definition makes no mention of the civil divisions into which the community is partitioned. These are omitted here not because they are unimportant but because this analysis is deliberately limited to a consideration of only the economic and spatial aspects of community life. To go beyond this would necessitate treating not only the spatial pattern but, as Professor Robert E. Park has expressed it, the "moral order" as well, which would complicate the problem. The object here is to stress the aspects of economic interdependence rather than of political independence. Furthermore, the activities of the market have, historically, been somewhat contemptuous of political boundaries; for,

[1] The classic statement of this is in the conceptual scheme presented by von Thünen in *Der isolierte Staat.* There, interestingly enough, the ecological and the geographical centers are identical. But von Thünen's primary interest was not in geographical position but rather in position measured in terms of transportation costs from concentric zones to a center —or, in other words, in ecological position.

although men have often aimed to achieve for their civil division complete economic independence, this end has more often appeared as a political slogan than as a historical actuality.

The position which the central business district takes within the pattern of the central city can likewise be described with more meaning in ecological than in geographical terms. Ecologically, its boundaries are fixed by the terminal properties of the transportation systems which converge upon it. For the inland city these will be rail and bus terminals; for the port city, both of these and water terminals.[2] These terminals represent breaks in transportation. It is such breaks which have, both historically and causally, been associated with the location of human settlement and the rise of the commercial city and the market. Frederick Ratzel, Adna F. Weber, and Charles H. Cooley have developed this point well. Sir Henry Maine has treated the origin and location of the market in a manner which leads to the same conclusion, for, as he has remarked, the market originated "where the domain of two or three villages converged."[3] This, in principle, holds true for the modern metropolitan market place as well. In the modern city, however, high-speed and long-distance communication facilities permit the convergence upon a central market place of the activities of communities, which communities are, unlike those to which Maine referred, non-contiguous. The location of the market place is, in the modern city, determined not so much by geographical *place* as by technological *process*.

But if transportation facilities fix the margins of the business district, communication facilities fix its center, which is the point of convergence of the telephone and telegraph systems which serve the metropolis. If modern transportation facilities rendered its posi-

[2]   In the present stage of aviation, landing fields must be located on the periphery of the community; the development of the helicopter may permit the arrival and departure of planes from points within the central business district. The helicopter may also be used more extensively as a kind of "air taxi" between the peripheral landing fields and the business center of the city.

[3]   *Cf.* Ratzel, *The History of Mankind* (3 vols.) ; Weber, *The Growth of Cities in the Nineteenth Century;* and Cooley, "A Theory of Transportation," *Sociological Theory and Social Research;* also Maine, *Ancient Law.*

tion less dependent than formerly upon geographic factors, facilities for communication, through their almost complete annihilation of space, have all but completely emancipated it from them. Buyers and sellers may now meet in the market via the telephone, the telegraph, and the radio. This is not to deny that face-to-face relations are still necessary and important, for there appear to be many types of market transactions in which the personal presence of the contracting parties is still indispensable to the consummation of the transaction.

But this distinction between the carrying of persons and goods and the carrying of information in connection with the activities of the market suggest that the central business district has two centers: one defined by the focus of lines of communication, the other by the focus of lines of transportation. With the first center is associated the merchandising of credits; with the second is associated the merchandising of consumers goods and services at retail. Which of these is to be taken as the most significant center depends upon which of the two associated functions—namely, financial control or retail distribution—characterize the economy of the central city. In the sense in which Sombart treats the metropolis in the advanced stage of capitalistic society—namely, as the financial rather than as the industrial or commercial city—the communication center, upon which the financial institutions depend and converge spatially, would constitute *the* center.

Thus, whether it is considered in its local, regional, national, or international setting, the central business district is the focal point of an elaborate transportation and communication structure. Chicago, which is more or less representative of American cities, serves to illustrate this. Except for Lake Michigan on the east, it is, like the city in von Thünen's figure, surrounded by a flat plain. The twenty-odd railroads which converge upon it have pushed their passenger (and less-than-carlot freight) terminals as close as was physically and economically possible into the center of the city. Thus, their inner terminal properties actually define the margins of central business district on three, if not on all four sides. From these passenger terminals more than two hundred thousand persons daily enter the central district; these include suburban commuters, who, from these points of entry, are within walking distance of their places of work. Over these roads, likewise, almost one-half of the population of the United States could, if it cared to, reach Chicago in a journey of overnight or less duration. With respect to the somewhat more strictly local transportation pattern it may be observed, first, that although the street pattern of the city is gridiron in general design, on it are superimposed thirteen diagonal streets, all of which are oriented toward the business center. In addition, this district is the point of convergence of thirty-six surface-car routes, which, through the transfer privilege and by the payment of extra fares, makes the district almost hourly accessible to millions of people. The central core of the larger central business district, the "Loop," took its name from the fact that here was established the transfer point for the elevated rapid transit lines which route every train into this area and form an iron ring around it. The bus system of the city is likewise oriented toward this central area, and here also are the terminals of the national passenger-bus lines.

The Chicago central business district is also the area of greatest daily traffic. For a twelve-hour period on a typical business day in 1926, pedestrians excepted, about one and three-fourths million people entered the district, of whom more than 80 per cent came by common carrier. In 1931, during a twenty-four-hour period on a summer week day, over one-half million vehicle trips (by passenger autos and trucks) were exchanged between the central business district and the city and the surrounding metropolitan area. Of these, seventy-two out of every hundred had either an origin or a destination within the district. It is such a network of transportation as this which permits a land area, comprising less than 1 per cent of the total area of the city, to serve as the market place for a regional population of almost five million people.

But the central business district in Chicago, as in every metropolis, is the center of an even more sensitive network, namely, the web of communication lines. From this area originates only slightly less than one-half of the total telegraph traffic of the city. Beneath the pit of its Board of Trade are 2,700 miles of telephone and telegraph wires, while from it wires run directly to scores of offices throughout the building and the city and to 540 cities scattered

from coast to coast—in all, over 150,000 miles of wire. In addition
to land telegraphic connections, 75,000 miles of nautical cable tie
this district to every important market on the face of the earth. To
a message sent from this district a cable reply from Europe is only
five minutes away.

An analysis of the telephone calls originating in an area almost
coterminous with the central business district serves as another significant index to the control functions which the institutions located
here perform. This telephone district contains less than six out of
every hundred of the total telephone accounts of the city, but from
these are made one-fourth of the total number of local calls—
slightly less than one-third of the total regional calls and one-seventh
of the total long-distance business transacted by the telephone company in Chicago. The ratios which the small number of phones
bear to the great volume of the various types of calls originating
from them express the degree to which the functions centered in
this district depend for their existence upon this form of communication.

The total machinery of transportation and communication devices therefore fixes the central business district at the ecological
center of the entire metropolitan community. Furthermore, they
bound the district and locate its centers. Associated with the boundaries and with each center are certain market organizations and
institutions. Some of the most representative of these deserve
mention.

With the transport of goods from these inner terminals, rather
than from those farther out which serve the heavier industrial
plants, are associated light manufacturing, warehousing, and wholesale distribution. Shipments from these manufacturing concerns
are, for the most part, in less-than-carlot quantities. These inner
terminals deal generally in this form of freight consignment, hence
they and the factories which occupy the zone immediately outside
the central business district stand in a symbiotic relation. The
warehouse, which is essentially a "bank of merchandise," is also
located with reference to these transportation terminals. The railroad carries goods in *space;* the warehouse carries them in *time.*
The wholesale establishment is the regional rather than the local

store since its customers are middlemen in strategic locations in the region from which they supply the retail demand of the "ultimate consumer." Actually it serves both the regional and the local middlemen as its spatial position near both the freight terminals and the department-store area suggests.

But the metropolitan market is, ideally, the money market rather than the goods and services market. Here are concentrated the bankers' banks, the great insurance companies, the branch of the Federal Reserve System, the investment houses, and the great stock and commodity exchanges. It is at this point that the spatial identity of the central business district with the communication center takes on significance. If it is the center of communication it is, by the same token, also the news center, in both the journalistic and the market sense of what news is. The relation between news and speculation has, historically, been not only close but causal. The rise of the great insurance firm of Lloyd's of London cannot be understood aside from the relation which risk-bearing bears to the availability of reliable news. As Karl Bücher has suggested, it was not accidental that the booth of the independent news bureau on the Venetian Rialto was located between the booths of the changers and the goldsmiths. Furthermore, the fact that the Fuggers were perhaps the greatest bankers and likewise the leading news-gatherers of their day is no less significant in this connection.[4] The central business district as the locus of the market is then the place where both news and credit are created and concentrated and from which both are distributed. Furthermore, it is the area whose risk-taking enterprises depend for their very existence upon the news.

The extreme centralization of men, institutions, and services which rapid communication and transportation have made possible is also expressed in modern industrial organization and control. This is not unrelated to the function of furnishing credit. In the territorial division of labor which has developed in the modern metropolitan community the industrial activities have tended to be-

[4]   For a comprehensive account of the evolution of Lloyd's see Wright and Fayle, *A History of Lloyd's;* also Bücher, *Industrial Evolution,* and Jacob Strieder, *Jacob Fugger the Rich.*

come reallocated to the satellites, while the financial and executive controls have tended to remain in the central city. Policy-making and executive functions have become concentrated at the focal point of lines of communication. The functional breach between the businessman and the machine, developed so ably by Veblen, here receives its spatial expression, which may in this case, as in others, turn out to be significant for understanding the social processes which underlie and explain it.[5]

This centralization of control and decentralization of fabrication have implications for the distinction between labor and capital and between industrial and civil politics. Theoretically, in a democratic society policy-making and its execution are divided between the electorate and the executive; in modern industrial organization, in contrast, in the absence of any adequate equivalent to the electorate, both the making and the execution of policy have tended to become the vested rights of the executives, or, as they have come to be properly designated, the "captains of industry." Irrespective of what is held to be true in history, the organization of the industrial community is, in fact, based on something other than the democratic principle. If, then, the metropolitan community may be considered as an economic or industrial rather than as a civil-political order, the central business district is its capital and its governors the finance capitalists.

The creating and supplying of credit, the primary functions of the metropolitan market, constitute not one but a whole bundle of functions as the foregoing description properly implies. But it, in turn, depends on another bundle of functions. These, among which may be cited accounting, auditing, bookkeeping, insurance, legal counsel, promotion, advertising, and management, have frequently been referred to as the ancillary or secondary functions of the market. Each, whether it be primary or secondary, represents a high degree of specialization, the corollary of which is the need for close integration. The nature of the interrelations dictates, furthermore, that this integration be close both in time and in space. The telephone and the telegraph have effected their temporal integration,

[5]   See *The Theory of Business Enterprise.*

but it is chiefly through a special form of housing, and the provision within it of rapid vertical transportation, that their spatial integration has been made possible. The skyscraper, which piles floor upon floor and office cubicle upon office cubicle and connects them by high-speed elevators, has done this. Thus does the division of labor in the metropolitan market place help to explain what is probably the most uniquely urban and at the same time the most uniquely American-urban device—the multistoried office building.[6]

But the need for the spatial integration of many specialists in the central market district is, as has been indicated, but one of a number of the factors with which the appearance of skyscraper is associated. The rise of the great industrial and financial corporations, the separation of executive management and control from the fabrication of the products, the increase in the division of labor in the market place, the complex organization of the marketing machinery, keen competition for the use of the limited land supply at the city's center, the undirected growth and unplanned nature of American cities, the invention of the steel skeleton construction, and the perfection of the electrically operated passenger elevator— all these have converged to make the skyscraper both possible and necessary.

But while the most significant center of the central business district in a metropolitan city is that which fixes the location of the financial and office district, the complex of retail establishments constitutes the second most significant center. This is the point on which all local and regional passenger transportation systems, except in some cases of the steam-railroad lines, immediately converge. It is a secondary center not in the sense of its occupying cheaper sites but because in the metropolis retail distribution is secondary in importance to the furnishing of credit. Here, then, is the retail market organized on a grand scale which differs from the provincial market in the extreme specialization of its marketing organization and in its anonymity, which is expressed in the substi-

---

[6]   The question of the indispensability of the multistoried structure to the efficiency of the market activities is a real one when it is noted that London, the world's greatest money market, is without a single such building.

tution of the "standard price" for the price reached through "higgling."[7]

Some measure of the degree of specialization in the central retail market in Chicago is furnished by the United States Census of Retail Distribution made in 1929. In the downtown shopping district were but 7 per cent of the total number of stores in the city, but these enjoyed a sales volume in excess of one-fourth of the total retail sales made in the entire city. For the department stores the ratio of establishments in this district to the total number in the city was 11.5 per cent, but these did only slightly less than one-half of the total business done in all the department stores in the city. For apparel stores the contrast was even more striking. Only 1.3 per cent of all such stores were located here, but these enjoyed 45 per cent of the total volume of business done in all the city's apparel establishments.[8]

Additional evidence of the specialized character of this retailing-transportation complex is furnished by the medical services in this district. Although these are provided by a professionally trained personnel, they are nevertheless part of the total retailing activity. The Chicago Loop showed an increase of but 17.6 per cent in its total medical personnel in the fifteen-year period between 1914 and 1939. This is not a large increase when compared with other indices of change in this area, such as in daily traffic, retail sales volume, or added office space. This relatively slight increase indicates, as regards *total* medical personnel, that this area was approaching a saturation point. The *selective* or specialized character of the change in medical personnel is, however, highly significant. In the same period the area lost 33.8 per cent of its general practitioners and gained 68.5 per cent in part-time specialists. But for physicians who devoted their full time to the practice of a single specialty, the gain was 118.4 per cent. In other words, the Loop had become less a local and more a regional medical market place,

[7]   In Chicago the "provincial market," where the price is in part by "higgling" or bidding, may be found on Maxwell Street just east of Halsted Street.
[8]   For more recent data see *Geographic Distribution of Retail Trade in Chicago, Illinois* (Bureau of the Census, June, 1939).

for such an increase in *specialized* medical services could be explained only by reason of the extension of the size of the area from which patients would come with their demand for medical services.[9] The spatial and temporal integration of these highly specialized medical experts is similar to that in the office section of the market place, effected through the skyscraper. In several instances medical practitioners are housed in buildings designed especially for their occupancy.

The central business district in every metropolitan city has, since its original settlement, been undergoing a process of slow and constant change—a process involving a selection of functions. The basis of this process was indicated earlier, namely, that those enterprises remain whose books, so to speak, still show a profit after the high charges for site rent are subtracted from the gains which accrue by virtue of their location at this strategic communication and transportation center. This is true in large part for the institutions which represent the more cultural or noneconomic aspects of metropolitan life as well as for those which are distinctly economic or profit-seeking in character.

The selective and specialized character of some of these noneconomic institutions may be briefly indicated. The downtown church represents a special form of religious institution. If it was established here when the city was young, the descendants of its original members have perhaps all fled to the residential areas of the central city or to the suburbs. But through its strategic position at the center of transportation and by virtue of its having frequently become self-supporting through its function as landlord, it can still survive without either the financial support or the spiritual cooperation of the descendants of its original members and founders. In the respect that, not infrequently, its drawing-power is due to the dramatic character of its ministerial personnel, a famous pulpit orator or a sort of weekly "headliner type" of speaker, it can continue to carry on even in competition with its more secular neigh-

9   Increased specialization is equivalent to an increase in the division of labor. Since the time of Adam Smith it has been axiomatic that "the extent of [the division of labor] must always be limited by . . . the extent of the market" (*The Wealth of Nations*).

bors, the legitimate theater and the movie palace, some of whose essential techniques it tends to employ. The Chicago Temple, the Central Church, and the Sunday Evening Club tend to approximate the characteristic forms of the downtown church.

The central business district is, furthermore, the natural habitat of the esoteric cult which, owing to its strange and unconventional beliefs, must recruit its devotees from an area wider than that of any local community. Here too are the theaters, the legitimate, and the gala and gigantic movie and vaudeville houses. Neither could be supported by anything less than a large regional population. Both provide, one might say, a luxury type of retail service in the field of leisure-time pursuits and are therefore to be found not far away from the great retail distributing center and focus of transportation lines. This location is necessary because they must be accessible to not only a large but in many cases a discriminating clientèle.

The great hotels of the district provide a specialized form of housing not primarily for a local but for a regional and national clientèle made up of wholesale buyers and sellers, out-of-town shoppers, tourists, and many others. These institutions also serve an important function as headquarters for the conventions of regional, national, and international business as well as professional and scientific organizations. The modern metropolitan hotel is now an auditorium as well as a dormitory and dining establishment. In this district also are to be found that complement of cultural institutions which can be supported only by the population of a great metropolitan community. These are the opera, the symphony, the public forum, the scientific library, the museum, and the art gallery.

This inventory of central business institutions and functions is of course not complete. Attention must, however, be given to a complex of institutions of which no mention has yet been made—the governmental institutions of the central city. They alone of all the institutions in the district are purely local in the scope of their activity and influence. They symbolize one of the major problems of the metropolitan region, namely, that it constitutes not a *de jure* but a *de facto* community. For this reason it fails frequently to achieve a more complete unity since it lacks a political and administrative machinery of its own. This is not to argue that political controls are necessary first in importance. It is however, to argue that the socioeconomic order which has evolved in the metropolitan community has proved that it is no longer self-regulatory. There is at present much talk about the relation of the national state to the activities of its traders in the national and international market. Although on a somewhat more complicated level, this relationship represents exactly the problem that exists in the metropolitan community as well. The automobile, rapid transit, the organization of modern industry, and many other technological and social changes have rendered the older set of political implements not only obsolete but also grossly inefficient. Its present socioeconomic organization suggests, furthermore, the anachronism of the old phrase, "the rural-urban antithesis." What exists in its place is well indicated by the more comprehensive concept—the metropolitan community. This provides us with a picture of a co-operating and mutually interdependent set of social and economic processes which, in large part, gives the lie to the old country-city dichotomy and, as suggested above, within which framework the older figure of speech can hardly be imagined.

The central business district has been treated thus far mainly from the ecological point of view. But it is the locus of not only a spatial but also a social order as well, and hence it cannot be thoroughly understood until the dual nature of its organization has been pointed out. To this a brief consideration will be given.

In Chicago, for example, the central business district happens to be an area identical with one of the seventy-five local communities into which the city has been tentatively divided for purposes of social investigation. But the designation of the area as a local community rests only on whatever analysis has been given it as a place of residence, that is, as the home of man rather than his place of work. The study of the local community has, traditionally, included the collection and analysis of such data as the total population, its age and sex composition, nativity, size of family, and similar data. The enumeration of this area in the 1934 municipal census showed that it contained but 3,530 legal residents. Of these, 80 per cent were males; 61 per cent were single; and, most striking of all, among the total population there were but 33 persons under the age of five years. But, in addition to these so-called legal residents, the area contained another population—the one-half million or more daily workers with whom, as such, the census had no concern. It is then only in terms of its 3,530 residents that the area has been designated as a local community. There is, however, little evidence that this population constitutes, in the vicinal and parochial or strictly moral sense of the term, a community. Its hotel and club population is characteristically united, if at all, on the basis of narrow and separate professional or business interests. It possesses little of what Durkheim has called "the patriotism of the parish." Its lodging-house population, which constitutes the bulk of its total number, is largely individualistic, inarticulate, and highly mobile in character. Within it there is little consensus. Likewise, between these two population groups, socially and economically disparate as they are, hotel and club dwellers, on the one hand, and flophouse denizens, on the other, there exists no significant community of interests.

But there is, in this district, another spatial and moral order, namely, the so-called business community. As to its age and sex composition, nativity, marital status, or even its total number but a meager little is known. But this population is the more important for understanding the nature and function of the area as a business district, and this despite the fact that it is, on the average, less than an eight-hour-per-day population. In contrast with the twenty-four-hour population of the area there is within it a marked degree of consensus, some features of which have been indicated above. This is based not upon kinship or geographical propinquity but upon the common professional or business interests generated in the activities of the market place. This consensus is not "all of a piece," but its various segments go to make up a whole which has, undeniably, a common pattern both as to its origin and as to its orientation. This population aggregate is, for the want of a better term, a secular society, but one which, like all secular societies, has its sacred aspects, such as, for instance, the codes and creeds of its business and professional groups. Perhaps its most representative individual is the business executive whose place of business and place of residence are miles apart and frequently under different municipal jurisdictions. His place of residence, on the periphery of the central city or in one of its dormitory suburbs, constitutes his *milieu natal;* the central business district is his *milieu professionel.* In addition he exerts an influence, not infrequently, upon a third *milieu*—the industrial community which responds to his will through the production and wage policies of his corporation. Such a definition of his area of influence, however, takes no account of the national and international range of the industrial and financial policies emanating from this central district.

In an analysis such as has been here presented the institutions of the market place have been made an object of a social, economic, and political theory. This theory should in its turn make for a more comprehensive understanding of the organization of the metropolitan community and, in turn, permit the forging of a set of adequate political tools for its more effective social control.

6

Cecil C. North

THE CITY AS A COMMUNITY:
AN INTRODUCTION TO A
RESEARCH PROJECT

IF IT IS TRUE that the city is the most characteristic phenomenon of modern life it is because in the city the outstanding
forces of present-day society are working out their logical consequences in more complete form than elsewhere. Here the operations
of capitalism, mobility of population, democracy, individualism,
and group action are all found in full swing. And here are displayed
their end results in the extremes of luxury and poverty, of civic
virtue and crime, of stable social organization and appalling disorganization.

Whether or not the city is a community is, obviously, largely a
matter of how we define a community. And this seems to be a matter over which there is the usual difficulty which appears when we
undertake to give definite scientific meaning to a term of popular
usage. There is, however, in all the connotations of the term "community," both popular and scientific, the fundamental notion of a
group of people inhabiting a prescribed geographical area who have
a considerable degree of unity in meeting the more important concerns of life.

The chief reason for casting the modern large city outside the
community fold is that many observers have been more impressed
with the evidences of absence of unity in the city than with the signs
of its presence. There can be no gainsaying the evidences of disorganization in the modern great city. National and racial groups

Reprinted from *The Urban Community*, ed. Ernest W. Burgess (Chicago:
University of Chicago Press, 1926), pp. 233–37.

gathered from the four quarters of the globe here live in close physical proximity, but with little similarity of tastes or habit or language
and little sympathy for, or understanding of, one another. Varieties
of religious groups either spend much of their energies in attempting
to neutralize the efforts of one another or go their respective ways
with indifference and mutual disdain. Warring economic groups,
through violent conflict or long-continued competition, wear out
one another's resources and at the same time deny their constitu-
ents the convenience or utility of their needed services. Opposing
ethical standards divide the city into warring factions concerning
law enforcement, Sunday observance, race-track gambling. It is
not strange that the spectacle of such a discordant medley of hundreds of thousands of individuals without any personal relations except in small selective groups should impress many observers with
the lack of any essential unity that might be described as communal.
Professor Sanderson, for example, says that the large metropolitan
city "is a mere aggregation of people living together under a city
government."[1]

Such a point of view, however, fails to take account of certain
aspects of social unity that are exceedingly significant for modern
society. To think of group unity as confined exclusively to situations
where simple, face-to-face relations prevail is to neglect some of
the most important phases of the present social order. Professor
Snedden has well pointed out the highly co-operative nature of
much of our mechanized impersonal relations.[2] Mail delivery, road-
building, protection from internal and external enemies, are now
carried on in a highly impersonal manner devoid of conscious co-
operation, but would not be possible if there did not exist a very
vital co-operative relationship between the citizens of the nation as
well as between states and local groups.

There are several distinctive marks of all modern local groups
that should be recognized as applying to cities as well as to rural
groups. First, the locality is decreasingly self-sufficient. Government, economic organization, and cultural organization, all are developed on national, or in some cases on world, lines. The citizen of

[1]   *Publications of the American Sociological Society*, XIV, 85.
[2]   *American Journal of Sociology*, XXVIII, 681 ff.

the local group is also a citizen of the state and of the nation, and he consequently relies on these outside agencies for a part of his life-needs. The economic life of the locality practically always reflects the economic conditions of the nation and, largely, of the civilized world. Hence the economic interests of the citizen look far beyond the boundaries of his city. His religion, his intellectual life, and practically all other aspects of his culture are fed by many streams whose sources are far beyond the confine of his locality. The modern local group, whether small rural community or metropolitan area, can in no sense satisfy the life-needs or claim the exclusive loyalty of its members.

In the second place all modern society is highly individualistic as compared with primitive society. That is, much larger place is given for variety of taste and habit and belief. No dead level of uniformity is pressed down on the lives of its members by any modern social group. Specialization and division of labor have been accompanied by differentiation of thought and interest. This means that the unity that exists within any modern group must be an organic unity, a functional cohesion of unlike parts, whether we have in mind economic organization, political organization, or culture. As Professor Cooley has well shown, the unity of opinion or thought or belief, in a modern group, is a unity that permeates many differences.[3]

In the next place, since the areas over which contacts take place are large, and since our unity is a functional cohesion of unlike parts instead of one of uniformity, the greater part of the relations maintained in modern society are impersonal. Our cultural contacts are through books and magazines and newspapers, and we have no fellowship of the personal sort with thousands who are daily helping to mold our thoughts and shape our personalities. We have very significant business relations with the tea-growers of China, the coffee-growers of Brazil, the diamond-miners of South Africa. The farmer of Montana has definite business relations with the banker of New York. But all this is so mechanized and carried on through such tortuous channels that the personal element has no place in it.

[3]   Cooley, *Social Organization*, pp. 121–28.

Now, the reason the city is looked upon as a confused mass of people without essential social unity is because in it these characteristics of modern society are seen in their most typical form. The citizens of the city are not bound together by any unique loyalty to a self-sufficient locality. They are highly diverse in their culture and in their interests. Their co-operative relations, except in small selective groups, are highly mechanical and impersonal. Bue we cannot deny that there is in the city an essential unity. The economic interdependence of city dwellers is certainly greater than is found in the rural community. In the maintenance of the public schools and all the departments of the city government we see a group of common objectives and essentially co-operative activity. The like response to intellectual and emotional stimuli is frequently much more marked over the whole metropolitan area than it is within the rural community.

The question may now be raised, Is a city a community in any sense in which a state or the nation is not one? Do not practically all modern political or locality groups have the sort of unity which we are claiming for the city? The essential difference lies in the number of the interests of the population which have been reduced to a co-operative basis, and in the degree to which the co-operative process is complete. Thus, if we compare the city with the state we find that the urban population is co-operating in many more things than are the citizens of the state. The functions of city government, for example, are much more numerous than those of the state. And governmental activities are not the only field in which the comparison is to be made. In intellectual and aesthetic pursuits, in religion, in voluntary civic and philanthropic activities, in business and industrial affairs it cannot be doubted that a larger number of co-operative projects is carried on by the urban population than by the state or nation.

When we compare the degree to which the co-operative process is complete in the city with the degree attained in the functions of the state or of the national group we find the same difference. For example, the co-operative process with respect to the schools is much more complete in the school district than in the state or nation, as are also the local public-health functions as compared with those of the state and nation.

There are undoubtedly striking differences between cities in these respects, as also between rural communities. These comparisons suggest that we may have here a measure of the communal process. All locality groups have a certain degree of communal process. That is, all have a number of co-operative activities, each of which has attained a certain degree of co-operative completeness. But the number and the degree vary greatly. Instead, therefore, of attempting to answer the question whether this or that locality group constitutes a community, we have to determine the extent to which the group is communal, and we have, as means of determining this extent, these objective units of measurement. The adoption of such an objective measure of communal unity frees us from much of the metaphysical character that has permeated our discussion of the community during the past decade. It also eliminates the futile search for the answer as to just what types of locality group are entitled to the designation of community. Any locality group may properly be called a community, or at least a potential community, but the degree to which it has attained the communal character is a matter of quantity and subject to measurement.

We may, in fact, isolate any particular phase of a city's life and undertake to study the degree to which it has attained a communal character. It rarely is the case that the same degree of progress has been attained in this respect in all the different aspects of the life of the city. Within recent years the community movement has been expressed in a number of separate efforts in American cities. The chamber of commerce movement is an attempt on the part of the mercantile and the employing interests to strengthen their position through co-operative effort. The Protestant churches have undertaken a similar project in the church federation movement. The organized labor interests have created the local trades council. The women's club movement has achieved city federations of clubs. Within the same city considerable progress may have been made toward realizing a business community or a religious community, while other aspects of the city life are still highly unco-operative.

The project in which I am engaged is a study of the community movement among the welfare activities of American cities. One question to be answered by such a study is, to what extent are American cities becoming communal in the development of those activities pertaining to the physical and moral well-being of the population? It seems apparent that this can be measured by determining the number of these activities that are being put upon a co-operative basis and the extent to which this co-operation is effective. Such a study should reveal, with respect to any particular city, the extent to which it has become a community in its welfare activities, and, with respect to the national life, what the tendency is in this field.

7

Paul Frederick Cressey

POPULATION SUCCESSION

IN CHICAGO: 1898–1930

THE POPULATION OF CHICAGO doubled from 1898 to 1930, amounting at the latter date to more than three million people. This rapid growth was accompanied by marked changes in the distribution of the city's population. Not simply did the population expand over a larger area, but certain sections of the city grew more rapidly than others and various cultural groups moved at different rates of speed.

In order to measure these movements, data for census tracts in 1910, 1920, and 1930 were used, as well as material from an 1898 census taken by the Chicago School Board. These census tracts and the precincts of the 1898 census were grouped into a series of ten concentric mile-zones radiating from the center of the city. The last, or tenth, zone is not directly comparable with the other zones, since it includes all the area from the ninth zone to the city limits and is quite irregular in shape. The large industrial community of South Chicago lies within this tenth zone.

In 1898 Chicago was relatively compact, half of its population living within a radius of 3.2 miles from the center of the city. In subsequent years this median point has steadily moved outward, being located at 4.1 miles in 1910, 5.0 miles in 1920, and 5.8 miles in 1930.[1] One of the most striking aspects of this general expansion

Reprinted from the *American Journal of Sociology* 44, no. 1 (July 1938): 59–69.

[1]   The medians for each year were calculated from the distribution of the population in the ten mile-zones into which the city was divided, and

has been the loss of population in the areas near the center of the city. In 1898, 45 per cent of the city's population—a total of 824,-000 people—lived within the first three mile-zones; but in 1930 this area housed only 14 per cent of Chicago's population, or 474,000 people.[2] This region includes most of the slum area of the city and corresponds roughly to what E. W. Burgess has designated as the "zone in transition."[3] During the years from 1898 to 1930 the population of the fourth to sixth mile-zones, inclusive, increased at approximately the same rate as that of the city as a whole. The greatest increase occurred in the outlying zones. In 1898 the seventh, eighth, and ninth zones included but 10 per cent of the population, whereas in 1930, 33 per cent of the population lived in this area. The population of the tenth zone increased from 5 to 14 per cent of the city's total during this general period, a considerable part of this increase being due to the rapid growth of industry in South Chicago.

This outward movement of population has continued beyond the limits of the city into a large number of suburbs. Between 1900 and 1930 the population of Chicago increased 99 per cent, whereas the population of fifteen of the larger suburbs, for which data are available, increased 329 per cent.

A more detailed picture of these movements may be had by studying the figures for specific cultural groups. This is particularly revealing because of the heterogeneous character of Chicago's population. Chicago is, in fact, one of the most European cities in America. Persons of native-white parentage constituted but 21 per cent of the population in 1900 and 28 per cent in 1930, the latter figure, according to available records, representing the highest percentage of American stock in the city's history. In 1930 one-quarter of the people were of foreign birth, and an additional 40 per cent were the children of foreign parents. Only two cities in Poland have more Poles, and but two cities in Ireland have more

rested on the assumption that the population was evenly distributed within each zone. The medians for the specific cultural groups in the city were calculated on a similar basis.

2   For the sake of simplicity these and subsequent population figures are expressed in terms of the nearest whole thousand.

3   R. E. Park and E. W. Burgess, *The City* (Chicago, 1925), p. 51.

Irish than are to be found in Chicago.[4] In addition Chicago is the third largest Swedish city in the world, the third largest Bohemian, the third largest Jewish, and the second largest Negro. There are seven immigrant groups in Chicago, each composed of over one hundred thousand people, in addition to which there are nearly a quarter of a million Negroes. This great diversity of population is one of the reasons why succession has been so conspicuous a phenomenon in the city's history.

The distribution of these various groups reflects a definite process of succession. Immigrant stocks follow a regular sequence of settlement in successive areas of increasing stability and status. This pattern of distribution represents the ecological setting within which the assimilation of the foreign population takes place. An immigrant group on its arrival settles in a compact colony in a low-rent industrial area usually located in the transitional zone near the center of the city. If the group is of large size several different areas of initial settlement may develop in various industrial sections. These congested areas of first settlement are characterized by the perpetuation of many European cultural traits. After some years of residence in such an area, the group, as it improves its economic and social standing, moves outward to some more desirable residential district, creating an area of second settlement. In such an area the group is not so closely concentrated physically, there is less cultural solidarity, and more American standards of living are adopted. Subsequent areas of settlement may develop in some cases, but the last stage in this series of movements is one of gradual dispersion through cosmopolitan residential districts. This diffusion marks the disintegration of the group and the absorption of the individuals into the general American population. The relative concentration or dispersion of various immigrant groups furnishes an excellent indication of the length of residence in the city and the general degree of assimilation which has taken place.

The distribution of the American groups has also followed a rather definite pattern, though their movements are more difficult

---

[4]   The statements in this paragraph referring to nationality groups in Chicago include those born in a specific country, together with the children of foreign-born parents.

to trace since they lack the conspicous cultural traits of the various immigrant groups. The American groups have tended to locate in the areas having direct access to the Loop, the business center of Chicago. The most desirable American residential districts have always been located along the main avenues running north, south, and west from the Loop. As the wealthier Americans have moved out along these main axes of transportation, other American groups of lower economic and social standing have generally followed in their wake. Along these main thoroughfares, near the Loop, is the rendezvous of the hobo—and the hobo is almost always an American. A little farther out are the rooming-house areas whose population is predominantly of native parentage, and then follow apartment-house areas with their cosmopolitan American population.

The immigrant and American groups follow rather different patterns of distribution, but behind these differences there is a striking similarity in the way in which these changes take place. This common process of succession involves a cycle of invasion, conflict, recession, and reorganization. These successive stages are interrelated, and they recur in the movement of all groups in the city.

The first stage in this cycle, that of invasion, usually begins with a few pioneers whose entrance into a new area may be unnoticed by the older residents. These pioneers tend to be individuals who have achieved a little greater economic success than their neighbors and who desire to improve their social status by moving into an area of greater prestige. Mass invasions set in after the initial invaders have established themselves in the new area. Such movement may involve merely a gradual transition which slowly replaces the older population, or it may take place with such rapidity as to be thought of in terms of a stampede. The area invaded may either be contiguous, or considerable distance may intervene. The direction of such movement is influenced by ecological barriers and by the main arteries of transportation which connect the two communities. The relative importance of various streets in Chicago in effecting group movement was determined statistically by comparing the population of specific groups in the census tracts adjacent to these streets with the total population of these groups in the sectors through which the streets ran. Once a mass movement is under way individuals are caught up in its spirit and often move with no other apparent reason than that everybody else is moving.

Conflict may accompany invasion, varying in intensity with the cultural differences and prejudices of the groups involved. Where the groups are of a similar social and economic level with no particular dislike for each other, the supplanting of one group by another usually involves only a minimum of friction. But where marked prejudices exist and there is a fear that the invading group will cause a serious loss in real estate values, violent opposition may develop. This situation has arisen particularly in the expansion of the Negro population into white communities and has been the reason for numerous bombings and other types of violence. Less extreme forms of hostility have developed over the entrance of Jews into gentile areas, and the movement of immigrants into American neighborhoods.

The correlative of invasion is recession, or the departure of the older population. The entrance of unwanted "outsiders" lowers the desirability of the area in the eyes of the older inhabitants. Community life begins to deteriorate and sooner or later there is a search for a newer and more respectable place to live. Recession, however, may sometimes precede invasion, for as an area grows old the housing accommodations become obsolete, street-paving and other public improvements may deteriorate, or there may be encroachments from trade or industry. Under such circumstances, as the area becomes less attractive, the older residents depart leaving unoccupied houses behind them, and this encourages the entrance of some new group into the area. Thus in some cases the normal sequence may be reversed and recession may precede rather than follow invasion. In such circumstances there is usually little or no conflict between the two groups.

The final stage of the cycle involves the reorganization of the social life of the invading group as it acquires dominance in the new area. It usually takes considerable time to transfer the institutions of the group, such as its churches, lodges, and other social organizations. Movement into a new community often creates a crisis in the life of a group. The established routine is interrupted, the "cake of custom" is broken, and opportunities are presented for the adoption of new ways of life. Immigrants frequently take advantage of entrance into a new area to change their names to more American forms, changes such as the following being not uncommon: Garskovitz to Groves, Smallovitz to Small, Abrahamson to Abrams, Weinstein to Weston. The organization of the family seems to change with movement from one area to another, especially in the case of the newer immigrant groups. Patriarchal patterns of authority and control which often characterize the area of first settlement give way to greater equality in family relations in secondary areas of settlement. This modification in family organization is illustrated in the case of a family, of which it was said, "After Mr. F. moved into this more American community he even allowed his daughter to marry the man she fell in love with." The adoption of more liberal forms of worship by the older synagogues in Chicago has always coincided with their movement and the construction of new houses of worship. Even after the invading group has established its dominance, a few of the older residents may still remain in the area. Such marooned families, surviving from earlier groups of inhabitants, may be found in many communities in Chicago and often furnish a clue to the past history of the area.

In time the invaders will become old residents. Another cycle may set in, with a new group of invaders entering the area and the older residents or their descendants moving on to other parts of the city. This cyclical process, with minor variations, has occurred repeatedly in the life of various cultural groups and in the history of different sections of the city.

Among the various groups in Chicago, the old American stock, because of its superior wealth and prestige, has been in the forefront in the outward movement of the city's population. In 1910 persons of native-white parentage were distributed at a median distance of 4.7 miles from the center of the city, and in 1930 at 6.6 miles, nearly a mile farther out than the median for the total population of the city.

The two most American sections of Chicago are the North and South sides. On the North Side in 1920, 25 per cent of the population was of native stock. This rose to 38 per cent in 1930, making this sector the most American part of the city. The "Gold Coast," the wealthiest and most fashionable area of the city, is located along the lake shore in this sector. North of the city limits and adjacent to the lake there sketch a series of well-to-do American suburbs, five of the most important having quadrupled in size between 1900 and 1930, at which time 52 per cent of their total population was of native stock. The South Side in 1900 was more American than the North Side, but by 1930 it had lost this leadership, at which time its native white stock amounted to but 28 per cent. On the West Side the American population has moved outward in large numbers to suburbs beyond the city limits, eight of which communities had a total population of 154,000 in 1930, 50 per cent of which was of American ancestry.

European immigrants first arrived in Chicago in large numbers during the decade following 1850. The Germans were the most important group in this early movement and by 1860 they constituted approximately one-fifth of the city's population. They settled in a compact colony on the North Side, where today two small concentrations still remain, located several miles north of the original area of settlement.[5] The outward movement of the German population is shown by the shift in the median point of their distribution from 3.2 miles in 1898 to 5.7 miles in 1930.[6] On the North Side this movement has been directed primarily along the main arteries of travel. In 1930, 36 per cent of the Germans in Chicago were located on the North Side, and an additional 31 per cent lived in the adjacent Northwest Side. The great majority of the group has ceased to live in specific German communities and is scattered through more or less cosmopolitan residential areas. This widespread dispersion is an index of the decline of social unity among the Germans and of their gradual absorption into the general life of the city.

The Irish began to arrive in Chicago about the same time as the

---

[5]   H. W. Zorbaugh, *The Gold Coast and the Slum* (Chicago, 1929), pp. 18–20; 149–50.
[6]   These medians and other statistical data in the remainder of this article referring to immigrant groups are calculated only for individuals of foreign birth, as no detailed data were available, prior to 1930, for the distribution of native-born persons of foreign parentage.

Germans, settling primarily in the general vicinity of the Stock Yards on the Southwest Side of the city. At the present time only a very small settlement remains in this area of initial concentration, and the group as a whole is widely scattered through more desirable residential districts farther from the center of the city. This outward movement of the Irish is indicated by the change in the median of their distribution from 3.2 miles in 1898 to 6.4 miles in 1930, a point over half a mile farther from the Loop than the median for the total population of the city. On the Southwest Side, where 35 per cent of the Irish still reside, the main axis of movement has also been along a main transportation artery. The Irish are even more widely dispersed through the city than the Germans, a fact which reflects the more complete disintegration of their group life and a greater degree of cultural assimilation.

The third large group of early immigrants was composed of Swedes who began arriving in considerable numbers during the 1860's. Their main center of settlement developed on the North Side where they became close neighbors of the Germans. In 1930, 37 per cent of the Swedish population lived in this section where two small colonies still remain from their original settlement. The great majority of the Swedish population has reached the final phase in the pattern of succession, that of widespread dispersion and assimilation. This is seen in the fact that for some years the Swedes have been located farther from the center of the city than any other specific group, the median of their distribution being 3.9 miles in 1898 and 7 miles in 1930.

The newer immigrant groups, from eastern and southern Europe, began to arrive in Chicago during the last decade of the nineteenth century. As they increased in numbers they displaced the older immigrant groups from their original areas of settlement. Most of these newer groups, despite considerable movement in recent years, still remain concentrated in distinct settlements relatively close to the center of the city.

The Czechoslovaks in Chicago are largely of Bohemian or Czech stock, there being only a relatively small number of Slovaks in the city. Their center of settlement has always been on the West Side, where in 1930, 50 per cent of the group resided. The median for the distribution of the Czechoslovaks has shifted from 2.7 miles in 1898 to 5.3 miles in 1930. Their movement on the West Side has followed the transportation lines into various suburbs west of the city limits. Cicero and Berwyn, the two most important of these suburbs, had a combined population of 114,000 in 1930, 34 per cent of this total being persons who were born in Czechoslovakia. The dispersion of this group has taken place more rapidly than that of any other group of recent immigrants. In part this may be due to their slightly longer residence in the city, but probably it also reflects their somewhat more rapid economic and cultural adjustment to urban American life.

The largest immigrant group in Chicago at the present time is composed of Poles. They have settled primarily on the Northwest Side, where in both 1898 and 1930, 48 per cent of the Poles lived. In addition to this main colony several minor areas of first settlement have developed in other parts of the city. As the group has grown in size there has been some outward movement, with the development of a few areas of secondary settlement. In 1898 the persons born in Poland were located at a median distance of 2.8 miles from the center of the city, and in 1930 at 4.6 miles. This latter figure is over a mile nearer the center of the city than the average for the total population, and represents the smallest amount of movement of any important group in the city during this period. The Poles still remain, on the whole, closely concentrated in areas of first settlement and they have not as yet made great progress in economic advancement or cultural assimilation.

The chief center of Italian settlement has been on the West Side, although there are a few small concentrations near industrial areas in other sections of the city. Until 1920 the Italians were even more compact and immobile than the Poles, the median of their distribution being 1.5 miles in 1898 and 2 miles in 1920. In the decade following 1920 there was considerable movement out to areas of secondary settlement, these new areas being connected with the old settlements by important through-streets. As a result of these movements the Italians in 1930 distributed at a median distance of 3.3 miles from the city's center. In spite of this recent expansion the majority of the Italians still live in areas of first settlement and the group as a whole is located closer to the center of the city than any other large immigrant population.

The Russians who have come to Chicago are almost entirely Russian Jews. They settled originally in a compact ghetto on the West Side, just south of the main Italian colony and far removed from the older group of German Jews living on the South Side. The decade from 1910 to 1920 witnessed a mass movement into an area of secondary settlement several miles west of the original ghetto area.[7] From 1898 to 1930 the median for the distribution of this group shifted from 1.6 to 4.8 miles, a movement covering a greater distance than that of any other group of recent immigrants. This mobility reflects a considerable amount of economic success, but the group as a whole, nevertheless, remains concentrated in rather definite settlements. The bonds of a common religion and culture and the external pressure of gentile prejudice have tended to give cohesion to the group and thus, despite its rapid movement, to retard the general dispersion and assimilation of its members.

Negroes have resided in Chicago since the earliest days of its history, but until the period of the World War they were relatively few in number and were widely scattered through the city. During the past twenty years, however, they have come to Chicago in such numbers that they now constitute one of the largest distinct groups in the city. Their chief area of settlement has been on the South Side where they now occupy an area approximately four miles long and a mile wide. This "Black Belt" of Negro population increased from 17,000 in 1898 to 91,000 in 1920, and in 1930 amounted to 189,-000, a figure which approaches that of New York's Harlem.[8] Negro settlements are also found in the abandoned Jewish ghetto area on the West Side, and in a few additional localities. Like other groups in the city the Negro population in recent years has moved out from the center of the city, the median for its distribution changing from 2.5 miles in 1898 to 4.5 miles in 1930. The unusual aspect of their history is that as they have moved and as their numbers have increased they have not become more widely dispersed through the

[7]   Louis Wirth, *The Ghetto* (Chicago, 1928), pp. 241–46.
[8]   In 1930 Harlem had a Negro population of 202,000. The total Negro population of Manhattan was 224,670.

city, but rather have come to be more highly concentrated in a few specific areas. There has, in fact, been an actual decrease in the number of Negroes in many sections of the city. As a result of their poverty and the pressure of white prejudice, the Negroes, particularly on the South Side, have come to live in a more compact community than any other important group in the city. One of the effects of this growing concentration has been to increase the racial consciousness and intensify the social and political solidarity of the Negroes in Chicago.[9]

The phenomena of succession have been so striking an aspect of Chicago's history largely because of the rapidity with which the city has grown and the great diversity of its cultural groups. These groups have moved through the city at varying rates of speed, reflecting different stages of economic and cultural advance. This process of succession has provided the framework for the distribution of the city's population and represents the way in which immigrant groups have escaped from their slum settlements and become assimilated into the general life of the city.

[9]   Harold F. Gosnell, *Negro Politicians: The Rise of Negro Politics in Chicago* (Chicago, 1933), chap. ii.

8

W. I. Thomas

THE IMMIGRANT COMMUNITY

THE COMMUNITY comprised of a number of families is the simplest form which society has assumed in the universal struggle against death. All the primary human needs can be satisfied in the community. Polish peasant communities, before 1860, lived as practically self-sufficient groups. They knew by report that there was a great world, and they had some relations with it, through Jews and manor owners; they had a priest and the religious-magical traditions of Christendom. But practically the extent of their world was the "*okolica*," "the neighborhood round about," and their definition of this was, "as far as a man is talked about." Their life was culturally poor, and they showed no tendency either to progress or to retrograde, but *they lived*. The peasant did not know he was a Pole; he even denied it. The lord was a Pole; he was a peasant. We have records showing that members of other immigrant groups realize first in America that they are members of a nationality: "I had never realized I was an Albanian until my brother came from America in 1909. He belonged to an Albanian society over here."[1]

The immigrants here tend to reproduce spontaneously the home community and to live in it. Letters show that they frequently reply

Reprinted from *Old World Traits Transplanted*, ed. Robert E. Park and Herbert A. Miller (New York: Harper and Brothers, 1921), pp. 145–59, 195–213.

1   Menas Laukas, "Life History," recorded by Winifred Rauschen-busch (manuscript).

to inquiries from home for a description of America, "I have not yet been able to see America." There are immigrants on the lower East Side of New York who have been here for twenty years and have never been up town. Even the intellectual immigrants feel painfully the failure to meet cultivated Americans.

The Italians

Among the more important immigrant groups the Italians show perhaps the strongest *wish* to remain in solitary communities. They settle here by villages and even by streets, neighbors in Italy tending to become neighbors here. . . .

The colony, from the village of Cinisi, Sicily, in the vicinity of East Sixty-ninth Street and Avenue A, New York, may be taken as typical. There are more than 200 families at this point, and there are other groups from Cinisi in Brooklyn, Harlem, and on Bleecker Street. . . .

The colony is held together by the force of custom. People do exactly as they did in Cinisi. If some one varies, he or she will be criticized. If many vary—then that will become the custom. It is by the group, collectively, that they progress. They do not wish the members of the colony to improve their economic conditions or to withdraw. If a woman is able to buy a fine dress, they say: "Look at that *villana* [serf]! In the old country she used to carry baskets of tomatoes on her head and now she carries a hat on it." "Gee! look at the daughter of so and so. In Cinisi she worked in the field and sunburnt her black. Here she dares to carry a parasol."

So strong is this influence that people hesitate to wear anything except what was customary in Cinisi. Everywhere there is fear of being "*sparlata*"—talked badly of. A woman bought a pair of silk stockings and the neighbors talked so much about her that her husband ordered her to take them off. . . . To dress poorly is criticized and to dress sportily is criticized. In this way one had to conform or be ostracized.

A number of families moved from the central group of Brooklyn. There they have combined and rent a whole two-story house. They are living better than those in the other groups and I often hear the East Sixty-ninth Street people say: "Look at those *paesani* in Brooklyn. When they were here they were in financial straits. One of them had to flee from the criticism here. He did not have the money to pay his moving van and crowded all his furniture into a small one-horse wagon. He even put his wife on to save car fare. He left a pile of debts and now he dares come around here with a horse and buggy."

If a wife is spied by another Cinisaro talking to a man who is known as a stranger—that is, who is not a relative—she is gossiped about: she has the latent willingness to become a prostitute. They say: "So and so's wife was talking with an American. Eh! She has the capacity to do wrong."

Nothing in the American women surprises them. They have already made an unfavorable judgment. My mother, for instance, was about to say that my wife, who is an American, was an exception to the rule, but when my wife went to Central Park with the baby she said, "They are all alike."[2]

Until 1914 the Sicilian colony in Chicago was an absolutely foreign community. The immigrants were mostly from villages near Palermo, though nearly all of the Sicilian provinces are represented. The most important of the village groups are those from Alta Villa Milicia, Bagheria Vicari, Cimmina, Termini-Imarezi, Monreali, and the city of Palermo. These groups retained their identity, living together as far as possible, intermarrying and celebrating the traditional feasts. Immigrants who settled in Louisiana came up to join their village colony. Those who had been leaders in Sicily retained their power here and, having greater force and intelligence, made contracts with local politicians, police officials, labor agents, and real estate dealers, and became the go-betweens for their colony and the outside-world labor agents.

Women continued to live as they had in Sicily, never leaving their homes except to make ceremonial visits or to attend mass. The presence of several garment factories in the district made it possible for them to earn by doing finishing at home. In later years hundreds of women went into the garment factories to work, some taking the street cars out of the district; but they went to and from work in groups, their shawls carefully wrapped about them.

In the entire district there was no food for sale that was not distinctly foreign; . . . but in season artichokes, cactus fruit *(fichi d'India)*, pomegranates, cocozella, and various herbs and greens never

[2]   Gaspare Cusumano, "Study of the Colony of Cinisi in New York City" (Manuscript).

sold in other parts of town were plentiful. There were no bookstores. Italian newspapers had a limited circulation, and the Chicago daily papers were sold at only two transfer points on the edge of the district. There were no evidences of taste in dress or house decoration. This group seemed to have had no folk music, but took great pleasure in band concerts when spirited marches and melodies from Verdi's operas were played. There was no educational standard; the older people were almost all illiterate; they accepted this as natural and explained it by saying, "We are *contadini*, and our heads are too thick to learn letters." Some of the younger ones had had a little elementary training, but with very few exceptions no one in the colony had gone beyond the *"quarto elementario."* Few had seen military service or learned trades except, of course, the tailors, barbers, and shoemakers. One heard of an occasional cabinet maker, harness maker, solderer, carpenter, or mason, but none followed his trade here, as the training did not fit him to American methods. Many who had worked in the orchards in Sicily found their way to South Water Street and worked as truckers and fruit packers and, becoming familiar with the way produce was handled, started their friends out as fruit and vegetable peddlers, thus establishing a wholesale business for themselves. Most of the men, however, were sent by their leaders to the railroads and building contractors as laborers. . . .

Individually, Sicilians seem to vary as much in their manner and ideals as Americans, but as a group they have certain very marked characteristics—reserve, suspicion, susceptibility to gossip, timidity, and the desire to *"fa figura."* Intense family pride, however, is the outstanding characteristic, and as the family unit not only includes those related by blood, but those related by ritual bonds as well (the *commare* and *compare*), and as intermarriage in the village groups is a common practice, this family pride becomes really a clan pride. . . .

During the last four years there has been a great change, the colony is slowly disintegrating, old customs are giving way. Contacts with the outside world, through work and school, have given boys and girls a vision of freedom and new opportunity. They are going to night schools and making their friends outside the old circle. They are out of patience with the petty interests and quarrels of the older group and refuse to have their lives ordered by their parents, whom they know to be ignorant and inexperienced. Families are not being broken up, the deep affections still persist, and though the old folks have misgivings, in their indulgent way they are letting the new generation take the lead and are proud of their progressive sons and daughters. Young married couples are making their homes north of the old district, within easy reach of their parents, but away from the old associations. Evidences of refinement are seen in their homes and in their manner, and their children are dressed and fed according to most modern standards.[23]

It appears from these statements: (1) that the Sicilian heritages are so different from the American that the members of this group feel no original interest in participating in American life; (2) that this difference is accepted in America as a natural fact, somewhat as an outlying herd of animals would be accepted and tolerated or exploited, without thought of its social incorporation; (3) that this solitary group is almost as inaccessible to superior individuals of its own nationality who might be its leaders as to American influence; . . . and (4) that, nevertheless, the mass begins to dissolve and change, owing to informal contacts with American life, made especially by the younger generation, and certainly largely through the public school, which is the one point at which contact is formal and inevitable. . . .

The Jews

The Jews tend even more than other immigrant groups to settle in cities. It is estimated that there are 3,320,000 Jews in America, and of these 1,500,000 are in New York City.[4]

The Jews come to this country more definitely as settlers than any other group, but they come from many countries: Russia, Rumania, Poland, Galicia, Germany, Turkey, etc. Most of them speak Yiddish in addition to the language of the country from which they come (Russian, Polish, Rumanian, Hungarian, and so forth), but there are various dialects of Yiddish, and the Jews from the Near East do not know Yiddish, but speak Greek, Ladino (Judæo-Spanish), Turkish, Arabic, and so forth. In their religious

[3] Marie Leavitt, "Report on the Sicilian Colony in Chicago" (manuscript).
[4] *Jewish Communal Register of New York City* (1917–18), p. 82; *American Jewish Yearbook* (Oppenheim reprint), p. 66.

ritual they may be orthodox, conservative, or reform. There are among them members of the pietistic, mystical, magical Chassidic sect; and at the other extreme are the freethinkers. Consequently the differences and mutual prejudices between different groups of Jews may be as great as those between members of different nationalities, and these inner divisions affect both their institutional life and their personal relations.

The Spanish and the Portuguese Jews found it difficult in the first half of the last century to admit whole-heartedly the German Jew to a close kinship with them—a difficulty which the German Jews experienced almost half a century later with the Jews hailing from Russia, and the Russian Jews in their turn only a decade later with the Jews coming from Galicia and Rumania. Because of this clannishness, several Jewish communities sprang up practically side by side in New York City: a Spanish-Portuguese community, a German community, a Russian community, an Oriental community, and a Galician, a Hungarian, and a Rumanian community. Almost every one of these communities was self-sufficient, with its own synagogues, charitable and educational institutions, and, what was inevitable, with its own politics. Under such conditions, the least untoward act, fancied or real, on the part of one group, led inevitably to strong separatistic tendencies in other groups. So, for instance, did the ascendancy of the German community result in the struggle of the so-called Downtown against Uptown, a struggle in which the combatants were mainly Russian and German Jews. In the same way did the sense of grievance which the Galician, Rumanian, Russian-Polish, and Bessarabian Jews felt against the ascendancy of the Russian Jewish community find its outlet in the formation of separate Verbands. For the Verbands, in spite of their voluble protestations of good intentions, were invariably organized as offensive and defensive alliances, a sort of *Verein zur Abwehr des Anti-Galizianerismus* or *Anti-Rumanierismus*, as the case might be. Only subsequent conditions changed their original plans and induced a new course of development.[5]

The Levantine Jews are very much isolated from the great Yiddish-speaking mass of Jews all about them. According to one of their spokesmen, Joseph Zedalicia, president of the Federation of Oriental Jews, the Levantine Jews "feel more discrimination from the other

[5]   S. Margoshes, *Jewish Communal Register*, p. 1286.

wings of the Jews than they do from the non-Jews." Part of the problem is that the Jews themselves, especially those of the lower East Side
communities—at least up until recently—did not actually realize that
these very new immigrants were also Jewish. They looked on these
"Spanioles" among them as "dagoes." Instances of street disturbances
and neighborhood disputes and complaints have been numerous. Some
years ago a group of residents in one section petitioned the mayor at
the time, Mr. Gaynor, to remove the "Turks" in their midst. When
they found that these people were Jews they hastened to settle the matter "among themselves."[6]

I am a Galician Jew and . . . God destined me to have a Russian
[Jewish] wife and it is a misfortune for me—not because she feeds me
with their Russian dishes, which are not bad, but the Russian company
she brings up to our house is unbearable . . . [detailed complaint].[7]

The Jew, like the peasant, first settled here in a colony, the
ghetto. This is not a new experience. Indeed he may have lived in
several ghettos, Vilna, Budapest, London, before he makes his way
to America.We call the territories in which the Jews and other immigrants first settle here areas of first settlement. The lower East
Side, the upper East Side, in the neighborhood of 110th Street and
Central Park, Brooklyn, Brownsville, East New York, are such
areas for the Jews.

Within an area of first settlement are found the customs and institutions of the home country; language and social ritual, dress and food
habits, the familiar notions of neighborly relations, the traditional
sanctions in family and personal conduct. Here are set up in their essential forms the patterns of community and family organization under which the individuals of the group lived in their European homes;
the synagogue as it exists in the towns of the Pale, the primitive forms
of burial and mutual aid societies, unmodified by the transplanting to
a new geographical environment. Spiritually, the old environment itself is transplanted. The greater number of the synagogue and benefit
society groups, among all of the several divisions of the Jews of the

6   Renee Darmstadter, "The Jewish Community of New York City"
(manuscript).
7   Letter to *Forward*, December 6, 1914. The editor replies humor-
istically, and advises him to thank God his wife is not a Rumanian.

East Side, are organized on the basis of common origins in Europe. The name of such a synagogue or aid society indicates that it has been formed by a group of persons who emigrated from the same village or city in the Old World; its purpose and organization is the same as it would be in the home village; coming together to pray, visiting the sick, caring for the burial of a member who has died, etc. The pattern of action is the same as it would be in the home village, and the feelings which keep it alive are those traditional sentiments of neighborly kinship and religious responsibility to which the same organization in Europe answered.[8]

As the Jews become more prosperous they begin to move to better quarters of the city, and the neighborhoods of Fourteenth Street and Second Avenue, the Bronx, are areas of second settlement. Finally the Jew may separate himself completely from his original colony and repudiate it. The contempt of the ghetto Jew for the *allrightnick* . . . is connected with this movement.

I visited a friend of mine in Riverside Drive—a Russian-English Jew who spent the last few years in Palestine. We took the bus. He . . . began to talk to me in Jewish and in a loud voice. . . . At Thirty-fourth Street and Fifth Avenue we changed busses. My friend continued his loud conversation in Jewish. "Please, do not speak Jewish around here," we heard a voice behind us. . . . It was the transfer agent of the bus company. . . . And he repeats his request in Jewish this time. "Why?" my friend asks him. "Just so. They won't have it." "Who won't have it?" "These people," and he points to the great crowd who daily pass this corner in the afternoon. . . . But *they* consist of many Jews. . . .[9]

Although it has lost its hold upon great numbers, the synagogue, including the activities associated with it, remains the most important feature in the life of the Jewish community as a whole, with the possible exception of the newspaper. The "synagogue Jew" is passing away. He has become a descriptive phrase and a literary type, but the attitudes created by the synagogue remain. The char-

[8]   Darmstadter, "Jewish Community."
[9]   P. Hirschbein, "Impressions," *The Day* (Yiddish newspaper), January 6, 1917.

acter of the Jew is the joint production of the hostility of the Gentile world and the communal life of which the synagogue was the center. . . .

The function of the synagogue was not limited to that of defense. Like the moated mediæval castles, which outwardly with their bastions and moats have all the appearance of fortresses, but which from the inner courts present the aspect of palaces intended to house and enrich a life of peace, so the synagogue not only protected the Jewish faith from a hostile world, but was also for the Jew a home for the development of his strivings and ideals. It was a house of prayer, a *"beth tephillah,"* a house of study, a *"beth ha'midrash,"* and a meeting house, where communal undertakings were formulated, and where all plans for the communal good were discussed and adopted. The synagogue rendered possible the cultivation of the spiritual life in the Diaspora, and thus gave point to the truth that wherever the Jewish people went it was accompanied by the *"shekhina,"* or Divine Presence.

Establishing a synagogue or being affiliated with one was not considered a matter of option. It was an accepted principle that wherever there were ten Jews they were in duty bound to form themselves into a congregation, and to carry on all the customary Jewish communal activities. While the Jew is in a position to discharge most of his religious duties by himself, it was realized that detachment from communal life could not but eventually lead to complete severance from the faith. Hence the designation of "evil neighbor" for one who, though living near a synagogue, kept aloof from it. That accepted principle it was which, enforced by the sanction of public sentiment, brought every Jew within the influence of the synagogue. . . .

The synagogue has lost hold on more than one-half of the largest Jewish community in the world. The estimated Jewish population of this city is about 1,500,000, which is a very conservative figure. But taking into consideration the 30 per cent who constitute the child population up to the age of fourteen, and allowing 10 per cent for adolescent Jewish girls, who, unfortunately, have hardly any place in the synagogue, we should expect at least 900,000 seats to accommodate Jewish worshipers on the high holidays, when the maximum attendance is reached. We find, however, the total seating capacity to be 381,000. If we add to that the 30,000 to 35,000 seats to be found in the 120 small synagogues not yet investigated, we see that out of 900,000 Jews only about 415,000 are synagogue Jews.

Secondly, we observe the remarkable unevenness in the per cent of the population affiliated with the synagogues, when judged by districts. Whereas in the Delancey District 44 per cent are synagogue Jews, in Bushwick and in Richmond only 7 per cent, in West Queens only 2 per cent, worship in synagogues. It is evident that the density of population, economic conditions, and length of stay in this country have so rapid an effect upon synagogue affiliation that we cannot but infer that the synagogue owes its existence more to the momentum of the past than to any new forces created in this country that make for its conservation and development.[10]

The Poles

In Polish-American society the parish is the center of community life, but the formation of the colony precedes the formation of the parish. Wherever Poles are collected for work, other Poles join them from the old country, and the colony grows spontaneously. The first organization is a mutual aid society. It is only when the colony has grown in numbers that a priest is called. But when the parish is established in America, it has a much larger social function than it has in Poland. It assumes, to a degree, the character of a commune.

Just as the benefit society is much more than a mutual insurance company, so the Polish-American parish is much more than a religious association for common worship under the leadership of a priest. The unique power of the parish in Polish-American life, much greater than in even the most conservative peasant communities in Poland, cannot be explained by the predominance of religious interests, which, like all other traditional social attitudes, are weakened by emigration, though they seem to be the last to disappear completely. The parish is, indeed, simply the old primary community reorganized and concentrated. In its concrete totality it is a substitute for both the narrower but more coherent village group and the wider but more diffuse and vaguely outlined *okolica*. In its institutional organization it performs the functions which in Poland are fulfilled by both the parish and the commune. It does not control the life of its members as efficiently as did the old community, for, first of all, it seldom covers a given territory entirely

[10]   M. M. Kaplan, *Jewish Communal Register*, pp. 117, 120.

and is unable to compel everyone living within this territory to belong to it; secondly, its stock of socially recognized rules and forms of behavior is much poorer; thirdly, the attitudes of its members evolve too rapidly in the new conditions; finally, it has no backing for its coercive measures in the wider society of which it is a part. But its activities are much broader and more complex than those of a parish or of a commune in the old country.[11]

The priest and the parish committee are careful to select a site for the church as close as possible to the centers where Poles work, and in a locality where rent is low and land is cheap. There follows a further territorial concentration of Poles. The original population—Italians, Germans, Irish—slowly moves out as the neighborhood becomes predominantly Polish. The parish thus becomes the community. Polish business is developed, associations . . . are formed, affording their members economic advantages, social entertainment, a field for economic co-operation, educational opportunities, help in expressing and realizing their political ideals, and a congenial social milieu in which the desires for recognition and response are satisfied. Even Poles who are not religious are thus drawn into the parish institutions.

[11]   Florian Znaniecki, "Study of Polish Institutions in America" (manuscript).

9

Herbert Blumer

MOULDING OF MASS BEHAVIOR

THROUGH THE

MOTION PICTURE

FIRST, A WORD about the mass of "movie-goers"—the general motion picture audience. Its general attributes are those of the mass. It consists of individuals with the most heterogeneous backgrounds—differences in families, in communities, in local cultures, in occupations, and in class affiliations. This mass has no form or organization. It has no program, no rules, no traditions, and no culture. It has no group consciousness, no we-feeling, no bonds of loyalty. In it the individuals are anonymous, have no social positions, no designated functions.

Before considering how such a formless mass with such a heterogeneous background is influenced and affected by motion pictures it is advisable to treat briefly the communicative nature of the cinema.

The unique feature of motion pictures, of course, is its vivid visual presentation. The images which are given are already fully established, clean-cut, easily identified, and easily followed. The complete psychological significance of this vivid visual presentation has never been stated. It seems clear, however, that it is conducive to ready comprehension or, what amounts to the same thing, it makes it easy for the spectator to assume the role of the characters, to identify himself with them quickly and effectively.

Much of the peculiar effectiveness of motion pictures comes from the use of the "close-up." This interesting communicative fea-

Reprinted from *Publications of the American Sociological Society* 29, no. 3 (August 1935) : 115–27.

ture deserves a few remarks. In motion pictures, as contrasted with the theater, the physical distance between the spectators and the actors is not fixed. This distance may be varied at will. Through the close-up the audience may be ushered into the very midst of the scene of action. This undoubtedly increases their sense of participation, but the phase of the experience I wish to stress is that it establishes feelings of rapport and intimacy. Here I think we find a genuine case wherein a decrease of physical distance is marked by a decrease in social distance. The close-up brings the spectator into touch contact with the characters. It grants him the privileged position of closeness, and permits him to observe at intimate range the play of facial and bodily gesture. My belief is that the close-up inevitably induces a sense of intimacy and of privileged familiarity. (Thornton Wilder informs me that the fan mail of movie stars appears to be much more intimate in tone than the fan mail received by theatrical or opera stars. In the latter the adoration is distant, seemingly conforming to the physical separation set by the theatre.)

A third feature of motion pictures helpful to an understanding of their nature as a communicative agency is their dramatic character. What is presented has a plot, a development, and a climax. There is movement, progressive suspense, and sensed anticipation —all of which also facilitate ready identification on the part of the spectator.

This analysis should explain why motion pictures are such an effective form of communication. Where the objects of concern are presented vividly and distinctly, where they are brought into intimate and close touch with the spectator, and where they share the impelling movement of drama, they arrest attention, check intrusion, and acquire control. The individual loses himself in the picture.

To induce this absorption or identification on the part of the spectator is the avowed purpose of the producer; to have the experience is the desire of the average movie-goer.

It is significant to note that to achieve the experience, motion pictures depend on appeals to primary emotions and sentiments. This is inevitable, of course, in all drama. But in motion pictures it is inevitably true. Little use is made of abstract forms or of complicated and remote symbolism (a movement in this direction would occur, should motion pictures become a cultural institution) but, instead, there is an exploitation of what is primary and universal in human beings: emotions, passions, and sentiments. Since motion pictures are dealing with a mass of individuals with enormous differences in educative and cultural backgrounds, it is on this level that they find common responsiveness.

Let me summarize then by saying that as a form of communication motion pictures operate as a visual, dramatic presentation, appealing primarily to emotions and sentiments.

What is the general influence of motion pictures? My belief is that it is a *reaffirmation of basic human values but an undermining of the mores*. This statement is not as contradictory as it sounds. Since the appeal of motion pictures depends so much on touching primary sentiments, it is not strange that they should stress those human qualities which are man's universal possession. In the cinema, one finds the constant portrayal and approval of such qualities as bravery, loyalty, love, affection, frankness, personal justness, cleverness, heroism, and friendship. Practically all motion pictures are tuned to the old and simple theme of conflict between what has our sympathy and what has our antipathy, between the good and the bad, between the desirable and the reprehensible. In motion pictures the sympathetic, the good, and the desirable are compounded out of such human qualities as those mentioned above —out of those already having widespread allegiance, those whose value is spontaneously appreciated. The elevation of these qualities to points of virtue and the accompanying reinforcement of the sentiments for which they stand is what I have in mind in declaring that motion pictures reaffirm basic human values.

However, the social patterns or schemes of conduct inside of which these primary human qualities are placed are likely to be somewhat new, strange, and unfamiliar. The characters, the setting, the events, and the forms of life presented are novel—in varying degree, but always to some degree. In a sense they have to be novel in order to attract attention. Further, it is to be expected that they would be strange and different because of the heterogeneity of the cultural backgrounds from which the movie-goers come. Herein, motion pictures operate like all agencies of mass communication to turn the attention of individuals outward from their areas of locally defined life. This concern with the new, the strange, and the different, is not merely a direction of attention to the outside of local culture; it is an attack upon the local culture. For these new forms of life which are presented in the movies become attractive and understandable, and develop a claim on one's allegiance. This is done by these forms of life being colored, so to speak, by the basic human qualities which are placed in them and operate through them. The beneficent value of the sentiment is imparted to the form of life which carries it; what was originally alien becomes suddenly emotionally familiar. This penetration of basic human values into new social forms constitutes one of the most interesting features of motion pictures. It explains why and how they undermine the prevailing patterns of local culture.

The residue of this invasion of local culture by motion pictures is in the form of awakened appetites, impulses, desires, yearnings, and hopes which even though experienced only momentarily and given expression only in day-dreaming, orient the individual in directions different from those prescribed by his tradition and culture. In my investigations I have found this to be noticeable particularly in the case of adolescents.

In further elaboration of this view that motion pictures operate against traditional forms and the mores, I should like to add that movie-goers, by reason of being a mass in an undefined area have no culture which might interpret and order their cinema experiences, and integrate them with those of local life. Instead the experiences remain alienated with no scheme to bridge them. It is this absence of an intermediate defining culture which makes motion pictures a matter of moral concern. It is also at the heart of the problem of their control. Without an intervening scheme of interpretation, the problem is inevitably met on the basis of controlled selection—censorship or choice of which pictures are to be seen.

If motion pictures, however, tend to alienate people from local culture they also prepare people for the wider area of life. This is done by enlarging their acquaintance, making new forms of life familiar to them, providing them with definite and defining images of this life, and suggesting to them "techniques" for adjustment to it. Motion pictures not only bring new objects to the attention of people but, what is probably more important, they make what has been remote and vague, immediate and clear. By reason of this ability they are especially effective in establishing stereotypes. This effectiveness is greatest where the initial familiarity with the object is least, for in such situations the object now shown in a definitive and familiar way becomes a norm. By portraying life in clearly seen and easily understood form motion pictures lend themselves to imitation of "techniques," and sometimes by reason of the appealing presentation invite such imitation.

Much might be made of this point that motion pictures sensitize people to new areas of life and prepare them for action in these areas. They serve the adolescent, particularly, as an educative agency. The point is not new, is adequately documented by studies which have been made, and is, I think, of minor importance. I wish to turn from it to the discussion of a phase of motion picture influence which, although little understood, I regard as of central importance.

In the detachment of the mass from local culture and the turning of their attention towards an outside world, the influence of motion pictures seems to be felt most in the realm of reverie. The motion picture experience is, itself, a form of reverie—in turn it is a great stimulus and feeder to further reverie. We do not know how to interpret the meaning of this reverie nor are we able to trace its effects. Many have claimed that it represents a harmless satisfaction of disturbing and dangerous impulses and serves, accordingly, to keep the individual house in order. But there is plenty of evidence for the counter belief that, instead, it whets appetites and stimulates impulses, leading to tension and not relaxation, to excitement and not quiescence, to disequilibrium and not organic harmony. Each interpretation is probably correct, but we do not know under what given conditions.

What I think is quite true is that there is an intimate relation between reverie, awakened disposition, and basic taste. The play of reverie, whether ordered as in the motion picture or free as in individual day dreaming awakens various impulses, furnishes objects upon which they may fasten, sketches schemes of possible conduct, and launches the individual upon vicarious journeying in new social worlds. That this rich play of inner experience has important effects on dispositions and tastes is seemingly true even though the nature of these effects is obscure. My interests at this point is merely in stating that mass reverie not only reflects the spirit and feelings of people but also invigorates and moulds this spirit and these feelings.

In this respect motion pictures are akin to folk tales and serve a role in modern life similar to that played by the latter in folk life. There is, however, a difference between them which is important for this discussion. To state it vigorously: folk tales reinforce the folk culture by reason of being closely integrated with it whereas motion pictures are integrated with no culture. The first part of the statement, I take it, needs no defense; the second part needs to be made clear. In declaring that motion pictures are integrated with no culture I am saying again, in part, that they stand on the outside of local life and serve to detach individuals from it. In this sense they do not fit into and reinforce local life as is done by folk tales and folk legends. But, further in explanation of the point, motion pictures, I think, can be said to have no culture. They are the product of secular business groups with commercial interests. The motion picture industry has no cultural aim, no cultural policies, no cultural program. The schemes of life shown in motion pictures, the institutional values which are stressed, the latent philosophies of conduct which are implied—all these show great diversity and inconsistency. They are a strange and incongruous mixture, with no guiding ideal, with no unity, and with no consistent scheme of life.

For this reason the play of motion pictures on reverie assumes a different character from that of folk tales. Its stimulation of reverie is likely to be distractive and confusing, probably making inner experience more lively but more unsettled and chaotic.

These remarks are intended neither to point out defects of the work of the motion picture industry nor to suggest a point for reform. Were the motion picture industry to seek to become a cultural institution inside of a society of free masses it would probably quickly collapse. Like any secular institution operating in an area of shifting interest the motion picture industry is highly sensitive to the varying desires of its clientele. One need but point to the anxious attention paid by the industry to the box-office receipts to guide their program of production. The mass of movie-goers is the final arbiter—to seek to impose on them a cultural program would be very hazardous, financially, to the movie industry.

This backward control over motion pictures which is exercised by the selective acts of the individual movie-goers suggests the idea that the cinema, despite its lack of culture, may be operating unwittingly to help prepare an *order* of life in a free and secular society. This idea is purely speculative. But one might interpret the shifting play of motion pictures in response to the selective acts of the mass, as unconscious experiments in feeling out the developing tastes and aspirations of the people and helping to mold them into a consistent pattern of life. I mention this at the very end of the paper, because it may mean that the free play of the masses does not represent inevitably an endless period of disintegration and absence of discipline. It may be merely transitional and preparatory to a new order of life measuring to a newly developed taste.

10

Helen MacGill Hughes

FROM POLITICS

TO HUMAN INTEREST

NEWSPAPERMEN, though noted for their assurance, have never been able to decide whether the modern newspaper is a "news" paper or a daily magazine. The difference is understood to be between something important and something entertaining.

Publishers, the Tories of the Fourth Estate, cherish the traditional belief that the press somehow promotes the health of the body politic and that great newspaper circulation is the *sine qua non* of an informed electorate. But their circulation managers are remarkably silent about the political functions of journalism; they never use the phrase, "the palladium of our liberties," to stimulate sales. But they do buy billboard space to announce a comic strip or the confessions of a movie star. Yet these delights are hardly a public necessity. Like many another sales promoter, the circulation manager is hugely successful in selling a product that people, it seems, do not need—indeed, Whitelaw Reid, the great editor of the *New York Tribune*, once characterized a thriving class of newspapers as being written for men who cannot read—but which they can be made to want. Now, the circulation managers are realists in a business where realists, though seldom vocal, are far from uncommon. And the greatest support for their view of the matter is found in the newspaper's human interest stories.

As an outstanding characteristic of American newspapers, hu-

From Helen MacGill Hughes, *News and the Human Interest Story* (Chicago: University of Chicago Press, 1940), pp. 1–29. Reprinted by permission of Helen MacGill Hughes.

man interest is relatively new. It was discovered by newspapermen a century ago and, sometime later, given a name. Its invasion of the newspaper and final adoption as a policy of news-writing were accompanied by changes in every aspect of the newspaper's organization. In the course of a revolution which is, one suspects, related to the revolution in life itself, the newspaper of the nineteenth century discarded some functions and added others. It emerges, in the twentieth century, as a new form. The natural history of the newspaper, which, as with an organic phenomenon, is "the history of the surviving species,"[1] is the story of the expansion of the traditional function—originally the publishing of practical, important news—to include the sale of interesting personal gossip. In the long process of discovering and exploiting human interest the press, for the first time, became rich and powerful.

The Traditional Conception of News

Until a hundred years ago, news in Europe and the United States was conceived of in the way it had been ever since news was bought and sold. It was limited to commercial and political intelligence.

Whenever trade and government has taken men away from home, the successful prosecution of their affairs has required them to know what was going on in their head offices. This is the condition that makes news imperative and gives it value and which, in the first place, gave rise to its regular collection.[2] The political welding of extensive territory under the government of the Roman Empire made it necessary to establish official agents in distant parts. To these representatives the news was first sold systematically. It came to them as newsletters. Provincial officials hired slaves to copy the *Acta Diurna*, which was a public record of the proceedings of the Roman Senate, the law courts, and the army. The scribes added to the manuscript any other news of the Capitol that would be of

[1]   Robert E. Park, "The Natural History of the Newspaper," *American Journal of Sociology*, November, 1923, p. 273.
[2]   Karl Bücher, *Industrial Evolution*, trans. Morley S. Wickett (New York: Henry Holt & Co., 1901), p. 217.

importance to the subscriber, and sent it off to him. Such news was a practical necessity to absent agents of the government, and worth paying for. Business and politics, in so far as it affected trade, were the subject of the famous newsletters sent to agents of the financial house of the Fuggers, of Augsburg, in the seventeenth century. "Lloyd's List" of shipping news was a private circular that was distributed in the eighteenth century among those London importers and speculators who subscribed to it. The newsletter took a form that was dictated by the demands of the person paying for it. Its contents were confined to what was relevant to the pursuit of professional activity; it corresponds to the house organ and the special departments of the modern newspaper in being technical and related to practical affairs. But it was not a public record; it did not circulate indiscriminately. Eventually news was printed and offered for public sale. The new medium, the newspaper, continued to supply the practical, important tidings of business and politics that had been the subject of the newsletter.

Though printed, the news was still the exclusive possession of men of large affairs. The layman had no access to it. In the smaller world of local concerns, in the countryside, the village, and the neighborhood, gossip circulated the news of interesting events among the illiterate—and others. Its scope was smaller, being the geographical range of the peasant and the villager. Word of mouth was its natural and spontaneous medium. It had no superstructure of professional news-gatherer and purchaser, and no cash value.

The early American newspapers were of the historic type. The first newspaper, the *Boston News-Letter,* originated, as its name suggests, in newsletters which were sent by the Boston postmaster to the governors of the Colonies. There was no machinery for the regular collection of even local reports. Editors, as a rule, were either the postmasters, who took advantage of presiding at the source of news and who were in touch with other public servants, or booksellers and job printers who got out a news chronicle incidentally to their other business. The news was principally a belated account of political happenings in Europe. Its sources were travelers and the crews of packet boats, letters, and the English newspapers. Domestic news had to do with the official acts of the governor and the courts, with the arrival and departure of ships, and with a description of their cargoes. The dulness of the record was occasionally relieved by items of more general interest, such as:

Piscataqua, April 6th. On Tuesday last five of the Skulking Indian Enemy killed two men about Scotland Garrison at York, viz., Daniel Dill and Joseph Jenkins, the last whereof they also stript and scalpt and after the Enemy withdrew they supposing him dead Jenkins arose and marched to the Garrison, and gave an account of the Action and liv'd but about 10 hours afterwards.[3]

But this sort of thing was not in keeping with the current conception of news, and so the telling of it was discreetly brief and matter of fact.

The Political Party Press

With the growing enthusiasm for self-government that led to the Revolution, the newspapers became the instruments of public opinion as well as of news. Official printers, who enjoyed the government patronage, printed newspapers indorsed and subsidized by the administration, while Tory sympathizers and the patriots replied to them in their own organs. The few journals that tried to give both sides were short-lived because both sides mistrusted them. After the Revolution the Federalists and the Republicans sought to capture public support by the founding and subsidizing of newspapers, for newspapers had proved themselves more effective than pamphlets in stirring people to action.

The newspaper thus became the agency of a cause. To print the news was the editor's public duty, but, being a "kept" editor, he was not free to tell things indiscriminately; there were tabooed subjects. The qualification for editorship was partisan enthusiasm, for his office was confused with that of the politician; indeed, the reward for fighting a good fight was often a political appointment. The editor held what Will Irwin calls the "professional attitude" to the newspaper: that the press, like the pulpit, should point out to the

[3]   *Boston News-Letter* (an issue of April, 1711).

people where their duty lies, and do so in conformity with its own scheme of values.

The paper that is dominated by its duty to the public interest cannot by the nature of its sacred calling conceive its function as purely commercial. It places its doctrine of the public good above every other consideration—even that of popularity and revenue. Thus Horace Greeley of the *New York Tribune*, a latter-day example, who was said by a fellow-editor to sacrifice everything to principle, once wrote editorially: "We have not sought [advertisements of the theaters] mainly because we consider the Stage, *as it is*, rather an injury than a benefit to the community—vicious, licentious, degrading, demoralizing."[4] The news thus assumes secondary importance in comparison with the editorial; it is subordinated to the propagating of a political or social gospel. Indeed, little or no distinction was made historically between the account of an event and the editor's opinion of it. While the editor's views are now confined to modest dimensions on an inside page, they once pervaded the whole newspaper and, like the communist sheets and the political press of France and Germany,[5] the journal was the mouthpiece of the man or the party behind it. The news was thus turned into a sermon. Now, a sermon is a doctrinaire exposition built on premises on which the faithful agree. In the light of the premises a contemporary event is translated into the familiar moral issue. Although the hearers know it all in advance and are never taken by surprise, the exhorter is under an inner compulsion to speak his piece to the bitter end. . . .

The professional attitude was challenged by the penny press, but it persisted, nevertheless, until after the Civil War in the moral organs edited by the fighting editors—Greeley, Godkin, Manton Marble, and others. There are still editors and readers who, as Lippmann puts it, think of the newspaper "as if it were a church or a school." But the commercial penny press substituted the market for

4   *New York Tribune*, May 11, 1841.
5   For an account of the political press of Republican Germany, which essentially resembled the eighteenth- and nineteenth-century American papers, see the author's "The Lindbergh Case: A Study of Human Interest and Politics," *American Journal of Sociology*, XLII, No. 1 (July, 1936), 32–54.

the mission. Its object was to sell, not its influence, but the news, and its customers, therefore, were those who were more interested in the news than in the editor's interpretation of the news.

The Penny Press and Human Interest

The commercial press began with the penny papers of the 1830's. The *New York Sun*, founded in 1833 by Benjamin Day, a printer, was the first outstanding success.

"The Cheap Press," as Parton, a contemporary, observed, "had, first of all, to create itself, and, secondly, to create its Public."[6] Its public was described as artisans and mechanics, a relatively unlettered class that had never had a newspaper before. Day had no party subsidy and no annual subscribers. His paper had to be self-supporting, with advertisements and cash purchases as the only sources of revenue. The London system of selling papers by newsboy had never been known in America. Irregular purchases had to be made in the newspaper office, but almost all readers got their papers by subscription and delivery. It was Day who introduced street sales. His innovation was greeted with moral indignation, for in taking the news into the market place he was selling "in competition with cakes and apples," as Parton put it,[7] the thing that was called "the tribune of the people and the palladium of our liberties." Therefore he had to offer for sale something his humble clientele would buy. And this was something far removed from the foreign dispatches, politics, and shipping news of the sixpenny contemporary papers.

Giving up the customary public function of the editor, Day made himself a livelihood by selling personal gossip, anecdotes, animal stories, and news of the police courts, told in the main in graphic dialogue form. Reviewing early issues, Frank M. O'Brien discovered the following:

The removal of William J. Duane as Secretary of the Treasury got two lines on a page where a big shark, caught off Barnstable, got three lines, and the feeding of the anaconda at the American Museum a quarter of a column. Miss Susan Allen, who bought a cigar on Broad-

---

6   James Parton, *The Life of Horace Greeley, Editor of the "New York Tribune"* (New York: Mason Bros., 1855), p. 145.
7   *Ibid.*, p. 141.

way and was arrested when she smoked it while she danced in the street, was featured more prominently than the expected visit to New York of Mr. Henry Clay, after whom millions of cigars were to be named.[8]

These inconsequential items were the first human interest stories in the American press.

New York was too large for oral gossip to circulate everywhere, and the mechanics and artisans bought gossip in the *Sun* and enjoyed it. Day had no philosophy about the popular taste; he discovered it accidentally when he printed the only things he could afford, namely, items detailing the unconsidered trifles of local city life which better-established papers neglected. Economics and politics, which filled the sixpenny papers, were practically ignored in the *Sun*, whose readers had no mind for the abstruse and the remote.

The assassination of the Czar Alexander II of Russia did not sell an extra paper, but the hanging of Foster, the "car-hook" murderer, sent the sales up seventeen thousand. The deaths of Cornelius Vanderbilt and Alexander T. Stewart had no effect on the *Sun's* circulation, the passing of Napoleon III raised it only one thousand for the day, and the death of Pius IX caused only four thousand irregular readers to buy the paper, but the execution of Dolan, a murderer now practically forgotten, sent the sales up ten thousand.[9]

Day's little four-page journal met with instant success. Within four months its sales reached five thousand, which was five hundred more than the *Courier and Enquirer*, the strongest sixpenny paper. When, in two years, it had fifteen thousand readers, the *Sun* claimed it was a "circulation far surpassing that of any other daily paper in the Union, and with one, perhaps two exceptions in London, in the world."[10]

[8]   *The Story of "The Sun"* (New York: George H. Doran Co., 1918), p. 45. (Used by permission of the author and the publishers.)
[9]   *Ibid.*, p. 323. This is a retrospective account, mentioning later issues of the *Sun*, when figures were better kept. But the character of the earlier issues was the same (used by permission of the author and the publishers).
[10]   *Sun*, June 30, 1835 (quoted in Willard Grosvenor Bleyer, *Main Currents in the History of American Journalism* [Boston: Houghton Mifflin, 1927], p. 160).

Day's only assistant was a fellow-printer called George Wisner, whose duties were to attend police-court sessions daily and to write two columns of news of the cases. That may have been because Day suspected his readers would enjoy it, but more probably it was because he had no political connections, no correspondents, and no money, and turned to the police-court reports because they were accessible and cheap. As penny papers were established in other cities, it was usual for the editorial staff to consist of the owner, a collector of news—meaning general city news—and a police reporter.

Out of Day's discovery of the attractiveness of items of purely human interest there grew up, almost at once, a new and lucrative type of journal.

A second penny paper, the *New York Evening Transcript*, appeared in the same year the *Sun* was founded. It was staffed by an editor and a police-court reporter. The *Transcript* was the first paper to recognize the ordinary man's enthusiasm for prize fights, races, and other sporting events, and it created a demand for itself by reporting them. Thus, as though by accident, the newspaper invaded a department of the national life that for decades has yielded it its liveliest, most uproarious—and perhaps its most profitable—columns.

James Gordon Bennett founded the penny *New York Herald* in 1835. Having no financial backing, he proposed, like Day, to print an independent newspaper that would pay for itself. . . .

Bennett secured the *Herald* its first great leap in circulation in its first year when a young man about town, named Robinson, murdered Helen Jewett, a prostitute. The sixpenny papers reported it in the brief formal way that was conventional in covering crime news. The penny papers, on the other hand, were the only ones to tell people the things that really interested them about the murder. Bennett found out all that an inquisitive person would like to ask, if he dared, and shared it unreservedly with his readers in the columns of the *Herald*. To do so, as he frankly told his readers, he exploited the customary privilege conceded to editors:

I knocked at the door. A Police Officer opened it, stealthily. I told him who I was. "Mr. B., you can enter," said he with great politeness. The crowds rushed from behind seeking also an entrance.

"No more comes in," said the Police Officer.

"Why do you let that man in?" asked one of the crowd.

"He is an editor—he is on public duty."[11]

The fashionable vice resort where Helen Jewett was murdered was a place that his readers could not afford to frequent, but whose aristocratic sinfulness filled them with envy and wonder. When he came to write the story, Bennett abandoned the role of the responsible editor for that of a chattering gossip. He was just the person his readers would have loved to have a long talk with—one who had seen everything and was ready to tell all about it. Describing the scene of the crime, he wrote:

What a sight burst upon me! There stood an elegant double mahogany bed all covered with burnt pieces of linen, blankets, pillows, black as cinders. I looked around for the object of my curiosity. On the carpet I saw a piece of linen sheet covering something as if carelessly flung over it.

"Here," said the Police Officer, "here is the poor creature." He half uncovered the ghastly corpse. I could scarcely look at it for a second or two. Slowly I began to discover the lineaments of the corpse as one would the beauties of a statue of marble. It was the most remarkable sight I ever beheld. I never have and never expect to see such another. "My God," I exclaimed, "How like a statue! I can scarcely conceive that form to be a corpse." Not a vein was to be seen. The body looked as white, as full, as polished, as the purest Parian marble. The perfect figure, the exquisite limbs, the fine face, the full arms, the beatiful bust, all, all surpassed in every respect the Venus de Medici, according to the casts generally given of her.

He saw the woman who had discovered the body, asked her everything a curious busybody could think of, and recounted the conversation in dialogue form to his readers—the first interview. He reconstructed the life of the girl in that "wicked house" and gave a long, full account of champagne parties given in the garden at the back which were attended by some of New York's most notable businessmen.

The popularity of Bennett's *Herald* was as natural as that of a talkative sheriff or coroner. Trifling and gossipy though these re-

[11]   *New York Herald* (an issue of April, 1836).

ports appeared, they take on importance because, by exploiting the human interest angle in the news, they taught people to read newspapers and made the press popular.[12]

The name "human interest stories" was first used in the office of the *Sun* to designate the chatty little reports of tragic or comic incidents in the lives of the people. Charles Dana, who bought the *Sun* after the Civil War, made human interest, which Day had accidentally discovered, an essential feature of news-writing. Mitchell, his editor-in-chief, in estimating Dana's importance in the history of journalism, wrote:

> From his individual perception of the true philosophy of human interest, more than from any other single source, have come the new general repudiation of the old conventional standards of news importance; the modern newspaper's appreciation of the news value of the sentiment and humor of the daily life around us; the recognition of the principle that a small incident, interesting in itself, and well-told, may be worth a column's space, when a large dull fact is hardly worth a stickful's; the surprising extension of the daily newspaper's province, so as to cover every department of general literature, and to take in the world's fancies and imaginings as well as its actual events.[13]

Bennett was too ingenious to duplicate the field of the existing penny papers, but made a market for himself by extending the news to areas of life not hitherto reported and, by doing so, sought to interest all sorts of people in the news. He was the first to realize the news value of church meetings and of social functions among the wealthy, and the first to cover Wall Street. Occasionally he caused excited comment by illustrating the reports with wood engravings. The paper was pert and bright. . . .

The party papers were put to no great cost to obtain their news, but Dana's and Bennett's expenditure for news-gathering was high; sales at a penny did not cover it. Hence, advertising was necessary if the paper was to live. Bennett sent solicitors all over New York to

[12]   While the population increased 32 per cent in a decade (1830–40), the total sale of newspapers increased 187 per cent (O'Brien, *op. cit.*, p. 136).
[13]   *Ibid.*, pp. 416–17. (Used by permission of the author and the publishers.)

bring in advertisements, for which he insisted on cash payments, since credit had ruined many a newspaper. He not only made the paper the principal vehicle of personals, patent medicine, and classified advertising, but established its financial success at the same time. He was able to say: "At the end of the first three months of its existence, the receipts of the *Herald* pay its expenses, a fact which never happened before in any newspaper enterprise."[14]

The penny papers had now made themselves financially independent of political parties. . . . The whole complex of the penny press, its news and its marketing, signalized the commercialization of the newspaper. Contemporary editors called it prostitution. It was the beginning of the independent journal and of a time when, ironically, prostitution would mean the very thing that was the party paper's virtue—propaganda for a cause.

The Independent Press: News and Advertising

In becoming cheap and pervasive the press, as so often happens in a competitive world, grew immensely profitable. But its rich yield was not within the grasp of everyone. Bennett, it is true, had founded the *New York Herald* with no money at all. Ten years later Horace Greeley established the first political penny paper with a capital of a thousand dollars. But ten years after that Henry Raymond, when founding the *New York Times*, required one hundred thousand dollars, and to raise it he organized a company of stockholders. The newspaper was now a capital investment and the change was reflected in its internal economy. By the time the *Tribune* was four months old the traffic in advertising had so increased that Greeley could not direct it and the editorial work, too, and he added a business manager to the staff, dividing the newspaper work into two departments. This had not been necessary until now. It signalized a revolution in journalism. Control was henceforth divided between "upstairs," where the editorial staff wrote the newspaper, and "downstairs," where the counting house or business office solicited advertisers and readers.

What the advertiser bought was circulation, and his money

[14]   *Herald*, August 7, 1835 (quoted in Bleyer, *op. cit.*, p. 188).

paid the costs of publishing the paper. Sales of the newspaper to readers barely paid for the ink and newsprint paper. But to make advertising space worth paying for, there must be wide circulation. The circulation liar was an inevitable phenomenon in a period when, to survive, it was necessary to boast. Circulation was achieved through the news columns. "The great newspapers," wrote Whitelaw Reid, "are those which look for news, not advertisements. With the news comes circulation, and when circulation demands, the advertisements seek the paper, not the paper the advertisements."[15]

Department stores developed in the eighties from the retail dry-goods business, and they found the newspaper was far superior to the circular or signboard as a device for announcing their prices and bargain days. Their advertisements and those of patent-medicine firms, stove factories, and land agents were so extensively printed that the newspapers added pages indefinitely. They tried to undercut each other's rates, and the younger Bennett complained to Whitelaw Reid: "The growth of this advertising troubles me. Whole columns of it I print now at a loss and would gladly throw part of it out, if it were not that some of you fellows would pick it up."[16]

At that time production costs were high. But newsprint paper fell in price when pulp replaced rags as the base.[17] Then Richard Hoe perfected his quadruple press, which, by 1890, was printing, cutting, folding, pasting, and counting seventy-two thousand eight-page papers an hour. Expenses were lowered and newspaper establishments were stable businesses, soon to become Big Business.

When a newspaper is sold on the street corner, there is always the danger that a more interesting paper may usurp its market. Since the readers are not subscribers, they can change their paper every day. In order to live, then, the paper found itself drawn into a

[15]   Whitelaw Reid, "Journalism as a Career," *American and English Studies* (New York: Charles Scribner's Sons, 1913), II, 220–21.
[16]   *Ibid.*, p. 237.
[17]   The price began to fall in 1880. By 1897 large consumers bought paper at less than one-eleventh of the price in the last year of the Civil War; see *ibid.*, p. 292.

race for scoops or beats. Whitelaw Reid wrote his correspondent during the Franco-Prussian War:

> For the next two months, if the War should last so long, remember that we look to you to keep us ahead of any other paper in New York on war news, and place no limitation upon your expenditures. . . . The first battle will doubtless be the occasion for the sharpest competition. If we can make a hit on that, it will be of incalculable advantage to us, both for the actual news and as an advertisement. If we can give a complete account of the first battle in advance of everybody else we shall make the *Tribune* the recognized authority on foreign news. But with the *Herald* lies our greatest danger. If they see a chance to get ahead they will willingly spend $50,000 in doing it.[18]

But Reid never advertised, in the modern sense, the beats his paper scored. The *Tribune* capped the news with heads of one-column width and printed long paragraphs of close type. When Pulitzer, in 1883, entered the New York field by buying the *World*, the modern tricks of news treatment had their beginning.

The Yellow Press

Emboldened by his success with the *St. Louis Post-Dispatch*, Pulitzer bought the *New York World* from Jay Gould. It was, at that time, a decrepit, conservative little sheet overshadowed by powerful competitors. Pulitzer forced it upon general attention by means of unconventional devices, some of which he had developed in St. Louis.

He had learned, for one thing, that a newspaper crusade engrosses people's interest as though it were a horse race; they will buy the paper from day to day to follow its progress. In the *World*, he crusaded against political malpractices. But what brought the paper even more readers were sensational campaigns, such as a drive to expose an astrologer active in white slavery. They were typically to get justice for some obscure but representative individual. To be the people's champion used to mean to trumpet party philippics; now it signified sponsoring the claims of inarticulate

[18]   Royal Cortissoz, *The Life of Whitelaw Reid* (New York: Charles Scribner's Sons, 1921), I, 170–71. (Used by permission of the publishers.)

victims. People took an interest in this sort of thing and it advertised the paper. It was the first manifestation of that tendency to make the newspaper a personal document, close to the lives of the readers, which shows itself at present in the blatant inquisitiveness of the tabloids.

The staff filled the *World* with breezy news and features. Interviewing had become a common practice of the political press, but such interviews were pontifical in tone and substance, with the stress on some public issue. Pulitzer, recognizing that the ordinary man was curious about the personal characteristics of notable people, wrote to his managing editor:

Please impress on the men who write our interviews with prominent men the importance of giving a striking vivid pen-sketch of the subject; also a vivid picture of his domestic environment, his wife, his children, his animal pets, etc. . . . Those are the things that will bring him more clearly home to the average reader than would his imposing thoughts, purposes or statements.[19]

Another device to make the paper interesting and easy to read was illustrations. People were attracted to them, even when they could not read. Diagrams increased the lure of crime stories. To simplify complicated issues, pictures were used in the political field; this was the first series of cartoons.

In three years the *World* had two hundred and fifty thousand readers and was the most sensational newspaper in the country. Sightless himself, Pulitzer tried to resist the more spectacular innovations, but he was bent on making the *World* a Democratic power, which meant gaining the attention of the masses for his editorials. In doing so he found his paper turning into something which he never intended and which did violence to his notions of propriety.

Hearst bought the *New York Journal* in 1895. From the very beginning he recognized Pulitzer as his rival among New York publishers, for Pulitzer had the kind of market he coveted—the custom of the common people. He bought Pulitzer's cleverest men for his

[19]   Don Seitz, *Joseph Pulitzer: His Life and Letters* (New York: Simon & Schuster, 1924), p. 422. (Used by permission of the publishers.)

152   HELEN MAC GILL HUGHES

own paper and waged war against the *World* by using its own weapons. The term, "Yellow Press," was contemptuously coined to describe the freakish journalism developed by each, in competition with the other. To call attention to the wonders and horrors which filled the two dailies, headlines came into use that were larger than ever printed before. Dana had said that news was anything that made people talk—Chamberlain, a Hearst editor, defined news as something sensational:

I used to go home from the office in the wee, sma' hours on the Hyde Street cable car. At my corner, a starter stood all night on post. Often, he got his morning *Examiner* just as I descended. Sometimes as he looked at the front page by the light of the lantern, he whistled and said, "Gee Whiz!" Then I knew that we had hit it. I've kept my eye on that car starter ever since. The ideal of this paper is to raise that "gee whiz!" emotion every day.[20]

If what actually occurred was not exciting enough to build circulation, news was made to happen. This was called stunt journalism; Bennett had proved its effectiveness in 1872 when he sent Henry Morton Stanley to Africa to find Livingstone. The paper that causes the news is naturally sure of scoring a beat. The *Journal* engaged in a succession of stunts so that every issue might be a surprise when it came on the street. If not by manufacture, then by exaggeration, news could be made that would be big enough to float the headlines. . . .

In the evening edition Hearst developed the human interest angle to heroic proportions by dramatizing the big stories as the chief items were now called. . . . Winkler, one of Hearst's several biographers, states that the paper specialized in fictionized news because it had to compensate for the lack of an Associated Press franchise,[21] but, whatever might have been the reason at the time, an editorial at the end of the *Journal*'s first year maintained: "The

[20]   Will Irwin, *Propaganda and the News or What Makes You Think So?* (New York: Whittlesey House, McGraw-Hill, 1936), p. 91. (Used by permission of the publishers.)
[21]   John K. Winkler, *William Randolph Hearst: An American Phenomenon* (New York: Simon & Schuster, 1928), p. 111. (Used by permission of the publishers.)

public is even more fond of entertainment than it is of information."[22] The staff prescribed "sport for the men, love and scandal for the women."

With the feature stuff which they printed in their Sunday issues, Pulitzer and Hearst directly invaded the field of the magazines in the hope of capturing their readers. The feature story is inspired by something that is in the news, but it is an account in which the local and particular aspects are minimized and the subject is expanded to include similar instances so as to be of very general interest. Winifred Black, who became celebrated in the profession as Annie Laurie, the first sob sister, wrote features for the Sunday Magazine, as the feature section was called, on such subjects as "Why Young Girls Kill Themselves." An article of this sort interests all readers and has human interest, though it is not, strictly speaking, a human interest story, for nothing has happened. The oddest feature was the comic strip, which the *World* proved was a dependable circulation-holder. It was the first attempt to interest children in newspapers. Understandable to children, and—at least in the early days—amusing, it was also entertaining to adults and kept them buying the paper.

The layman sometimes speaks of the more lurid and spectacular features invented in this period as human interest or thinks of the latter as constituting the yellowness of the modern daily. But the newspaperman understands the human interest story as a special form of news-writing that has no relation to pornography and is quite as likely to be about law-abiding persons—or manlike behavior in animals—as about notorious characters.

The fundamental change in journalism brought about by the Yellow Press was the complete concentration on the production of a commodity, of something that would sell. The missionary conception of his profession that had fortified the political editor had given way to the business attitude, as Will Irwin calls it:

We are here to supply a commodity—news, and, to a certain extent, views upon that news. We are responsible for furnishing sound news. That is, we will not lie, exaggerate or pad, any more than we

22   *Journal*, November 8, 1896.

would, if we were manufacturing linens, cheapen our product with cotton threads. But we will give the public exactly what it wants, without bothering to elevate the commonwealth. If we find that people prefer murders, then murders they shall have.[23]

Every change in the newspaper, since, has been to perfect it as a commodity—that is, to make it responsive to its market. Sixty years before, "upstairs" had wholly dominated the newspaper, but the balance of power had now shifted in the direction of "downstairs."

The Tabloids

Every new kind of newspaper in the last hundred years was able to claim, for a time, that it had the largest circulation in the country. This happened again in the second decade of the present century when the tabloid appeared—and for the same reasons. For every experiment and technical advance in journalism has been to attain greater public favor or to reach a portion of the public previously indifferent or ignored. The tabloid, being a picture paper, has probably probed to the last level of potential readers. . . .

The tabloids specialized in confessions. Space and language are the commonest impediments to communication, but the newspaper by now had virtually overcome them by a sensitive news-gathering mechanism and a simple vocabulary. Yet there remains always the fact that people do not easily penetrate each other's minds. Artistic formulation, in poetry or fiction, supplies the entree through the author's intuition. But the newspaperman has no poetic license. Untimately, then, the most revealing and readable communications a newspaper can print are autobiographical: interviews, diaries, letters, and confessions. The commonest hoax that editors resort to in order to win readers is the ghost-written "Story of My Experience." Hoaxes are instructive just because they embody empirically reached conclusions about the readers' tastes—that is, about interest.

Macfadden required the news in his paper to be not merely big,

[23]   "The American Newspaper," *Collier's*, April 1, 1911, p. 18. (Used by permission of the author and *Collier's*.)

in form and substance, but "hot"—which means as near to the threshold of tabooed subjects as public morality allows. It specialized in crime and scandal in the city, making no effort to secure national and foreign news. Indeed, the typical reading matter except for confessions was not news at all, but feature stuff—and this is true of the *News* and of the *Mirror*. The features are written by columnists on sport, on the movies and radio, and their stars, on lovemaking, etiquette, cooking, and on the care of dogs and cats.

By making the columnist popular the tabloids seek to induce people to buy the paper day after day; that is, to stabilize circulation. He writes for that part of the public which Thomas, in discussing the readers of the Yellow Press, described as the "most ignorant, childish and numerous."[24] It is the class without professional interests in whom regular reading can be inculcated only by reference to the pursuits of its leisure time. The tabloid reader is possibly the last reader—the saturation point of circulation.

The Present State of the Press

Newspapers coexist side by side, but they are not all the same thing. The conception one has of itself varies enormously from that held by another, the reason being that the newspaper is not a unitary thing; it is an omnibus, offering editorials, advertising, news, and human interest stories, and each journal's character depends upon which of the four elements dominates. Thus, some publishers insist on the traditional character of the newspaper as a moral or educational agent, but the one and a half million New Yorkers who read the tabloid *Daily News*, and most of the half million who read the *Times*, want to be interested rather than edified; and when they pay two cents for a newspaper they do not expect their purchase to elevate or educate them. The range of types accounts for the confusion among laymen and within the press itself as to what the newspaper is. At the present time, too, the newspaper appears to be going through an era of transition, the effect of which is to cast doubt on most general statements about it. It is a natural

[24]   W. I. Thomas, "The Psychology of Yellow Journalism," *American Magazine*, LXVI (March, 1908), 494.

accompaniment of the transformation into a commodity that every aspect of it is re-examined to discover whether it might not be an uneconomic use of space—meaning, by uneconomic, inferior in its power to interest the reader. The experimental spirit dominates it. "The job," says Stanley Walker, "is run by organization, but it must be in some respects unconventional, for news itself is unconventional."[25] The accidents of its history united the four separate functions in the newspaper as we know it, and now the question arises whether under new conditions of competition it still pays to serve all four within the same organization.[26] . . .

The time has now come when the advertiser yields more than three-quarters of the income of the press.[27] Inevitably, then, though it is in a state of change, the press is unlikely to change in any way that would disturb this agreeable relationship. The newspaper once declared its financial independence of political parties; it has shown no disposition as yet to emancipate itself from business. Radicalism may be endured in the ranks but it is hardly to be expected in the owners and directors of the newspaper industry, which is itself a great capitalistic enterprise. As a matter of fact, advertisers are emancipating themselves from the press. The local advertisers, because they are unwilling to pay for space in several dailies, are bringing about a restriction in the number of newspapers. Their influence, pushed to the logical conclusion, would effect local monopolies, by which a single newspaper commands all the existing circulation.[28] Moreover, the advertisers have discovered that the reader's attention is easiest to hold in the evening, and so the afternoon

[25]   *City Editor* (New York: Frederick Stokes, 1934), p. 3. (Used by permission of the publisher.)
[26]   "A new type of newspaper" is announced for 1940 in New York. The publisher, Ralph Ingersoll, has been associated with *Time, Fortune,* and the *New Yorker,* publications which have revolutionized—each in its own way—the form and matter of the magazines (*Time,* April 10, 1939, p. 61). Whatever the new journal is, it will be the first innovation in newspapers since the tabloid *Daily News* began its successful career in 1919.
[27]   Malcolm M. Willey and Stuart A. Rice, *Communication Agencies and Social Life* ("Recent Social Trends Monographs" [New York: McGraw-Hill Co., 1933], p. 175).
[28]   Where once mere quantity was demanded, the advertiser now makes distinctions on the basis of the readers' purchasing power for specific goods. For some goods class, not mass, circulation is required.

papers outnumber the morning.[29] But in the evening the newspaper must compete for the reader's time with the radio and the motion picture. It meets the menace of these rivals by constant attempts to restrain the radio in announcing news and by exploiting telephoto news photography. . . .

The real barrier to greater circulations—if greater are possible —is interest. This is still the fundamental problem of journalism.

The newspaper's machinery for the gathering of news, at least in its mechanical aspects, can hardly be improved upon. What Will Irwin calls news efficiency—"getting the latest event to the further-most reader in the shortest possible time"—is so perfected now that it may be said that there is practically no physical hindrance to the diffusion of any piece of news from any part of the world to the United States. At times there are obstacles in the form of official censorship or voluntary suppression—such as the press agreed to while Lindbergh tried to communicate with his child's kidnapers —but newspaper competition makes it difficult for them to be in-tact for long; some paper will tell in order to get a beat. "In America," as the retiring German Ambassador said regretfully in 1917, "everything is told." Illiteracy is negligible as a limit to newspaper reading. On the other hand, the news weeklies, particularly *Time*, being more leisurely in their editing, are able to offer critical readers a more intelligible picture of the world than that of the dailies. To the meaner comprehension the newsreels and the news broadcasts address a less sophisticated version of events. In all these agencies, however, as in the newspaper, the truth is more or less at the mercy of pressure groups. This, at least, is the view of several critics of the press who see in the devious and unacknowledged influence of various industrial and moral interests a worse threat to democracy than in the open and constant bias of the old party organs.

In offering the public human interest stories the newspaper competes with the magazines. The latter, in particular the cheaper monthlies, specialize nowadays in fiction that closely follows contemporary events. The daily newspaper, however, still enjoys the obvious advantages of cheapness and diversity.

To decide categorically whether newspapers in general are "news" papers or literature is difficult and perhaps not vital. While

29   Willey and Rice, *op. cit.*, p. 160.

the first term describes a number of successful well-established sheets, the second characterizes a thriving class of daily publications whose popularity is affecting the constitution of all the others. There is no doubt that newspapermen tend to judge much of the news on its human interest—a policy whose effect goes far toward converting the press into a form of popular literature. They customarily print this literature on the front page.

The front page, like a clinical thermometer, has registered every change in the newspaper's constitution; its present form recapitulates the newspaper's natural history. An understanding of it reveals the editor's estimate of the news and human interest stories which he prints there.

11

Frederick G. Detweiler

THE NEGRO PRESS TODAY

"Negroes aid in landslide vote for Roosevelt," cries
a headline of the *St. Louis Argus* following the 1936 election, and
goes on to make the following observation: "It is a safe estimate
that at least 75 per cent of the Negro vote throughout the nation as
well as in St. Louis where the Sixth Ward went Democratic the first
time in its history was for Roosevelt and the New Deal." Even
though these figures may be due to enthusiasm more than to fact,[1]
it is apparent that there were many Negro newspapers in favor of
Roosevelt.

Certainly the large-city papers supported him. The *Argus*, for
instance, is credited by the Audit Bureau of Circulation with 13,000
circulation. The *Washington Tribune*, apparently with a circulation
over 10,000, printed two columns of quotations from other Negro
newspapers, all of which were enthusiastic for the New Deal. It was
felt that Roosevelt had made himself the champion of the American
Negro; and without citing figures, one would have no difficulty in
showing the huge burden of unemployment that was carried by the
colored group and the fact that F.E.R.A. and W.P.A. and other relief units were their only refuge. For a long time Negro leaders had
been advocating the abandonment of blind adherence to the Re-

Reprinted from the *American Journal of Sociology* 44, no. 3 (November
1938) : 391–400.

[1]   The figures are about right for Harlem; the First Congressional
District of Illinois elected a Democratic representative; that the majority
of colored people went Democratic is asserted by Earl Brown in *Opportunity*, XIV, 359 ff.

publican party and a "more intelligent" way of marking ballots. The Democratic Congressman from Chicago was elected over the Republican candidate; and several others were elected to seats in legislatures. The Rev. Marshall L. Shepard, colored minister who prayed at the Democratic National Convention in Philadelphia, was himself elected assemblyman in Pennsylvania. Even a cursory reading of representative Negro papers shows how widespread was the interest among Negroes in the East and the North in the national election. The *Washington Tribune* had been carrying a straw vote during the campaign, using a complete page to shout to its readers that there were disfranchised Negroes in Washington to the number of 160,000 but they could speak in a straw vote if in no other way.

This Democratic enthusiasm carried over to the local elections of November, 1937. Picking up the *Philadelphia Tribune* for November 4, we find a song of triumph over the election of a colored state athletic commissioner on the Democratic ticket with the claim that "Tuesday's election marked the eclipse of the type of Republican machine formed years ago by the Penrose, the McNichol and Vare dynasties." And the *Norfolk Journal and Guide* a few days later contained an article by Kelly Miller freely criticizing Landon's radio talk of October 19. The two papers just referred to are reported by the A.B.C. as having 16,000 and 17,000 circulations, respectively.

The Negro's interest in politics dates from reconstruction days, when he suddenly found himself very important in the eyes of his new friends of the North. This interest was nursed along by the national Republican conventions with their large numbers of Negro delegates from the South. There were also certain federal jobs given to Negroes. In northern cities, like Chicago, added importance came to all those precinct workers who helped to bring out the vote. But in 1936, says the *Argus*, "The axe fell heavier on these Negro delegates from the South at the last Republican convention in Cleveland . . . than at any other convention. . . . There were more Negro delegates and alternates in the Democratic National Convention at Philadelphia than ever before in the history of the Democratic party." The Negro's interest in the federal government (which often seems to him his only friend) is well explained by the paper just quoted. Here it is said that 83,000 colored people were taught to read and write by 23,000 others who were employed by the government; 150,000 others have been in the C.C.C., where colored reserve officers have been employed along with nearly 200 educational advisers; Negroes have been given positions in offices in Washington, some of them with Negro clerks under them; and so on.

How many votes the *Argus* turned from the Republican to the Democratic column will never be known. The editor of the *Journal and Guide* writes:

Up to 1928 the Negro electorate in Norfolk and throughout Virginia was 100 per cent Republican. In that year the *Journal and Guide* declared for the national Democratic candidates and in subsequent years has supported also the state and local Democratic administrations. At first there were thunderous repercussions of disapproval from its own group, but the newspaper persisted. Today 75 per cent of the Negro vote cast in Virginia is Democratic.

The *Afro-American* (home office in Baltimore), through its editor, Mr. Carl Murphy, writes:

We were the first of the larger weekly newspapers to advocate a division of the ballot among all the parties and used our editorial columns to urge the election of such men as Smith and Roosevelt. Locally we have been able to persuade 30,000 out of the 50,000 registered colored voters to support local Democratic candidates.

. . . Even if the claims made by these editors are only fairly well grounded, it would still be evident that we are dealing here with a rather articulate pressure group and very probably that this press is having more political effect with its readers than are the white man's papers with theirs. The latter, as is well known, were notoriously defeated in 1936. That there were still Negroes who voted Republican we know because they are scolded in the editorials. There are reasons, however, for saying that these large-city papers published by Negroes had something to do with the numbers of colored people who voted for the New Deal. Naturally those who had benefited directly from New Deal activities needed no newspaper to tell them how to vote any more than they required any improper partisan solicitation. But there were many others who could be told about these propitious activities. As will be seen below, the newspapers had already been able to boast of certain local political achievements. For many years now they had been looked up to as political spokesmen for their readers. Along with the humbler people who read their columns and occasionally found their own names when some Mrs. Elvira So-and-So left Atlanta for Athens over Sunday, the Negroes who served as leaders in their communities were regular supporters of their press. If you want to find copies of the papers go to the ministers, the school teachers, the political leaders, those who are prominent in "society," sports, and so on. The newspaper is generally closely allied with this class. Partly through them and partly by putting out into the daylight what it wants to put there, it has its influence.

. . . It is particularly worthy of note that early in November, 1937, these papers had extensive reports of the massacre of Haitians by Santo Dominicans, news which this writer and his neighbors did not see or observed only scantily represented in the white city newspaper. Naturally the news is kept up to date on such subjects as the Scottsboro boys, Angelo Herndon, the recent antilynching bill in Congress, and government policies (such as housing) involving Negroes. Father Divine is mentioned as news only, not to be defended. The papers carry a good deal of social service; advice on various matters, especially health is prominent.

A very significant phase of the journalism of Negroes in the cities is its interest in local improvements: better schools for Negroes, better attention to streets, fairer distribution of tax money for parks and other public facilities, efforts of colored people to be represented in jobs, especially jobs in stores run by white people in Negro communities.

One editor says that he enjoys the confidence of the governments of his city and state, so that he is frequently invited to confer with officials about matters affecting his group. The Negroes in his community have enjoyed the decided improvement of parks, playgrounds, schools, street-paving, and other such matters for which the paper has always spoken. The *Philadelphia Tribune* has successfully fought for a colored member in City Council and one on the School Board. These things are only samples of many such that have been achieved by this paper; among others could be mentioned the Pennsylvania Civil Rights bill recently signed by Governor Earle and the progress in having colored workers received in the unions. The work of the C.I.O. has had much to do with this last item; and the fact that both political parties are actively bidding for the colored vote has just as certainly speeded up the participation of Negroes in public jobs. In a similar vein the editor of the *Afro-American* recounts the successful campaigns to put colored and white schoolteachers on the same salary scale in Montgomery County and in Baltimore; it has the promise of the appointment of colored policemen.

A unique service rendered by the *Afro-American* is the "Clean-Block Campaign" begun in Baltimore in 1935 and continuing each year during the summer. The same effort was started two years ago in Philadelphia and in 1937 in Washington. Richmond has been having such a campaign also. This is an organization of Negro householders by blocks to compete with each other in cleaning and beautifying housefronts, yards, and streets. Children are brought into the movement; captains are commissioned; money is solicited for prizes; the campaign is featured in the paper; meetings are held; the support of white friends (particularly of the mayor) is enlisted. There are songs printed and numerous pictures taken. By-products were the organization of neighborhood improvement associations; additional paving done by the city; co-operation of the Pennsylvania Railroad; participation of Negro and white householders together in a block where both are living.

In Houston, Texas, almost twenty years ago, there was a C. F. Richardson who published a paper called *Informer* in the face of considerable hostility on the part of some whites. Three times advertisers withdrew their business, and one night somebody—was it the Ku Klux Klan?—entered the establishment and carried away an entire edition of the paper then ready for mailing. Evidently this situation is, for Houston, a thing of the past. The Negro editor's work in that city recently has been successful in obtaining better school facilities, including buildings, teachers, and two Negro doctors to attend Negro children, besides better streets and the addition of Negro policemen to the city force. Likewise, C. A. Scott, the manager of the syndicate above mentioned, with his office in the heart of the Atlanta Negro district (Auburn Avenue), believes that his work has been instrumental in adding 1,000 Negro voters to the list of those registered in the city, and has even decreased the number of Negro homicides. He is now campaigning for Negro police in Negro neighborhoods.

Results obtained in this manner are not to be thought of as the effect of propaganda directed upon the white rulers of these communities. The process is not so simple. Influential Negroes with some voting power behind them continually urge desired improvements upon the authorities; but in doing so they are reinforced by an enlightened group of newspaper readers who help to keep them on the job. We must remember that the Negro newspaper is not read by white people.

. . . It is better to say that they are putting into print feelings and demands and interpretations of events that come to the surface in the minds of their people. Their atmosphere is one of questioning, discussing, talk in back yards, talk in the streets, in lodge meetings, in poolrooms; and sermons in churches. The newspaper editorial thus becomes the articulate voice of an inarticulate interest. Conversely then the newspaper stirs up discussion in all the places referred to. The editor's horizon is at least as wide as that of the small-town white editor and often wider. Negro writers are interested in South Africa, where there is a huge race problem; in Brazil, where the color line is indistinct; in Soviet Russia, whither Robeson has gone to have his children educated; in the Virgin Islands, Haiti, Santo Domingo, Liberia. From Spain, toward the end of 1937, Langston Hughes was writing articles for the *Afro-American*, which sent a man to Russia to interview Stalin, to Berlin to see the Olympics, and to Geneva to witness the appearance of Haile Selassie before the League of Nations.

The Negro editor leads his group in being race-conscious. The value of reiterated discussion of the antilynching bill lies not so much in any changes it is likely to make in the lynching of Negroes, since the great majority of Negroes know that they are in no danger.

The value lies rather in the fact that the bill provides a definite issue about which race-consciousness can gather and become powerful. The *Philadelphia Tribune* tells us that the Institute of Public Opinion finds 65 per cent of southern people in favor of an anti-lynching bill, the result, according to the *Tribune*, of agitation by colored people. The truth probably is that the colored people, at least so far as their newspapers are concerned, have had little effect on the thinking of the whites. There is no question of the success of the papers in whipping up race-consciousness with this issue however. Of course when we say "little effect," we must admit that the National Association for the Advancement of Colored People has been the spearhead of the antilynching agitation. Their magazines, the *Crisis*, and the National Urban League's *Opportunity*, have been read by some white people.

Negro periodicals use keywords for certain great abstractions: "American citizen," "truth," "justice," "constitutional rights," and sometimes "race." The last term is synonymous with Negro, as in "people of the Race," or "John Doe, a race man." With the exception of this last, all the keywords are the same ones as are used by white people. Who among us would not respond to these slogans that appear as watchwords of certain newspapers: "Exponent of Truth and Justice," "A Square Deal for Every Man," "Equality to All," "Service," "Full Enfranchisement for All American Citizens," "A Right To Live as Men, Nothing More, Nothing Less; to This We Dedicate Our Lives."

As symbols to nucleate group sentiment, use is made of write-ups and pictures of prominent individuals. Joe Louis and Jesse Owens have this value. The first child born in Washington in 1936 and the first in 1937 were colored; these facts are reported on the first page. Cab Calloway gives a long interview after his return from a transatlantic tour. His success is that of his race. Mrs. Mary McLeod Bethune is photographed at dinner with Mrs. Franklin Roosevelt. An entertainer who was known to Edward VIII in England and said to have achieved some intimacy with the King is featured. So are Northwestern University's black football players. Symbolic value appears also in the large photographs of Princess

Kouka, a Sudanese of striking appearance selected as an African beauty to play in pictures opposite Paul Robeson. The Scottsboro boys become symbols.

Naturally a newspaper which is all editorial may have less success in influencing opinion than one which is known as a legitimate news organ. The Negro paper began as an extended editorial, but it has been gradually justifying itself as a newspaper.

12

Samuel C. Kincheloe

THE BEHAVIOR SEQUENCE

OF A DYING CHURCH

THE FOLLOWING CASE STUDY of a dying church is presented
for the purpose of describing the processes which go on as a church
fails in its effort to survive, and also to indicate a methodological
procedure in the study of churches.[1]

In the city of Chicago proper there is a great area of receding
white Protestants where the major reactions of churches are those
of moving, federating, "institutionalizing," turning to elementary
religious practices, and dying. Statistical studies indicate that the
peak of Protestant occupation for the area in which the Monroe
Park Church[2] is located was in 1895, and that there has been a
gradual decline in Protestant strength since that time. On the west
side of Chicago it is necessary to go well out toward the suburbs to
find many churches which are growing.

Community Background

Monroe Park Church is located on what might be called the
rear guard of white American Protestantism on the west side of
Chicago. The community is deteriorating and is spoken of as dirty

Reprinted from *Religious Education*, April 1929, pp. 329–45.

[1]   This is one of a number of cases from a study on the church in the
changing community. The author is indebted to Paul R. Griffith, George E.
Bottomley, Leslie L. Beaver, Guy L. Scuitema, and Donald Stewart for
valuable assistance.
[2]   This is not the real name of the church.

and dilapidated. Mixed indiscrimiately on every street are ancient two story frame houses with long flights of steps leading up to the front doors, squat frame cottages, houses built of part brick and part wood, and old two family brick flats, all in various states of disrepair. The streets are dirty, junk is piled on vacant lots, and uninviting stores are found here and there. Numerous mangy, unkempt dogs run the streets. The one word which characterizes the community is that it is "nondescript." Hollanders, Poles, and Negroes live side by side. In recent years more and more of the white population has been moving out of the community, and the Negroes have been moving in in large numbers.

A community worker says:

The homes in the community are not modern. A large percentage of them do not have electric lights and in some instances the tenants use coaloil lamps. A furnace is a thing to be marveled at, and bath tubs and hot water tanks only a select few possess. There are no screens in the summer time, hence flies and mosquitoes are free to torture the people. The streets are dirty and garbage is dumped in alleys and allowed to accumulate. The homes in which the Hollanders live have been kept in good repair, the ones occupied by the Polish are fairly clean inside but seldom if ever painted outside. Those buildings occupied by the Negro are typical, being those in which no one else would live, especially since they have once been occupied by the Negro. In some instances I have known lower class whites to live in the same building with the Negro, but that is not the ordinary thing. There are no large stores in the community, but the ordinary variety store where one may buy anything from safety pins to bologna predominates.

The community is a gang area, and the delinquency rate is high. The general area in which the church is located has a low percentage of home ownership, but a high one of family disorganization.

The old church building is at present being used as a bottle works and the congregation is meeting in a rented hall. The dingy, barn like brick structure standing flush with the sidewalk could never have been noted for its beauty, but in the olden days it could have prided itself on being neat and well taken care of. Old age and neglect have done their work, and the building appears forlorn and deserted. A block and a half further down the street, we find all who remain of the membership of the church, meeting in a one room store building. In the small room are a number of chairs, two pianos, a pulpit, a desk, and two old sheet iron stoves. With these articles comprising all of its worldly belongings, and with 49 active members on its roll, we have the Monroe Park Church of today.[3]

Efforts at Adaptation

The history of the church given below was prepared by a participating observer. It reveals how the church sought by various means to maintain itself in the changing community.[4]

The church began as a mission. It came to have a large Sunday school and at one time the church was "filled to overflowing." Evangelistic zeal led gospel teams of church members to go out over the city. The Scotch could not keep their own children in the church but won the German children of the community. The church sought to win the Bohemians to the south by supplying a Bohemian pastor. A large number of Yiddish New Testaments were bought and the church sought to win the Jews. A semi-socialistic work was tried. Boys' clubs were organized.

The Monroe Park Church was first started as a mission by the Third Church some fifty or sixty years ago in what was then rapidly becoming a home for people working in the stock yards, lumber yards, and factories to the south. To the west and northwest the well-to-do people of the time lived. The neighborhood was largely populated by German and Irish immigrants with a goodly sprinkling of native stock. The main street of the '80's and '90's was Blue Island Avenue. There large retail stores lined both sides of the street almost its entire length from Harrison Street to 21st Street, drawing a very lucrative trade from the hinterland of thrifty citizens. With the passing of the years Ashland Avenue became a very substantial thoroughfare, lined with beautiful homes of well-to-do business and professional men, and there finally the Monroe Park Church under the name of Ogden Church found its permanent abode. The neighborhood had several good

3   This was in the spring of 1927.
4   This document reveals the value of the data prepared by members of the congregation. Such a document becomes objective material in that different workers may check upon it and interpret it.

strong German Protestant churches, a large Catholic church that once boasted of having 25,000 communicants, and several English speaking Protestant churches.

The Monroe Park Church was always a small church and of no great wealth, for as the local people prospered they rapidly left the community to move to other parts of the city. My earliest recollection of any value was during the pastorate of Reverend Harry Farwell in the '90's. Farwell was a quiet kindly man who did his work without flourish, but with sincerity, and did it well. The church's great work was among the young people. It had a large Sunday school and young people's work, and the substantial element in the church came from the north on Ashland Boulevard and from the west, the children of the poorer people coming from the east and southeast.

The church even at this time could not meet its budget but had to be helped with grants from the denomination. In the late 80's the church called to its pastorate A. E. Parker, a new front was built on the old building, and the work flourished. The church was at its zenith of power in the community. A very large Sunday school and young people's society were taking care of the junior end of the field and Parker, who was a man of magnetic personality, filled the church to overflowing with his preaching, which was somewhat emotional and evangelistic. In the height of his work a scandal broke out which almost ruined the church and gave it a blow that was well nigh mortal, and it never after recovered its former place.

The church then called A. F. Quinlan in the early 1900's. Quinlan was a man of entirely different temperament from Parker, being a scholarly man of no mean ability. New difficulties arose, the Jewish invasion was commencing and Gentiles commenced to leave the field in increasing numbers as the years passed by. Several of the men who remained from the Parker regime started out visiting other churches to hold evangelistic revival meetings, not being content with their immediate field, which perhaps needed their efforts more than any other, and this hurt and hampered the work.

Through all of the years that I can recollect the church had quite a percent of Scotch, and be it said to their credit they were ever loyal, several families remaining with the church until their death, and supporting it even after leaving the community (both financially and with their presence at the service). They really developed the church out of the virgin prairie. I can't understand why it was they could never interest their children in the church. The old folks were loyal to death, but the children turned away. The church then began to reach the children of the German immigrants in the community, and a number of these young Germans joined the church and became active in it. The Lutherans were never reached this way; only the German Evangelicals.

During the Quinlan era, our city society was urged to do something for the Bohemians to our south. We had built up a very good work among them. We had a service in their native tongue by a Bohemian pastor, but we never could convince the Home Mission Board of the value of this work, and the Bohemians finally took the matter into their own hands and rented a hall further south and went along independently. In the interval the Jews were coming in thicker and thicker, but the church held on resolutely, and continued to do a large work among the children and young people. The young people as they married moved from the community and went to church elsewhere.

During Quinlan's ministry the work was carried on in a sound conservative way. It did not have large numbers in the adult membership, but it had good, sound, hard thinking people, no rich among them, but a loyalty that was admirable.

After Quinlan's departure around 1910 the church had several ministers who came and went after short intervals. About 1910 we experimented with a Jewish work.[5] We held a night school to teach the immigrants English, reading, and writing. The Jews took to this very eagerly and we had a very large enrollment in this work, but we could make absolutely no religious impression on them. This was finally abandoned.

A young man full of vigor by the name of Holmes was then called to the pastorate and he tried a semi-socialistic work among the foreigners in our neighborhood. He had a forum where they might come and debate their ideas and theories on religion and socialism. This was also a failure. He, however, developed a boys' club that did very good work and lasted for some time and helped to build up the Sunday school. During all of this time the church had only furnished two students to the ministry, one of whom stuck it out and is still a missionary in India. The other got into trouble and finally ended up in an Episcopal church.

[5]   A number of Yiddish New Testaments were found in one of the cabinets of the church (1926).

From interviews it was learned that the church came under the direction of the local Missionary Board about 1904.[6] A number of supply pastors, or student pastors, who remained only a year or two, furnished the church with its leadership. This transient line of inexperienced student pastors—13 in 26 years—did not help the church situation. Constructive work lasting over a number of years was impossible. During these years there was an average attendance at Sunday morning services of from 25 to 35, though sometimes running up as high as 50 or 60. Things seemed hopeless, and in 1910 the pastor said "let the old cat die." This attitude made the lay leaders of the church angry, and they got busy and kept the church running along as before. So far there had been no departure from the conventional church program.

The real break came during the pastorate of Reverend William Smithson, between 1919 and 1924. Reports indicate that at first everything went well. The church took on new life, and the Missionary Board said many encouraging things about the church. While the conventional program was not disturbed, the pastor saw the need of other activities, and organized a work for boys. The church was redecorated and repaired, and a chapel was added. In the report for the following year the pastor is hopeful, and launches out on a new program of activity. He says in his report:[7]

The officers of the church have caught the vision of community service and during this year we pass from the conventional type of church to one serving the community. An enlarged program is to be installed and from a scattered membership in various parts of the city, we shall have an intensified program for the community at its doors.

It is evident that the church had at last awakened to the fact that it was dying, and that unless some radical change was made the church would soon come to an end. They were stirred out of their self complacency and rallied around the idea of a community program. Here was a way of justifying their existence.

[6] Figures have been supplied by the Mission Board back to 1920 only.

[7] The annual reports of pastors, even though favorable, often reveal problems through which the church is going.

The following year the report was less optimistic. The church was running up against problems in its new undertaking. The pastor says in his report:

Other Protestant churches being unable to finance themselves have struck their colors and surrendered, but—"Our Flag is still there." The wonderfully efficient organization known as our Home Mission Board has made it possible for us to survive.

The third annual report has lost all of the optimism of the former reports, and much space is given to the difficulty of the field and to the fact that other nearby churches are failing. It ends with the statement that

The Monroe Park Church may be facing the test, but its members bravely go to the battle singing as it pours out its money and the lives of its volunteer workers.

Things were not going very well, and the members of the congregation were dissatisfied. Failure stared them in the face, and they began to assess the blame for their misfortune. They accused the Reverend Smithson of having "no push" and said he didn't get things done, and asked him to resign. The church officials upheld Mr. Smithson, but the congregation won out, and the pastor and one of the officials resigned.

At the close of this quarrel things were in bad shape, and it is very likely that within a year or so the church would have died a natural death had the Mission Board, which had been supporting the church, not decided that it should be closed. As they held a deed to the building because of having supported it for many years, they sold it to another congregation. This order to close and this selling of the building over their heads made the members of the church angry. They gathered together and resolved that the church should not be closed. All of their sentiment for the old church was aroused, and they pulled themselves out of the slump they had been in and went to work.

They rented the building from the group that bought it, and by interesting several men of the denomination in their case, they finally got the denomination to agree either to pay their rent in the present building, or to furnish them an adequate place in which to meet. The rent was therefore paid, but all other financial support was shut off. The congregation, through the Mission Board, secured a preacher and paid his salary out of their own pockets. Therefore, during the last three years, Monroe Park Church, aside from its rent, has been supporting itself and has kept a full time pastor for the first time in many years.

Enthusiasm was in evidence everywhere. The church realized that it was fighting for its life, and that if it was to secure recognition of the Mission Board it must prove itself worthy. A large number of the leaders of the church, and a good proportion of the members, live many miles to the west and north. The community, which had at one time been American (Scotch), had become first Jewish and then a mixture of Lithuanians, Greeks, Italians, Irish, Negroes, and a large colony of Hollanders. An active program of community service seemed to be the only door open to the church. Money was not available for extensive institutional work, though that was the thing desired, and the thing looked forward to as an ultimate end. Simple community work of the non-equipment kind was the only recourse.

Experience soon showed that it was impossible to do a large adult work in the community. There were very few American Protestant adults living in the community and it was impossible to reach the Catholics. Under the circumstances the church could do nothing but develop a children's work. The children were of various nationalities and religions—many of them children of Dutch parents, attending the Holland church in the morning and the Monroe Park Church in the evening. Many others were Poles and came from Catholic homes, while others came from homes where there was little religious life. As a result, there was always a question as to the value of the work being done and as to whether or not it was a duplication of work carried on by other churches. . . .

The Coming of Volunteers

There are in Chicago a number of institutes, training schools, and seminaries for the training of religious workers. These schools send their students into the churches of the city for experience. Some of these schools send their workers without charge. It is not an uncommon thing for churches which are declining in strength and in the number of their own workers to use these volunteer helpers. Sometimes the members of the church are not in complete accord with the teachings of these volunteer helpers, but they are willing to take them rather than have the church close. In some instances the character of the institution is changed by their presence. A prominent worker in a Bible training institute once remarked that they had two kinds of friends, one that used them openly and the other that used them, but kept quiet about it. These workers are not alone interested in securing training but often feel that they are under commission to do definite Christian work. The following document reveals the attitudes of one worker who came to Monroe Park Church from an institution which trains religious workers.

I came to Chicago to prepare for Christian work at the Albany Bible Institute in April, 1923, and although I had been prominent in church work in my home church for several years, I was not a Christian until January of the same year.

It is customary for the Institute to send students into the various churches to do Christian work—so of course I was sent out likewise. It was not until February 17, 1924, that I was privileged to go to Monroe Park Church.

At that time I went upon invitation of Rev. M. J. Atwood, a friend of our family, who was called to act as substitute pastor. He invited me to sing at the morning and evening services. I shall never forget that first trip! I took a street car downtown and then over to Twelfth Street. It was bitter cold, a snowy night, and I had never been out in the city alone, to say the least down through this district and at night! I had no fear, for whom God sends he protects.

I felt that it was a definite mission God had privileged me to perform because it was so unlike any other experience I had ever had. At last I arrived at the church, and after peering around and rubbing the snow off the sign I was able to make out Monroe Park Church so I decided I was right.

The door was not yet opened and I waited some time before one of the men of the church came who ushered me in and built a fire. By that time the congregation had arrived. It consisted of six or seven people, the majority being children. Rev. Mr. Atwood gave an inspiring message and I sang two or three solos.

Not much there to leave an impression was there? No? Ah, yes! It will never leave me. How I realized anew that just as the Christians of that community were turning away from the church by not supporting it, just as the non-Christians were turning a deaf ear and blind eye to the symbol of His only hope for salvation, so too the cruel world turned aside and spurned the love of our Lord! The church was in that community and many knew it not.

The people called for me as a special worker from the Institute, and I was then "officially" assigned to work at the Monroe Park Church.

My work at first was that of soloist and personal worker. It gradually increased until my duties covered the following: Soloist, choir leader (junior and senior), personal worker, Sunday school teacher, junior pastor (having organized out of the small group of children a junior church, myself a junior pastor, a work which has now grown to a membership of two hundred and forty under the able direction of Miss Watson), church visitor, vacation Bible school director and teacher, deaconess, Sunday school superintendent assistant, representative at many of the banquets, rallies and other West Side and union meetings of young people of the denomination. In fact, it has been my great joy to do any and all of the tasks in connection with the church from filling the pulpit in absence of the pastor on two occasions when he was not able to speak, to serving as janitor and helping clean out for special functions when our janitor "was not" or was unable to serve.

I name these things without boast or pride, but with the joy of doing the lowly tasks, as they are often called, for My Lord—experiences which have made me love the church the more. In this way my social life has developed, too, because of the good times we had when two or more of us gathered to clean or work for the social interests of the church.

As far as religious interests are concerned, I owe much to Monroe Park Church through the grace of God for my own spiritual development. Here it was I first served Him wholeheartedly in a consecrated service, where I saw the sinfulness of sin, the matchless mercy of the saving grace of God, wept and prayed, laughed and sang, all for the glory of God. Where I made my first confession of faith by rejoining church as a Christian, and not as a mere human effort to be better. Where I made my surrender publicly for God for the foreign field service should He so lead. Previous to this time I was an ardent opposer of foreign work. Where I met and led to Christ and loved and married the companion whom God had chosen to be my co-worker in His vineyard. Where trials and temptations almost too great to bear were shared and lifted through the prayers and fellowship of those faithful loyal friends whom I came to know and love so well in so short a time. Where it was my privilege to point and lead many to Christ and to help Christians along the way as God saw fit to manifest Himself in and through his servant. True, there were a few times when I was tempted to leave and give up the struggle, but oh, the joy I received as God had His way and by one means or another kept me where He wanted me and could use me best.

Monroe Park Church then and now!

Out of the dusk comes the dawn and out of the church comes Christian love and the message of salvation. A message the world needs, and Monroe Park Church is sending out in that community. God's word will not return to Him void!

I ride on the street cars to the church each time I go, which is at least three times a week and often more. My husband is also a faithful worker there and he too is a member. We spend about five hours on the street car on Sunday in order to attend all services.

Why do we go so often, so far, and so regularly?

Simply, because God has set us apart to work in that particular field. We have considered and attempted many others—even the foreign field—and always with failure, being forcibly (by direction of our Divine Guide) guided and steered back to the Monroe Park Church. In the two years I have been there I have not missed over six or eight services, rallies, banquets, socials, or other social or religious functions of the church. We stay there out of love for the lost who come there weekly seeking to know Jesus, for the Christian who comes hungry to learn more of Him, and for the Christian fellowship that so binds the hearts together. I have enjoyed the fellowship of this church all this time and have paid the last respects to her departed saints as I have sung their favorite hymns over their lifeless bodies while they sang songs and praised God in Heaven.

I trust that the influence of this old church and the indelible impressions I have received may be the means of a deeper faith and more earnest effort to put forth by some struggling church which will likewise prove one of the shining lights of Christian love in some dark, sinsick community.[8]

Why the Church Lives On—A Study in Attitudes

The principal reason for Monroe Park Church's continued existence in its critical community situation, is the loyalty and determination of its small group of members. There are now (October, 1926) only a hundred and eighteen names on the church roll, and many of these are not bona fide members. Forty-nine are all that can be counted upon to attend services and to take an active part. A map of the distribution of the membership shows that only a few of the active workers are in the neighborhood. About fifty percent of the entire membership lives in the community, but the majority of these no longer attend. Monroe Park Church, as far as control, personnel, and financial support is concerned, consists of a group of not over twenty-five people.

In order to understand the church it is necessary to study this small group of members and to observe their attitudes toward the church. . . . The method used in determining the attitudes of these people was that of the personal interview and of the written life history. The challenge was thrown out, "What does Monroe Park Church mean to you," and a number of answers were received.

Perhaps the best statement of the meaning of the church was found in the story of Miss Snyder, one of the mainstays of both the work and the finance of the church.

Having come to Chicago from a little village in the West when I was nine years old, I became a member of Monroe Park Sunday school. My sister, brother, and stepmother were members of this church but not active workers. They and my father attended the services. My oldest brother had heard the call to enter the ministry from this church and had gone away to school to prepare himself for this calling. He is now a missionary in India.

[8]   Mrs. Hughes, the author of the above note, and her husband dropped out of Monroe Park Church altogether a few months after this letter was written. It is not unusual that people who are about ready to quit an institution give the most dramatic rehearsals of the meaning of the institution. They have already begun to see the church in retrospect and to glorify its achievements.

I became a Sunday school teacher shortly after I joined the church and have continued to teach in the Sunday school up to the present time.

I united with the senior Christian Endeavor Society soon after I joined the church, for that was the only C. E. at that time, there being no junior or intermediate society. A few years later I felt that we ought to have a C. E. for the boys and girls. I continued this junior work for several years and God gave me the vision of an intermediate C. E. as a result of attending a C. E. convention. I came home and organized an intermediate society. I think I have held every office in our senior organization. I now have charge of both the junior C. E. and the intermediate C. E.

When I was in high school we moved out of the neighborhood about a mile and a half from the church, right near another church of our denomination. The rest of the family then attended this other church, but I would not leave Monroe Park. My heart and soul were in the work there. Our family tried their best to get me away but it was not accomplished. For several years at that time I was not allowed to be out in the evenings or to go so far from home after dark, so during that time I could only attend the Sunday school and morning service.

Later I moved to Cicero and am now living in Oak Park but I have never for a moment considered leaving the church I love. For one and surely the main reason, I feel that I am needed there. God still wants me to work for Him in that neighborhood. The missionaries leave their homes and travel far into unknown lands to carry the gospel to those who know it not. There are those in and about our church who need and want the gospel and need it just as truly as the so called "heathen."

It takes money to run an institution. Many of the people in the community cannot give very much—a dime a week means a great deal to them. I have no home obligations—I am living with my married sister and just supporting myself. I can give more than some in the neighborhood and my money is consecrated to God and I hear Him tell me to help carry on His work in that community where there is so much wickedness, so much "moonshine," so much crime.

My faith bids me be assured that God will provide for Monroe Park Church to continue to serve the community. He has overcome obstacles for us that humanly seemed impossible, and He will continue to use His power on behalf of His church as long as we are faithful to the trust He has committed to us.

Evidences of Change

One side of the picture has been given in this study of the attitudes of the membership. We get an entirely different picture from one man in the church who has recently returned after a long absence. Mr. Cowdry, a business man of middle age, was an elder in the church and church clerk in the early 1900's. In 1912 he left the church and went east. In 1926 he returned to Chicago and settled in Oak Park. It was only natural that he should be interested in his old church and he returned to Monroe Park to help out. His story of the change that has taken place, and his attitude toward the church when he returned, reveal the change which must have taken place. The following are extracted from a stenographic report of an interview with Mr. Cowdry.[9]

Well, I left in 1912. The field was getting pretty ragged then—it was tapering awfully fast. When I left, there were several Scotch families there. Two of these Scotch families—five adults—died since I left. That is where death and movement settled the problem of Monroe Park Church spiritually, for they were the backbone of the church. There was no one to take their place. None of the Johnsons' children made good church members. I never saw one of Fuller's children in the church. Yet these old members were as faithful as anything you can imagine. They would no more miss a Wednesday service than anything.

I was away for about fourteen years from the city and on my return went down to the old works to see what had happened in the interval, and found that the Jew was being pushed out by the Negro, and the people who had originally settled in the community were practically all gone. The church work was being carried on by a handful of young people who came from a distance. The church claimed a membership of about fifty and a Sunday school of one hundred. The preacher was a man from the South, from rural Kentucky, where he had been a minister in the Southern Church. The church services were of a highly emotional type so dissimilar from what I had been accustomed to that I was bewildered. Even in the congregational singing the

[9]   The stenographically reported interview as a sociological document has obvious advantages over an interview reproduced from memory or from notes.

old hymnal of the church with its fine type of inspiration and dignity had been supplanted with cheap editions of so called Gospel Hymns, such as "Tell Mother I'll Be There." The preaching was of a very low order of sentimentalism, with the preacher's desire to make his plea so gruesome that the women folk were often driven to tears. I talked with some of the people that I felt should know better, and their reply was that they could do nothing about it, as they were outnumbered by those that wanted such a service. On further observation covering about a year, I observed that those who were active in carrying on the work felt that they were doing a very important work, though they themselves had an inadequate conception of their religion, and other than carrying on a Sunday service were doing nothing really constructive in the community. They were simply hypnotizing themselves into the belief that they were martyrs in a great work.

It is an entirely different proposition now. I'll give you the reaction of some of the people who used to go there and still have business there in that neighborhood. I went to see one of the men the other day.

"What's going to become of that church? What's it coming to?" I asked him.

"Oh, I guess they're doing pretty good among the kids, but it's the street jargon proposition that I can't get used to." That man used to go there but now he goes to a church out west.

Turning to the Children

The most interesting service which Monroe Park Church conducts and the one of which it boasted the most was its junior church service. Originally the service was for both boys and girls, but in two years time this meeting became so large that it was necessary to divide it. Consequently, for the last few months the girls have come at 4:30 and the boys at 6:00.

These junior church services often had an attendance of 100 boys and 100 girls, though the average was probably 75 girls and 50 boys. The children were of different nationalities, but the large majority were either Polish or Dutch. Some Sundays both groups would be present, and other Sundays the Poles would be missing. The Dutch groups nearly all attended the nearby Holland churches in the morning, while the Poles were Catholic. There were a few children from Monroe Park Church Sunday school present.

Junior church was led by Miss Watson and Mr. Jacobs, two workers from a Bible institute. They were assisted in various ways by other students from the Institute and by one or two of the men of Monroe Park Church who came down to act as policemen and to try to keep order. . . .

The value of the junior church services has been open to serious question by various people associated with the church. The Mission Board heard that Monroe Park Church had had difficulty in enforcing order owing to its crowded conditions, and the fact that it had had to throw out a number of the boys from its services. The Board sent a man down to investigate what was going on and they found that all of the boys who were thrown out were members of the Dutch Reformed Church. So the Mission Board is now well aware of the fact that many of the members of this junior church are also members of the Holland church and that there is a duplication of effort. The leaders of the junior church recognize the situation and say they do not care how many of the Hollanders they throw out, for these boys have a church of their own to take care of their religious life. The leaders, however, hesitate to throw out the Polish boys, for that is the group they believe it is their duty to reach. The leaders are discouraged, but they do not know how to meet the problem. The elders of the church join in protest, and demand order. Serious attempts to keep order by toning down the meeting resulted in big drops in attendance. Many of the boys admittedly come for a big time, and look upon the junior church as "just like a show," as one boy expressed it. The meeting affords them a chance to get together with other boys and have a good time, along with an occasional gift of candy, popcorn or doughnuts.

Secularizing Church Activities

Some of the workers in seeking recruits brought into the church a group of boys who were in process of "ganging". Miss Watson says the boys were induced to come to the church through what she calls "street visitations" carried on by Mr. Jacobs and herself. "We walked through the streets and alleys and hailed every kid we saw, asking him enthusiastically to come over, telling them that we had the best thing going—no big people there."

The Chapinski gang of boys has taken its name from a Polish family whose three sons are members.[10] The oldest boy, John, is now in Parental School for petty stealing, but the other two are still active and supposedly leaders of the gang. There are about twenty boys in the group and they are all adept at the tricks of their "trade." The community is a bootlegging center and these boys have been coached by older criminals. They are usually at war with the "Fifth Street" gang and fighting between the two occurs on the slightest provocation. The boys of both gangs spend most of their time on the street and can usually be found at night playing in the Fourth Street School yard.

The gang originated about three years ago in the coal and wood shed in Chapinski's back yard. In the beginning there were only a few boys, John and Mike Chapinski and Tom Oachs and Jim and Harry Vittio. In a short time Roy Kostka and his brother Joe joined them and brought their friend Tommy Steinfeldt.

Previous to this time there had been a gang known as the "Black Cats," so called because they swiped milk in the evening and either drank or sold it. The boys in this gang were asked to pay dues and Peter Minsky and Jack Dooley left the gang and joined the Chapinskis. According to Mike the boys first met in the shed as a "club house" and sat around and talked. A bit later they learned to shoot dice and if there was money to be had they played for money. Mike and John say they first began to rob to get things with which to fix up the club, but later on they conceived the idea of selling what they stole for spending money. Until about a year ago they seemed to specialize in lead pipe and plumbing fixtures, varying their recreation in summer by stealing pop or beer. When nothing else presented itself the gang found entertainment in "beating up niggers." They have succeeded in almost eliminating negroes from the Fourth Street School playgrounds.

They moved from one shed to another for about a year and for the next two years they were without a club house. They congregated in the school yard, in doorways, on and around the bread boxes in front of the stores, and at the church every time they found the worker in.

The boys use the "L" exclusively for transportation. It is an easy matter to sneak a ride, and the whole gang goes regularly to the Oak Street beach in the summer time and never thinks of spending a cent for fare. They have often stolen rides on the "L" to Cicero to steal chickens. On one occasion Mike and his brother told of going on such

<hr>

[10]   From a student's report made in December, 1927. Assistance in the writing of this report was given by one of the community workers in Monroe Park Center.

an expedition and the only reason they could think of for taking the chickens was to throw them at the third rail on the "L" just to see if they could hit it. The store keepers in the community watch the boys with an eagle eye and whenever it is possible to prevent it never allow one of them in their stores. The boys have come to confide in the workers in the Monroe Park Center and often relate to them their experiences in thievery. The people in the community blame the gang for everything that happens, and there is no doubt that many times other boys are responsible, but are able to hide behind the reputation of the Chapinski gang.

At first the gang activities of the boys were not known to the church workers. In an interview with the writer one of the leading workers of the junior church remarked, "Yes, we raised them up but we did not know what we were getting and I hope we never raise another crop like that." Later when the activities of the gang became known to the church workers they sought by various means to have the boys correct their ways. The strength of the neighborhood traditions and the training by older gangs in the community seemed to triumph over the church influences. The boys used the features of the church for their own ends. They even used some of the workers as confidants and sought their help in escaping the penalties of their misbehavior. Last summer during daily vacation Bible school classes the boys were making small toy automobiles and tin was needed. Several gang members volunteered to find some and presently returned with a great heap of oil cans from a nearby junk yard.

There were times when the workers felt that they were influencing the boys, as during football season when a coach was supplied. Stealing dropped off but it might have been because time was otherwise occupied. When football activities were over they went back to their old forms of behavior.

The football team in the fall was coached by Mr. Jacobs, and won from everyone with whom they played. It occupied their time and several merchants remarked that they had been troubled less with the Chapinski's than formerly. An effort was made to secure a gymnasium where basketball could follow the football season, but the attempt was not successful. The gang meets in the church on Saturday afternoons as a club.

Only six or eight of the Chapinski gang attend Sunday school, but the Sunday evening meeting has been practically made for them. On the night of December 18, 1927, the number of boys present totalled eighteen, and only one boy there was not a member of the gang. . . .

The Church Disbands

For a number of years, the question of the future of the Monroe Park Church has been discussed by leading members of the church and representatives of the Missionary Society. For some time it has been difficult for the Missionary Society to see the justification of its expenditure in this place. Denominational headquarters had originally accepted the situation as presented by the Mission Board when the building was sold, and thought that the church should die. But after a lengthy fight, denominational headquarters voted that the Mission Board should furnish the church a place to meet, and consequently the Mission Board rented back the building they had sold. This situation continued for a while, and then the building was sold again, this time to a bottle works which demanded possession. Several "last meetings" in the old church house were held, and a number of former members came back for the farewell services.

A number of attempts were made to find a suitable home for the church, but without success. Finally the small, one-room store building mentioned in the beginning of this story was secured. Here the church has been holding all of its services since July, 1926.

The departure from the old building has caused the loss of a few of the members, and has made others more irregular in their attendance. They say that the church without its building "is no longer like home." Others believed that the church would die as soon as it had to leave its building, and so lost heart. The old guard still remained faithful, however, and the work with the children in the neighborhood continued.

Instead of killing the church, the move seemed to add new fuel to the flame. The places of those who dropped out were filled by others living in the community. The junior church and the Sunday school grew till the little store building would hold no more. Every-one was enthusiastic and more determined than ever that the church should not die. They glorified in their added hardships. The psychology of having a small building filled to overflowing rather than a large building with a seemingly small group present worked in favor of the church.

In the fall the Mission Board attempted to bring about a union of the four struggling churches on the Near West Side, under the leadership and in the building of an old established church of the denomination. It was intended that a preaching center would be maintained at this church and that neighborhood work would be carried on in the other three locations. A preliminary meeting was held to discuss the proposed merger, and all but Monroe Park Church seemed favorably inclined. Monroe Park Church stood out strongly against the merger, claiming that the work for the chil-dren in their neighborhood would be neglected and that they were unwilling to give up their pastor or their church organization. The meeting angered the members, for they realized their existence as a church hung in the balance, and hostility to the Mission Board was openly shown.

The matter of the merger was temporarily dropped by all of the churches in order that they might take part in the "Loyalty Cam-paign" with a united front.

Monroe Park Church entered with enthusiasm on the six weeks loyalty campaign, put on by the churches of the denomination in the city during November and December of 1926. It fought hard to get new members and boost attendance, in order to increase its strength, and its reputation with the denomination. It got some new members, and had a comparatively large attendance at its meetings. A little bulletin was published called the *Monroe Park Voice*, which was filled from cover to cover with advertisements of coming events, and with vigorous optimistic notes predicting the triumph of Mon-roe Park Church.[11] The *Voice* predicted for the final night of the campaign with this declaration:

[11]   Material from church papers often indicates the weaknesses or strength of a church. Such extravagant statements are signs of weakness rather than strength.

To the victor belong the spoils and now that we have reached our goal, let's climax this night with the greatest rejoicing we have ever experienced. On this day let it be said of our church—"That they rose up early about the dawning of the day, and compassed this section of the city after the new manner seven times, and blew their trumpets and the people of this section of Chicago shouted with a great shout the walls of the old and inadequate building crumbled and fell and Monroe Park Church is promised a new home so it can take this section of Chicago for God. It can be done! It must be done, and by God's Grace we will do it."

Monroe Park Church also took part in the Million Dollar Drive for funds, and went far over the top. The *Voice* remarks that:

Monroe Park Church not only accepted its quota but asked that its quota be raised and then more than doubled the increased quota with the understanding that the difference be retained as a Monroe Park Church Fund. This money is to be paid in the most convenient way for the subscriber, covering a three year period of time, the first payment not due till next April. With the present financial condition of our church it seemed next to impossible to expect them to give to this cause. Yet the consecration of this people arose to meet the challenging needs of our own denomination and will gladly assume their share.

All in all it was a very successful six weeks. New members were obtained and much enthusiasm was generated.

With the ending of the Loyalty Campaign and the beginning of the New Year, the church again came up against the problem of the future. Congregational meetings with representatives from the Missionary Society were again held to determine what the future of the church should be, and speeches were made by different members in behalf of the old church. The representatives of the Missionary Society stated that the church had outlived its usefulness, and that it was standing in the way of a work for the children of the community. During these numerous meetings a great deal of misunderstanding arose, and many arguments and statements were made for each proposition. It became evident that the Missionary Society would do no more for the church unless it were given complete control.

Monroe Park Center

Monroe Park Church formally disbanded July 3, 1927. The members were assured that a work for the children of the community would continue. Since that date, one of the earlier workers of the church has been continued by the Missionary Society in a community service work. The Society has not yet determined how extensive a neighborhood work should be conducted. Some of the religious features of the church life have been continued through volunteer help.

The program for the Center for the first few months of 1928 included clubs for mothers, and for older and younger boys and girls, a special group for the gang, game periods for boys and girls, manual training for boys, and handicraft clubs for girls. In the autumn of 1928 the schedule of activities listed boy scouts, pre-school kindergarten, doll clubs, and cooking.

Conclusion

The behavior sequence of this dying church may be summarized as follows:

The church began as a mission. It came to have a thriving Sunday school, and its services were described as "filled to overflowing." Movements of population and death finally took the leaders of the church. The children of incoming German immigrants were sought, and some of those who were won became leaders of the church as they became older. The church attempted to gain the incoming Bohemians and Jews. Various programs of clubs, forums, and week-day activities were attempted. The church sought and received home missionary aid.

As the church declined the members assessed the blame for their failure now upon the pastor, now upon unfaithful members, now upon the incoming groups, and finally upon the home missionary society. They quarreled among themselves and with outside groups.

There were periods of optimism and enthusiasm, and periods of despondency when the members would have closed the church had they not been angry at some one. They came to glorify the past, and to make much of the sacredness of the old church building, and of their own past fellowship.

A small group of people came to bear the burden of service for the church. When their own workers left, they accepted volunteer help from outside the congregation. These volunteer workers came to dominate the situation, and changed the character of the teaching of the church. The services became extremely informal and lacking in ritual.

The old church home was sold and the building turned into a bottle works, while the congregation moved to a rented hall. By means of rewards and entertainments, the children of the community were induced to attend an evening religious service in the rented hall. These children were of a different religious faith and background from the Monroe Park Church, and regarded it as a secular rather than a religious institution. The church even came to be a gathering place for a boys' gang, whose members attended these evening services.

Under the stress of circumstances, the workers came to emphasize play and recreation as a part of their program. The church finally dissolved, and a community center program was financed by the home missionary society. The staff is now seeking to meet specific community problems and needs by means of a social service program. Some volunteer religious work continues, although one transformation after another has taken place, until the character of the institution is now completely changed.

IV Social Worlds

13

Paul G. Cressey

THE TAXI-DANCE HALL

AS A SOCIAL WORLD

FOR THOSE who attend the taxi-dance hall, even irregularly, it is a distinct social world, with its own ways of acting, talking, and thinking. It has its own vocabulary, its own activities and interests, its own conception of what is significant in life, and—to a certain extent—its own scheme of life. This cultural world pervades many avenues of the habitué's life, and some of its aspects are readily apparent to even a casual visitor at the halls.

I had expected almost anything at this dance hall but even then I was surprised. It was the most speckled crew I'd ever seen: Filipinos, Chinese, Mexicans, Polish immigrants, brawny laborers, and high-school boys. More disturbing was the cynical look which the men directed at the girls and the matter-of-fact way they appropriated the girls at the beginning of each dance. The girls, themselves, were young, highly painted creatures, who talked little—and when they did speak used strange expressions to accentuate their talk. They spoke of "Black and Tans," "Joe's Place," "Pinoys," "nigger lovers," and used other terms with which I was not familiar. My attempts to get acquainted with several of the girls met with indifference on their part, while at the same time they each seemed very much alive to a few men and

Reprinted from Paul G. Cressey, *The Taxi-Dance Hall: A Sociological Study in Commercialized Recreation and City Life* (Chicago: University of Chicago Press, 1932), pp. 31–53. Earlier in the book Cressey explains that a taxi-dance hall is a commercial public dance institution attracting only male patrons, which seeks to provide them an opportunity for social dancing by employing women dance partners, who are paid on a commission basis through the ticket-a-dance plan, and who are expected to dance with any patron who may select them for as few or as many dances as he is willing to purchase.

several girls in the place. To everyone else they seemed polite, coquett-ish, but really quite indifferent. I left the place feeling that I had been permitted to witness but not to participate in the real life revolving around the hall.[1]

So well is the vital world of the dance hall veiled by conven-tionalized conduct that a person may attend regularly without perceiving it. Unless he is initiated into the meaning of certain ac-tivities, of certain words and phrases, of certain interests and standards of conduct, he may as well not try to understand the hu-man significance of the taxi-dance hall. For many factors aid in making the world of the taxi-dance hall a moral milieu rather com-pletely removed from the other more conventional forms of city life.

I. *Fundamental Wishes of Person Fulfilled*

Perhaps the most important aspect of this dance-hall world making possible its moral isolation is the completeness of the in-terests and satisfactions afforded in it. Especially for young girls removed from home influences and living with other taxi-dancers the dance-hall life proves sufficient to meet satisfactorily most of their dominant interests and wishes.

After I had gotten started at the dance hall I enjoyed the life too much to want to give it up. It was easy work, gave me more money than I could earn in any other way, and I had a chance to meet all kinds of people. I had no dull moments. I met bootleggers, rum-runners, hijackers, stick-up men, globe-trotters, and hobos. They were all different kind of men, different from the kind I'd be meeting if I'd stayed at home with my folks in Rogers Park. . . . After a girl starts into the dance hall and makes good it's easy to live for months without ever getting outside the influence of the dance hall. Take myself for in-stance: I lived with other dance-hall girls, met my fellows at the dance hall, got my living from the dance hall. In fact, there was nothing I wanted that I couldn't get through it. It was an easy life, and I just drifted along with the rest. I suppose if something hadn't come along to jerk me out, I'd still be a drifter out on the West Side.[2]

1   Impressions of an investigator on his first visit to a taxi-dance hall.
2   Case No. 11.

Not only economic gain, but opportunities for excitement, masculine conquests, intimacies, and masculine affection are all provided in the taxi-dance hall. The dancers may even identify themselves with the dance-hall life so completely that when they return after an absence they experience a feeling of joy and satisfaction in "getting back home again."

You can't imagine how happy I felt to get back to the "school" again after two weeks at home in Wisconsin. Of course I was glad to see my mother, but then you know we don't have so much to talk about any more. And as for that old German stepfather of mine—the less I see of him the better. I don't feel like I belong back in Wisconsin any more. But up at the "school" I just feel at home. . . . I know how things go, I have my friends who are always glad to see me come back, and who are really interested enough to spend their money on me. There are a lot of fellows up there who don't amount to much, but—just the same—I have more real friends there than in all the rest of the world put together.[3]

The fundamental desire for recognition, for status, along with the desire for intimacy or response, and for new experience and excitement, all find some satisfactions in the taxi-dance hall. In fact, the desire for security is the only one of Thomas' "Four Wishes"[4] which does not have a place in the life of the efficient taxi-dancer.

II. *Unique Activities and Vocabulary*

A second fundamental aspect of the world of the taxi-dance hall helping to maintain its moral isolation is its distinctive patterns of behavior and vocabulary. Even minor characteristics of a person's behavior and manner may become, to the dance-hall world, the means for identifying him as either an "insider" or an "outsider." Thus a taxi-dancer suggests some of the clues which she used to identify an outsider:

---

[3]   Case No. 10.
[4]   See W. I. Thomas' statement of the "Four Wishes" in *The Unadjusted Girl*, chap. i.

The first time I saw you I knew right away you didn't belong on West Madison Street. You didn't act like the other white fellows who came up to the hall. The other strange men would come in and be very quiet or act like they weren't sure of themselves. They wouldn't talk very much. But you did. You'd even go up and talk straight out to the boss, but none of the others would have done that until after they'd known him.

Then when you'd come over to me you'd first ask me to dance— not just hand me a ticket like the others did. Then you danced differently. . . .

I also discovered right away you talked differently, used different words, and while you didn't brag about yourself like most of the others do, I got the feeling that you thought you were somebody, and yet you weren't ashamed to be caught in the hall. That's the way I got the idea you were a "professional" of some sort.[5]

The special vocabulary of the dance-hall world is itself a means of identification, as well as communication. It reflects the special interests, judgments, and activities which center about the establishment. To a considerable extent the vocabulary is constructed from common slang and from the "West Side dialect." But in addition there are other picturesque words and phrases which have their chief usage in the dance-hall world. Many of these words or phrases find almost universal usage among all patrons, but others are used exclusively by one group. The Filipinos, for instance, have their own words and phrases; while the white youth of the West Side also has his special vocabulary. Likewise, the taxi-dancer has her words and phrases by which she describes both the Filipino and the West Side youth. This whole special vocabulary, however, blends together and reveals a unique world of interests and activities, in which the focus of interest is sensual and commercial. . . .

III. *Unique Meanings of Conventional Activity*

Not only have a new vocabulary and a distinct type of personal behavior in the world of the taxi-dance hall developed, but old,

[5]   Comment of a veteran taxi-dancer to an investigator.

well-established phrases and customs have acquired new meanings and purposes. An outward conformity to well-established customs often cloaks conduct in conflict with the moral standards of society. Such thoroughly acceptable conventions as courting and "dating" take on new meanings. The date, a conventionally accepted means for young people to become acquainted, comes to have, in the environment of the taxi-dance hall, a suggestion of immorality. While the first date with a taxi-dancer may only give rise to speculation concerning its significance, several dates together are accepted by many as proof that an illicit relationship has been established.

They've been going together now for two weeks. . . . You don't suppose he's spending his evenings up here, and taking her home every night, unless there's something doing? . . . Say, listen Big Boy, there ain't no Santa Claus![6]

Not only the date itself, but many other forms of conventional behavior come to have new meanings in the taxi-dance hall.

"Well, of course they're sweet on each other," Mildred exclaimed in answer to my suggestion that Hazel and Arthur seemed well acquainted. "Haven't you noticed she gives him all her free dances, and that he's jealous whenever any fellow dances more than two dances with her? Art doesn't dance with anybody else now, you notice. He just comes up and sits around and gives her his tickets. . . . I don't suppose you've noticed that new dress she's got, and her new fur coat. Well, a girl doesn't get a fur coat at a nickel a dance," she concluded sardonically.[7]

The taxi-dance hall has its own body of judgments and experiences by which the activities revolving about the establishment are interpreted.

IV. *The Taxi-dancer Dominant in Taxi-dance Hall*

The most distinguishing aspect of the taxi-dance hall is the position of prominence and prestige occupied by the successful

[6]   Case No. 12.
[7]   Records of an investigator.

taxi-dancer. Far from feeling herself exploited commercially, the taxi-dancer responds to the stimulation of the situation and the admiration of the patrons and for a time finds satisfaction in them.

Of course it's an easy life, no work, sleep late in the morning, more money than I could earn by day work—and all that. But that's not all that makes me like it. There's something about the hall that makes me feel good. I may be as blue as indigo when I go down there but before long I feel all peppy again. I don't think it's the music. I like to be with people and up at the hall the fellows—especially the Filipinos —treats me real nice.[8]

Especially where the patrons are seeking to win a girl's favor, with the hope of securing late night engagements, they are polite and courteous. Since the girl's society outside the dance hall—so much sought after by many of the patrons—can be secured only through the dubious process of courtship rather than through the more dependable method of bargaining, the popular taxi-dancer has a favorable status in the taxi-dance hall which seems to arise in part from the very uncertainty of her favors. Even with those patrons who very evidently have no desire or expectation of securing a date, the taxi-dancer usually has satisfactory associations. Their contacts are of either an impersonal character or a friendly comaraderie.

More completely even than in other types of dance establishments the taxi-dancer dominates the social world, because of the peculiar organization of the taxi-dance hall. The patrons are, for the most part, transient and casual in their attendance. The girls, on the other hand, have a definite and rather permanent economic relationship to the establishment. In their contacts with one another and with the patrons they set the mode, provide a certain scheme of life, and set the immediate standards of conduct for both taxi-dancers and patrons. External standards of conduct may be maintained by the management, but the most direct control remains with the group of girls who dominate the life of the establishment and who have evolved certain codes and techniques of control. These are transmitted from experienced girls to newcomers through casual contacts in the dance hall. Naturally enough, the restroom

[8]   Case No. 12.

during intermissions provides one place for the transmission of this code.

I'll never forget my first night at the hall. As you know, I wasn't much of a Sunday-school kid when I hit that place, but they sure made me think I was. During the intermission I went back to the restroom and found the girls powdering, painting, using lipstick, swearing, smoking, and drinking. One girl was pretty drunk, and she was cussing and saying the worst things I'd ever heard. The others were listening to her and laughing at everything she said. The whole thing made me sick and I left.

I didn't go back to the restroom for almost a week. When I did, one evening, a tough-looking Polish girl yelled out at me, "Big Blond Mamma thinks she's stuck up, don't she?" I was so mad I didn't know what to do, so I just turned and walked out.

But it didn't take long to get used to things. I gradually got to using their talk and now when I go back there I talk just like the rest of them.[9]

V. *The Exploitation Motif*

Another basic characteristic of the social world of the taxi-dance hall—already implied in much of the previous discussion—is the existence in it of unique "schemes of life." The schemes of life typical of the taxi-dance hall are in part products of the establishment itself and of the type of life necessary because of its social structure and the interests of its personnel. They represent the ways by which the people most closely identified with the taxi-dance hall seek to achieve through it what they consider significant in life. Their methods are somewhat standardized, and when fully matured are associated with a certain "philosophy of life" or "rationale" by which these activities, and the methods used, are justified. The dominant scheme of life for both patrons and taxi-dancers grows out of the combined commercial and romantic interests and the necessary casual intimacies with many patrons. It is represented in the motive of exploitation towards the other sex, prominent in the minds of most seasoned taxi-dancers and of not a few patrons.

[9] Case No. 13.

An important aspect of the scheme of life is the attitude which taxi-dancer and patron adopt toward each other. The impersonal attitudes of the market place very soon supersede the romantic impulses which normally might develop. Under the spur of commercialism the taxi-dancer, for instance, very soon comes to view the patrons, young or old, not so much as *ends*, but rather as *means* toward the achievement of her objectives—the recouping of her personal fortunes. Romantic behavior, along with other less desirable forms of stimulation, becomes merely another acceptable method for the commercial exploitation of the men.

The patron's point of view is the complement of the taxi-dancer's. He is interested in securing an attractive young woman with whom he may dance and converse without the formality of an introduction and without many of the responsibilities entailed at other social gatherings. Frequently he desires a young woman who gives promise of other contacts later in the night. Thus, from the special interests of the patrons and the commercial aims of the taxi-dancer a competitive struggle develops between man and woman for an advantage over each other. In many instances the struggle is a conscious one in which any means, fair or foul, are used in exploiting the other.

All these girls are after is the money they think they can get out of a fellow. They'll "gyp" a guy if they can. But they don't get far wid me. I'm on to them. . . . But it's not that I care about. I can take care of myself. I'm not just trying to keep them from putting something over on me; I'm trying to put it over on them. I know what I'm after and I'm out to get it. That's me all over.[10]

With the seasoned taxi-dancer this philosophy of exploitation, the zealous practicing of her techniques, the revengeful impulses arising from blasted dreams and romances, and her honest though carefree view of her own unconventional conduct blend together to make her a distinct personality type, interesting in itself. While individualized and somewhat egocentric, able quickly to find the character faults in others who would seek to take advantage of her, she is unable, apparently, to discover the major faults in herself. But

10   Conversation of a patron with an investigator.

neither taxi-dancer nor most patrons perceive that the most basic explanation for these unfortunate associations, these unpleasant experiences, is to be found not so much in the original character of the individuals themselves as in the very social structure of the present-day taxi-dance hall.

Unable to perceive these basic yet unseen social forces which shape her life, the taxi-dancer becomes something of a drifter, gaining what satisfactions she can from the transient thrills of the day and from the skilful practicing of her devices for exploitation. . . .

VI. *Orientals as "Fish"*

The motive toward exploitation is seen most clearly in the attitude toward "dating" and dancing with Orientals. These young men, frequently because of the absence of satisfactory young women of their own races in the United States and because they are denied free social contacts with white Americans, find their problem of social contacts with young women a distracting one. Frequently this restriction reaches such a point that it becomes a matter of absorbing curiosity and even a mark of pride to secure contacts with white American women. Under such circumstances many Orientals are willing to pay exorbitantly for even casual contacts with taxi-dancers. The girls, however, often regard them as "fish," as persons to be exploited.

I was invited into the parlor of the Malowiski home where Sophie was entertaining a rather uncouth Chinese fellow who claimed to be a waiter in a chop-suey restaurant. They did not converse. He merely sat and looked. Nor did he dance. . . . Sophie and I began moving toward the doorway but in an instant she hesitated. "We mustn't get so far away. My 'fish' might get jealous!" "Your fish?" I asked. "What is that?" "Oh, that Chinaman over there." "Why do you call him your 'fish'?" I persisted. "Oh," she replied, "he gives me about twenty dollars every time I ask him, and he only spends two evenings a week up here."[11]

Orientals, and especially Filipino young men, prove to be such lucrative sources of income that many young women, under the

11   Report of an investigator.

spur of opportunism, lay aside whatever racial prejudices they may have and give themselves to a thorough and systematic exploitation of them. They may even develop techniques for exploitation.

Lila . . . told me that the Filipino boys were good suckers and spent a lot of money on the girls, providing the girls act jealous and start a fight over them once in a while. "If I had to live on the money I made in this joint I'd starve to death. But you can always get money from these Filipinos.

"My sister works here too, but she is sick tonight. She tried to drink everything she could get her mits on . . . and then fought with a couple of girls over her Chink. He goes to the university and works as a waiter. He gets a little money from home, but my sis keeps him busy so she can get a lot of bucks out of him.

"I keep my bozo busy, too. He is an interne at a hospital and works in a barber shop, too. He bought me this dress last week after I told him I would cut his throat if he danced with any other dame. These white guys that come up here are all the bunk. They wouldn't give a girl a dime if it killed them, so don't waste your time.

"I'll introduce you to a new one that just came over. He still has a little cash from home and you can take it away from him if you're smart. One girl that used to work up here went with a Filipino who was a boxer. She took $1200 away from him and then blew to California. When she got there she wrote him and told him to go to hell, that he was a dumb sucker and that she was going into the movies."[12]

Among her own white friends it is necessary for the taxi-dancer to explain her interests in Orientals. Here the justification is found again in terms of exploitation.

"Oh, these "Niggers" [Filipinos] and "Chinks" [Chinese] are just "fish" to the girls. They say to us fellows, "You don't mind if I play around a little with these fellows, do you? They're all right, and give us presents, too. We don't mean nothing with them."

The girls just keep them on the string for what they can get out of them. One girl told me she had three of them. She'd get Christmas presents from them, see? These guys are mostly Filipinos. They have a lot of jack [money]. Most of them go to college, I guess.[13]

12   Logan, *op. cit.*, January 30, 1930.
13   Comment of a Polish youth to an investigator.

However, there are many taxi-dancers who will not accept dates from Orientals, and occasionally one may even object to being in the same dance hall with them. For these girls "staying white," as it is called, is of supreme consideration.

The "Flips" [Filipinos] are all right for anybody that wants them. They're a lot more polite than most of the other fellows who come up here. But they're not white, that's all. Of course, I'll dance with them at the hall. But I won't go out with them. I'm white, and I intend to stay white.[14] . . .

VII. *Sensual Dancing and Exploitation*

The motive of exploitation even extends to the type of dancing which many taxi-dancers find it profitable to practice and encourage. Many girls who are anxious to increase their earnings adopt a standardized form of sensual dancing commonly practiced in many halls. The individual's decision as to whether or not to engage in this practice is more completely an economic adjustment —and less a moral decision—than is commonly thought. A typical attitude is expressed in the following excerpt:

Up here you might as well sit in the corner if you don't dance that way. I stood on the side with thirty cents for the first two nights because I wouldn't, but now I'm like the worst of them. Two girls up here won't speak to me now, but I don't care. It's the money I'm after.[15]

From a frank accommodation to the economic situation in which the girl finds herself to a justification of her conduct on the basis of exploitation is a transition very easy to make. In the taxi-dance hall, where exploitation is thought of as any means of gaining money and gifts short of overt immorality, the idea of exploitation very readily affords a satisfactory rationalization for sensual dancing. Such conduct appears as but another means for "fishing" or exploiting the men.

14   Case No. 10.
15   Case No. 20.

VIII. *The "Sex Game"*

The exploitation motive which is characteristic of so many aspects of the life of the taxi-dance hall also has its place in the personal sex philosophy and practices of the taxi-dancer. The "sex-game," a term applied to this scheme of life,[16] denotes the battle of wits in which there is a careful stalking of the other sex and in which the woman frankly utilizes her sex attractions as an aid in winning the game.

This game arises very naturally as a fortuitous adjustment of the unattached woman in a world of transient contacts. In these casual associations utilitarian interests tend to take precedence over all others. For the girl trying to make her way in such a world a readjustment in her code may seem mandatory. The philosophy of the sex game is the natural result.

Though often thought of and described as "gold-digging," the sex game is the characteristic scheme of life not only of the seasoned taxi-dancer but of many other groups of women who seek to make their way in a world of transient associates. The waitress, according to Frances Donovan,[17] finds it expedient to avail herself of some such practice. Were the information available, it is probable that it would also be found that the chorus girl, the cabaret entertainer, and even many salesgirls find some form of the sex game immediately advantageous.

While there is perhaps no basic pattern of life on which there is more agreement among seasoned taxi-dancers than in their sex philosophy, the uniformity cannot be said to be wholly a result of their dance-hall activities. It is, rather, a product of their very similar experiences prior to entrance upon dance-hall life. Even though from widely different cultural backgrounds, most of them have gone through very much the same experiences before entering the taxi-dance hall and have arrived at similar schemes of life. For the most part they have been young girls set adrift in a careless money-mad city life with little effective moral instruction to guide

[16]   See Frances Donovan, *The Woman Who Waits*, pp. 211–20.
[17]   *Ibid.*, p. 213.

them and with no money-making skill or training, who have come to accept uncritically the standards of achievement represented in the shop windows and on the boulevards.

In the quest after the material equipment of life which seems of such prime importance, the girl becomes not only an individualist but also—frankly—an opportunist. Unable to buy many of the stimulations and material things which she craves through the money earned in conventional occupations, she has, in her resourcefulness, discovered financial possibilities in her own personality and feminine charm. This adjustment is merely a matter-of-fact adaptation to the exigencies of the situation in which moral considerations, in a surprising number of cases, have only secondary importance. In the words of one taxi-dancer, the problem becomes simply one of "making the most of what you've got."

I don't go to the hall to make friends. I go there to make money. I've been up there only a month, but I already know how to make the cash. I've got to look peppy and fast, but a girl doesn't have to dance immodestly to make the money. I get all the dances I want without, but maybe it's because I've got a good figure and wear the right kind of dresses. . . . It's just a question of making the most of what you've got. All I've got to work with is my "sex appeal."[18]

IX. *Forms of Sexual Alliance*

The sex game very naturally results in considerable sexual irregularity. From these experiences have arisen several forms or patterns of sexual alliances which, although imported from the outside, nevertheless have become an integral part of the world of the taxi-dance hall. In some cases these importations have been considerably altered to meet the economic necessities of the situation. This is strikingly true in the case of the "plural alliance," an anomalous adjustment which has been reported from but a few circles outside the taxi-dance hall, though it might develop equally well in other detached worlds.

The mistress. The highest in point of status of these various extra-marital alliances is that of the mistress. Like the other forms of

[18]   Case No. 15.

illicit sex activities associated with the taxi-dance hall, there is a considerable amount of personal interest and sympathy in the attitudes of paramours toward each other. Likewise there are rather definite and well-understood standards of loyalty and faithfulness. Very often there is little bargaining. It is rather a co-operative association in which the man, in the terminology of the dance hall, either "pays the rent" or "buys the groceries," or both. These alliances may last for some months.

The plural alliance. A less frequent arrangement is what might be called the "plural alliance." Instead of being "true" to one man, the girl enters an understanding by which she agrees to be faithful to a certain three or four men, who may even come to know one another. Through separate arrangements with each man the financial requirements are met.

Ann wasn't what you'd call promiscuous. She had an understanding with four fellows by which she'd restrict herself to us four. She picked us out and then invited us into the arrangement. We each contributed something. Two of us paid her rent, another paid her groceries, and the fourth fellow bought some of her clothes. There never was any jealousy among us. Often we'd meet at her apartment and sit around together. It got to be quite a joke who'd get to stay. When midnight came she'd turn to the unlucky fellows and say, "Well, it's about time for you guys to go on home." Then the next night she'd pick on the other fellow. Nobody got jealous, because—we all knew Ann. . . . As far as any of us ever knew she was faithful to this arrangement as long as it lasted—for over four months.[19]

The overnight date. There is, finally, the overnight date—a rather frequent practice. However, activities of this sort, it should be noted, quickly take on the character of clandestine prostitution.

X. *The Romantic Impulse*

It has been pointed out in the last pages that the taxi-dancer's scheme of life involves an emphasis, fundamentally, upon exploitation. Whether in the girl's attitude toward the patrons, the Orientals, attendance at night resorts, or in the "sex game," the

[19]   Case No. 27.

attitude of exploitation—of getting as much as possible for nothing —is clearly seen. This is not only the taxi-dancer's own point of view, but—in its more conservative form—it is no doubt the attitude the proprietors desire that the girls take. In practice, however, the motive toward exploitation is constantly being checkmated by another force—the romantic impulse. Whether desired or not, the romantic impulse flowers forth with increased vigor in this setting —to such an extent that the proprietors have accepted it as an inevitable handicap in doing business.

For the first years that we ran our school we tried to keep the girls from leaving with the patrons. We even made it a rule that any girl who met a man at the foot of the stairs would be fired. But it did no good. They'd just meet them on a corner a block away. And if we told them they couldn't meet them on a corner they'd meet in a restaurant. So we gave it up. As long as boys are boys and girls are girls they're going to get together somehow.[20]

Toward the patrons the taxi-dancer's general attitude may be that of exploitation, but before long she comes to make certain "exceptions." She comes to "like" certain men, and the rigid commercial system of the dance hall breaks down. Instead of demanding a ticket from her more favored suitors she frequently gives them "free dances," voluntarily renouncing her income from those whom she favors. Even the extensive system of "ticket-collectors," who circulate among the dancers during each dance number demanding from every taxi-dancer a part of each ticket, is not sufficient to check this tendency. By one ruse or another the taxi-dancer finds a way of circumventing the system and succeeds in giving up at least part of the income received from dances with her special friends.

The romantic impulse also functions in the attitude of the girls toward Orientals, and especially Filipinos. At first regarding the Filipino as an object of exploitation, many before long come to take an entirely different attitude.

The Filipinos are nice fellows. I don't know whether you know I'm engaged to a Filipino. I love him, too. Right now, I'm trying to make up my mind whether I love him enough to give up everything

[20]   Statement of a proprietor.

else for him. And if I marry him, I won't quit. Even if I find I've made a mistake, I'll stick by him just as long as he'll stick by me. I'm either going to marry for good or not at all.

If we do marry we'll go to the Islands to live. There won't be so much prejudice over there, will there? . . . I wouldn't mind having a baby a little brown. I've seen some of them. They're not so very different and they look awfully cute to me.[21]

The acceptability of the Filipino, in preference to other Oriental groups, is explained by such factors as his Occidental culture, represented in the Spanish influence in the Philippine Islands; his suave manners, dapper dressing, and politeness; and the romantic Spanish-lover role which it is possible for him to play. For the young girl with a limited knowledge of the world the Filipino especially appears as an attractive and romantic figure.

I didn't know much when I started at the hall. I didn't even know what a Filipino was. I thought they were movie actors or something. They were always well dressed, and treated me nicely; I fell for them hard. They took me out to nice places, and took me riding in taxicabs all the time. I thought they must be rich.[22]

Especially when the girl is dissatisfied with her past, with the type of opportunities which her other men friends afford, or with their treatment of her, the politeness and deference of the Filipino help to give her an enhanced conception of herself. Under such circumstances the taxi-dancer very frequently becomes romantically interested in him.

In some instances the romantic impulse in its reaction to the sordid emphasis in the taxi-dance hall takes on additional strength, and may even extend to a naïve acceptance of an individualistic philosophy suggestive of "freedom of love" doctrines.

I believe in love, even though I've really never had any. . . . I know I've had a lot to make me not believe in it, but if I really didn't believe it was possible for me to have a real true love I believe I'd want to die. . . . I wouldn't care what kind of a man he was, just so I loved him. I wouldn't care what he did for a living either. I don't

21   Case No. 21.
22   Case No. 19.

like drinking, but if he was a bootlegger, or even a garbage collector, and I loved him, I'd marry him. It wouldn't be anybody's business what my husband did. He'd be my husband, nobody's else's. . . .

Love is a lot more important than getting married. What does marriage amount to anyway? A preacher says something over your head but it doesn't mean anything unless you love your man.[23]

The romantic interests cut across and negate, quite extensively, the impersonal commercial system of the taxi-dance hall. Yet the personal romantic interest of one day may become the utilitarian interest of the following. If the object of a taxi-dancer's affection is believed to attempt exploitation, disillusionment, cynicism, and resentment quickly supplant her sincere romantic interest.

Out of these conflicting impulses and disorganizing activities the taxi-dancers and patrons shape their standards and practices, their own schemes of life. The wide range of satisfactions in the taxi-dance hall, the distinct vocabulary and ways of acting, the interpretations of activities, the code, the organization and structure, and the dominant schemes of life are the basic factors in the social world of the taxi-dance hall, by which the activities, the conception of life, and philosophy of life of taxi-dancer and patron are molded.

[23]   Case No. 12.

14

St. Clair Drake and Horace R. Cayton

LOWER CLASS: SEX AND FAMILY

BABY CHILE crawled into the bed with Mr. Ben. She cried
and cried and stroked the bulky dressing on his shoulder. "Honey, I
didn't mean to do that. I love you! I love you!"

Mr. Ben didn't say a word. The needle was wearing off and his
shoulder hurt. But he wasn't gonna let no woman know she'd hurt
him. He bit his lip and tried to sleep. He pushed her hand away
from his shoulder. He cursed her.

"Hush up, dammit, shet up!" he growled. "I wanna sleep."

Baby Chile kept moaning, "Why'd I do it? Why'd I do it?"

"Shet up, you bitch," Mr. Ben bawled. "I wisht they'da let them
creepers take you to the station! Cain't you let me sleep?"

Baby Chile didn't say another word. She just lay there a-thinking and a-thinking. She was trying to remember how it happened.
Step by step she reconstructed the event in her mind as though the
rehearsal would assuage her feeling of guilt.

She'd been living with Mr. Ben six months now. Of course he
was old and he hadn't ever got the country outa him yet. But he
had a good job s'long as he kept the furnace fired and the halls
swept out. And he got his room free, bein' janitor. She had a relief
check coming in reg'lar for herself and her little girl. They could
make it all right as long as the case-worker didn't crack down on
'em. But Mr. Ben was so suspicious. He was always watching her
and signifyin' she was turning tricks with Slick who helped him

From St. Clair Drake and Horace R. Cayton, *Black Metropolis: A Study
of Negro Life in a Northern City* (New York: Harcourt, Brace, 1945),
pp. 567–70. Copyright 1945 by St. Clair Drake and Horace R. Cayton.
Reprinted by permission of Harcourt, Brace & World, Inc.

with the furnace and slept in the basement. She wouldn't turn no tricks with Slick. He had bad blood and wouldn't take his shots reg'lar. But you couldn't convince old Mr. Ben. Ben didn't treat her little girl right, either. 'Course, it wasn't his child. But he oughta act right. She cooked for him and slept with him and never held her relief check back on him. He could treat her child right. That was the cause of it all, anyhow.

Baby Chile had come home near dark after a day of imbibing Christmas cheer. She must have been a little slug-happy. All she remembered was chasing her little girl outa Mamie's kitchenette next door, telling her to stay outa that whorehouse. "I ain't raisin' you to be a goddammed whore! Why I send you to Sunday school? Why I try to raise you right? For you to lay up there with them whores?" You just couldn't keep her outa that place listening to the vendor playing boogie-woogie and seein' things only grown folks oughta see. Then she remembered stretching out on the bed. Just before she lay down she'd asked her daughter, "What Ben get you for Christmas, chile?"

"Nothin', Mother Dear."

"Nothin'?"

"No, ma'am."

Her eyes fell on the sideboard covered with new, shiny bottles of whisky and beer and wine—plenty of "Christmas cheer." A turkey was cooking in the stove. "An' that no-'count bastard didn't get *you* nothin'?" She remembered throwing herself on the bed in a rage. The radio was playing Christmas carols—the kind that always made her cry because it sounded like the church back down in Mississippi. She lay there half drunk, carols ringing in her ears from the radio, boogie-woogie assailing them from the juke-box across the hall, the smell of turkey emanating from the kitchen, and her little girl whimpering in the corner.

She recalled the "accident" vividly. She was dozing on the bed in the one large room which along with the kitchen made up their home. She woke up when Ben came into the room. She didn't know how long she'd been sleeping. Whisky and beer don't mix anyhow, and when you been in and outa taverns all day Christmas Eve you get enough to lay you out cold.

When Mr. Ben opened the door near midnight she was almost

sober, but mad as hell. Her head ached, she was so mad. Ben grunted, walked into the kitchen, and started to baste the turkey. She challenged him:

"You buy Fanny May a present?"

"Naw," he grunted, "I spent my money for the turkey and the drinks. Tomorrow's Christmas, ain't it? What you do with yore relief check? Drink it up? Why'n you get her a present? She's yore chile, ain't she?"

Ben wouldn't have been so gruff, but he was tired and peeved. That damn furnace hadn't been acting right and everybody was stayin' up all night to see Christmas in, and pestering him for more heat. And all the time he was trying to get the turkey cooked, too. Baby Chile oughta been doing it—she had been sashayin' roun' all day drinking other men's liquor. How'd anybody expect him to think about a present for Fanny May? That girl didn't like him and respect him, nohow—always walling her eyes at him, but polite as hell to "Mother Dear." Crap! Mr. Ben didn't say any of this out very loud. He just mumbled it to himself as he bent over the stove basting the turkey.

Baby Chile stood up and stared at him. She felt her hell arising. She didn't say a word. She walked deliberately to the kitchen table and took up a paring knife, studied it for a moment, and then— with every ounce of energy that anger and frustration could pump into her muscles—she sank it between his shoulders and fled screaming into the hall. "Oh, I've killed Mr. Ben! I've killed my old man! I've killed him!"

Her little girl raced over to the noisy room next door and asked Miss Mamie to call the doctor. And Mamie interrupted her Christmas Eve business to help a neighbor.

Now Baby Chile was in bed with Mr. Ben. His shoulder was all fixed. She squeezed him tight, kissed him, and went to sleep.

Everybody had a good time on Christmas Day at Mr. Ben's. Fanny May went to church. The old folks began a whist game in the morning that ran continuously until midnight, with visitors dropping in to take a hand, eat a turkey sandwich, and drink from Mr.

Ben's sideboard. The janitor sat in his rocking chair like a king holding court, as the tenants streamed in and out and Baby Chile bustled about making him comfortable. Baby Chile was "high" enough to be lively, but was careful not to get drunk. No one mentioned the tragedy of the night before. Only Slick was uncomfortable.

15

William Foote Whyte

SOCIAL STRUCTURE, THE GANG,

AND THE INDIVIDUAL

THE CORNER-GANG STRUCTURE arises out of the habitual association of the members over a long period of time. The nuclei of most gangs can be traced back to early boyhood, when living close together provided the first opportunities for social contacts. School years modified the original pattern somewhat, but I know of no corner gangs which arose through classroom or school-playground association. The gangs grew up on the corner and remained there with remarkable persistence from early boyhood until the members reached their late twenties or early thirties. In the course of years some groups were broken up by the movement of families away from Cornerville, and the remaining members merged with gangs on near-by corners; but frequently movement out of the district does not take the corner boy away from his corner. On any evening on almost any corner one finds corner boys who have come in from other parts of the city or from suburbs to be with their old friends. The residence of the corner boy may also change within the district, but nearly always he retains his allegiance to his original corner.

Home plays a very small role in the group activities of the corner boy. Except when he eats, sleeps, or is sick, he is rarely at home, and his friends always go to his corner first when they want to find him. Even the corner boy's name indicates the dominant importance of the gang in his activities. It is possible to associate with a group of men for months and never discover the family

Reprinted from William F. Whyte, *Street Corner Society: The Social Structure of an Italian Slum* (Chicago: University of Chicago Press, 1943; 2d ed., 1955), pp. 255–76. Copyright 1943, 1955 by The University of Chicago.

names of more than a few of them. Most are known by nicknames attached to them by the group. Furthermore, it is easy to overlook the distinction between married and single men. The married man regularly sets aside one evening a week to take out his wife. There are other occasions when they go out together and entertain together, and some corner boys devote more attention to their wives than others, but, married or single, the corner boy can be found on his corner almost every night of the week.

His social activities away from the corner are organized with similar regularity. Many corner gangs set aside the same night each week for some special activity, such as bowling. With the Nortons this habit was so strong that it persisted for some of the members long after the original group had broken up.

Most groups have a regular evening meeting-place aside from the corner. Nearly every night at about the same time the gang gathers for "coffee-and" in its favorite cafeteria or for beer in the corner tavern. When some other activity occupies the evening, the boys meet at the cafeteria or tavern before returning to the corner or going home. Positions at the tables are fixed by custom. Night after night each group gathers around the same tables. The right to these positions is recognized by other Cornerville groups. When strangers are found at the accustomed places, the necessity of finding other chairs is a matter of some annoyance, especially if no near-by location is available. However, most groups gather after nine in the evening when few are present except the regular customers who are familiar with the established procedure.

The life of the corner boy proceeds along regular and narrowly circumscribed channels. As Doc said to me:

Fellows around here don't know what to do except within a radius of about three hundred yards. That's the truth, Bill. They come home from work, hang on the corner, go up to eat, back to the corner, up a show, and they come back to hang on the corner. If they're not on the corner, it's likely the boys there will know where you can find them. Most of them stick to one corner. It's only rarely that a fellow will change his corner.

The stable composition of the group and the lack of social assurance on the part of its members contribute toward producing a very high rate of social interaction within the group. The group structure is a product of these interactions.

Out of such interaction there arises a system of mutual obligations which is fundamental to group cohesion. If the men are to carry on their activities as a unit, there are many occasions when they must do favors for one another. The code of the corner boy requires him to help his friends when he can and to refrain from doing anything to harm them. When life in the group runs smoothly, the obligations binding members to one another are not explicitly recognized. Once Doc asked me to do something for him, and I said that he had done so much for me that I welcomed the chance to reciprocate. He objected: "I don't want it that way. I want you to do this for me because you're my friend. That's all."

It is only when the relationship breaks down that the underlying obligations are brought to light. While Alec and Frank were friends, I never heard either one of them discuss the services he was performing for the other, but when they had a falling-out over the group activities with the Aphrodite Club, each man complained to Doc that the other was not acting as he should in view of the services that had been done him. In other words, actions which were performed explicitly for the sake of friendship were revealed as being part of a system of mutual obligations.

Not all the corner boys live up to their obligations equally well, and this factor partly accounts for the differentiation in status among them. The man with a low status may violate his obligations without much change in his position. His fellows know that he has failed to discharge certain obligations in the past, and his position reflects his past performances. On the other hand, the leader is depended upon by all the members to meet his personal obligations. He cannot fail to do so without causing confusion and endangering his position.

The relationship of status to the system of mutual obligations is most clearly revealed when one observes the use of money. During the time that I knew a corner gang called the Millers, Sam Franco, the leader, was out of work except for an occasional odd job; whenever he had a little money, he spent it on Joe and Chichi, his closest friends, who were next to him in the structure of the group. When Joe or Chichi had money, which was less frequent, they reciprocated. Sam frequently paid for two members who stood close to the bottom of his group and occasionally for others. The two men who held positions immediately below Joe and Chichi were considered very well off according to Cornerville standards. Sam said that he occasionally borrowed money from them, but never more than fifty cents at a time. Such loans he repaid at the earliest possible moment. There were four other members with lower positions in the group, who nearly always had more money than Sam. He did not recall ever having borrowed from them. He said that the only time he had obtained a substantial sum from anyone around his corner was when he borrowed eleven dollars from a friend who was the *leader* of another corner gang.

The situation was the same among the Nortons. Doc did not hesitate to accept money from Danny, but he avoided taking any from the followers.

The leader spends more money on his followers than they on him. The farther down in the structure one looks, the fewer are the financial relations which tend to obligate the leader to a follower. This does not mean that the leader has more money than others or even that he necessarily spends more—though he must always be a free spender. It means that the financial relations must be explained in social terms. Unconsciously, and in some cases consciously, the leader refrains from putting himself under obligations to those with low status in the group.

The leader is the focal point for the organization of his group. In his absence, the members of the gang are divided into a number of small groups. There is no common activity or general conversation. When the leader appears, the situation changes strikingly. The small units form into one large group. The conversation becomes general, and unified action frequently follows. The leader becomes the central point in the discussion. A follower starts to say something, pauses when he notices that the leader is not listening, and begins again when he has the leader's attention. When the leader leaves the group, unity gives way to the divisions that existed before his appearance.

The members do not feel that the gang is really gathered until the leader appears. They recognize an obligation to wait for him before beginning any group activity, and when he is present they expect him to make their decisions. One night when the Nortons had a bowling match, Long John had no money to put up as his side bet, and he agreed that Chick Morelli should bowl in his place. After the match Danny said to Doc, "You should never have put Chick in there."

Doc replied with some annoyance, "Listen, Danny, you yourself suggested that Chick should bowl instead of Long John."

Danny said, "I know, but you shouldn't have let it go."

The leader is the man who acts when the situation requires action. He is more resourceful than his followers. Past events have shown that his ideas were right. In this sense "right" simply means satisfactory to the members. He is the most independent in judgment. While his followers are undecided as to a course of action or upon the character of a newcomer, the leader makes up his mind.

When he gives his word to one of his boys, he keeps it. The followers look to him for advice and encouragement, and he receives more of their confidences than any other man. Consequently, he knows more about what is going on in the group than anyone else. Whenever there is a quarrel among the boys, he hears of it almost as soon as it happens. Each party to the quarrel may appeal to him to work out a solution; and, even when the men do not want to compose their differences, each one takes his side of the story to the leader at the first opportunity. A man's standing depends partly upon the leader's belief that he has been conducting himself properly.

The leader is respected for his fair-mindedness. Whereas there may be hard feelings among some of the followers, the leader cannot bear a grudge against any man in the group. He has close friends (men who stand next to him in position), and he is indifferent to some of the members; but, if he is to retain his reputation for impartiality, he cannot allow personal animus to override his judgment.

The leader need not be the best baseball player, bowler, or fighter, but he must have some skill in whatever pursuits are of particular interest to the group. It is natural for him to promote activities in which he excels and to discourage those in which he is not skilful; and, in so far as he is thus able to influence the group, his competent performance is a natural consequence of his position. At the same time his performance supports his position.

The leader is better known and more respected outside his group than are any of his followers. His capacity for social movement is greater. One of the most important functions he performs is that of relating his group to other groups in the district. Whether the relationship is one of conflict, competition, or cooperation, he is expected to represent the interests of his fellows. The politician and the racketeer must deal with the leader in order to win the support of his followers. The leader's reputation outside the group tends to support his standing within the group, and his position in the group supports his reputation among outsiders.

The leader does not deal with his followers as an undifferentiated group. Doc explained:

On any corner you would find not only a leader but probably a couple of lieutenants. They could be leaders themselves, but they let the man lead them. You would say, "They let him lead because they like the way he does things." Sure, but he leans upon them for his authority. Many times you find fellows on a corner that stay in the background until some situation comes up, and then they will take over and call the shots. Things like that can change fast sometimes.

. . . I once asked Doc and Sam to tell me who was the leader of a corner gang that was familiar to both of them. Sam commented:

Doc picked out Carmen. He picked out the wrong man. I told him why he was wrong—that Dominic was the leader. But that very same night, there was almost a fight between the two of them, Dominic and Carmen. And now the group is split up into two gangs.

Doc said:

Sometimes you can't pick out one leader. The leadership may be in doubt. Maybe there are a couple of boys vying for the honors. But you can find that out.

The leadership is changed not through an uprising of the bottom men but by a shift in the relations between men at the top of the structure. When a gang breaks into two parts, the explanation is to be found in a conflict between the leader and one of his former lieutenants.

This discussion should not give the impression that the leader is the only man who proposes a course of action. Other men frequently have ideas, but their suggestions must go through the proper channels if they are to go into effect.

In one meeting of the Cornerville S. and A., Dodo, who held a bottom ranking, proposed that he be allowed to handle the sale of beer in the clubrooms in return for 75 per cent of the profits. Tony spoke in favor of Dodo's suggestion but proposed giving him a somewhat smaller percentage. Dodo agreed. Then Carlo proposed to have Dodo handle the beer in quite a different way, and Tony agreed. Tony made the motion, and it was carried unanimously. In this case Dodo's proposal was carried through, after substantial modifications, upon the actions of Tony and Carlo.

In another meeting Dodo said that he had two motions to make: that the club's funds be deposited in a bank and that no officer be allowed to serve two consecutive terms. Tony was not present at this time. Dom, the president, said that only one motion should be made at a time and that, furthermore, Dodo should not make any motions until there had been opportunity for discussion. Dodo agreed. Dom then commented that it would be foolish to deposit the funds when the club had so little to deposit. Carlo expressed his agreement. The meeting passed on to other things without action upon the first motion and without even a word of discussion on the second one. In the same meeting, Chris, who held a middle position, moved that a member must be in the club for a year before being allowed to hold office. Carlo said that it was a good idea, he seconded the motion, and it carried unanimously.

The actions of the leader can be characterized in terms of the origination of action in pair and set events. A pair event is one which takes place between two people. A set event is one in which one man originates action for two or more others. The leader frequently originates action for the group without waiting for the suggestions of his followers. A follower may originate action for the leader in a pair event, but he does not originate action for the leader and other followers at the same time—that is, he does not originate action in a set event which includes the leader. Of course, when the leader is not present, parts of the group are mobilized when men lower in the structure originate action in set events. It is through observation of such set events when the top men are not present that it is possible to determine the relative positions of the men who are neither leaders nor lieutenants.

Each member of the corner gang has his own position in the gang structure. Although the positions may remain unchanged over long periods of time, they should not be conceived in static terms. To have a position means that the individual has a customary way of interacting with other members of the group. When the pattern of interactions changes, the positions change. The positions of the members are interdependent, and one position cannot change without causing some adjustments in the other positions. Since the group is organized around the men with the top positions, some of the men with low standing may change positions or drop out without upsetting the balance of the group. . . .

One may generalize upon these processes in terms of group equilibrium. The group may be said to be in equilibrium when the interactions of its members fall into the customary pattern through which group activities are and have been organized. The pattern of interactions may undergo certain modifications without upsetting the group equilibrium, but abrupt and drastic changes destroy the equilibrium.

The actions of the individual member may also be conceived in terms of equilibrium. Each individual has his own characteristic way of interacting with other individuals. This is probably fixed within wide limits by his native endowment, but it develops and takes its individual form through the experiences of the individual in interacting with others throughout the course of his life. Twentieth-century American life demands a high degree of flexibility of action from the individual, and the normal person learns to adjust within certain limits to changes in the frequency and type of his interactions with others. This flexibility can be developed only through experiencing a wide variety of situations which require adjustment to different patterns of interaction. The more limited the individual's experience, the more rigid his manner of interacting, and the more difficult his adjustment when changes are forced upon him.

This conclusion has important implications for the understanding of the problems of the corner boy. As we have seen, gang activities proceed from day to day in a remarkably fixed pattern. The members come together every day and interact with a very high frequency. Whether he is at the top and originates action for the group in set events, is in the middle and follows the origination of the leader and originates for those below him, or is at the bottom of the group and always follows in set events, the individual member has a way of interaction which remains stable and fixed through continual group activity over a long period of time. His mental well-being requires continuance of his way of interacting. He needs the customary channels for his activity, and, when they are lacking, he is disturbed.

Doc told me this story:

One night Angelo and Phil went to the Tivoli to see a picture. They didn't have enough money for Frank, so they had to leave him behind. You should have seen him. It's a terrible thing to be left behind by the boys. You would have thought Frank was in a cage. I sat next to him by the playground. Danny was holding the crap game in the playground. Frank said to me, "Do you think Danny would have a quarter for me?"

I said, "I don't know. Ask him if you want to."

But Frank didn't want to ask him. He asked me, "Do you think Long John has a quarter?"

I said, "No, I know that Long John is clean." Frank didn't know what to do. If he had got the nerve up to ask Danny for the quarter right away, he could have run after the boys and caught up with them before they reached the theater. I knew that he would run if he had the money. But he waited too long so he wouldn't be able to catch up with them. It was nine-thirty when the crap game broke up. Frank went into the playground with me. He wanted me to ask Danny for something, but I told him to ask himself. He didn't want to. He said he thought he would go home, and he started, but then he came back. He asked us when we were going down to Jennings. I told him ten o'clock. We always go at ten now. He said that was too long to wait so he went home. Danny, Long John, and I went down to Jennings. We had been there about fifteen minutes when in walks Frank, and he sits down at a table next to us and starts reading the paper. Danny says, "What's the matter, Frank, no coffee?"

Frank says, "That's all right. I don't feel like it."

Danny says, "Go ahead, get your coffee." So Frank got coffee. We were ready to go before Angelo and Phil had come in. I could see that Frank didn't want to leave, but he had to because you're supposed to go out with the man that takes care of your check. He walked home with us, and then I guess he went back to Jennings' to meet Angelo and Phil.

Frank had a very high regard for Danny and Doc, and at an earlier period he would have been perfectly happy in their company, but since Angelo had become the leader of the group he had seldom interacted with them and he had been interacting regularly and frequently with Angelo and Phil. When he was deprived of their company, the resulting disturbance was strikingly apparent.

A man with a low position in the group is less flexible in his adjustments than the leader, who customarily deals with groups outside of his own. This may explain why Frank was so upset by events of only a few hours' duration. However, no matter what the corner boy's position, he suffers when the manner of his interaction must undergo drastic changes. This is clearly illustrated in the cases of Long John's nightmares and Doc's dizzy spells.

Long John had had this trouble on certain previous occasions, but then the fear of death had gone, and he had been able to sleep without difficulty. He had not been troubled for a long period up to the time that he experienced his latest attack. I do not know the circumstances surrounding the earlier attacks, but on this occasion Long John's social situation seemed clearly to explain his plight. He had become adjusted to a very high rate of interaction with Doc and Danny. While he did not have great influence among the followers in the Nortons, they did not originate action for him in set events, and he occasionally originated action for them. When the Nortons broke up and Doc and Danny went into Spongi's inner circle, Long John was left stranded. He could no longer interact with Doc and Danny with the same frequency. When he went over to Norton Street, he found the followers building up their own organization under the leadership of Angelo. If he was to participate in their activities, he had to become a follower in set events originated by Angelo. The members who had been below him in the Nortons were constantly trying to originate action for him. When his relationship with Doc and Danny broke down, he had no defense against these aggressions.

Doc brought about the cure by changing Long John's social situation. By bringing him into Spongi's inner circle, Doc reestablished the close relationship between Long John, Danny, and himself. In so doing, he protected Long John from the aggressions of the former followers. When Long John was once more interacting with Doc and Danny with great frequency, his mental difficulties disappeared, and he began acting with the same assurance that had previously characterized his behavior.

Doc's dizzy spells came upon him when he was unemployed and had no spending money. He considered his unemployment the cause of his difficulties, and, in a sense, it was, but in order to understand the case it is necessary to inquire into the changes which unemployment necessitated in the activity of the individual. While no one enjoys being unemployed and without money, there are many Cornerville men who could adjust themselves to that situation without serious difficulties. Why was Doc so different? To say that he was a particularly sensitive person simply gives a name to the phenomenon and provides no answer. The observation of interactions provides the answer. Doc was accustomed to a high frequency of interaction with the members of his group and to frequent contacts with members of other groups. While he sometimes directly originated action in set events for the group, it was customary for one of the other members to originate action for him in a pair event, and then he would originate action in a set event. That is, someone would suggest a course of action, and then Doc would get the boys together and organize group activity. The events of Doc's political campaign indicate that this pattern had broken down. Mike was continually telling Doc what to do about the campaign, and I was telling him what to do about seeing Mr. Smith and others to get a job. While we originated action for him with increasing frequency, he was not able to originate action in set events. Lacking money, he could not participate in group activities without accepting the support of others and letting them determine his course of action. Therefore, on many occasions he avoided associating with his friends—that is, his frequency of interaction was drastically reduced. At a time when he should have been going out to make contacts with other groups, he was unable to act according to the political pattern even with the groups that he knew, and he saw less and less of those outside his circle of closest friends. When he was alone, he did not get dizzy, but, when he was with a group of people and was unable to act in his customary manner, he fell prey to the dizzy spells.

When Doc began his recreation-center job, the spells disappeared. He was once again able to originate action, first for the boys in his center, but also for his own corner boys. Since he now had money, he could again associate with his friends and could also broaden his contacts. When the job and the money ran out, the manner of interaction to which Doc was adjusted was once more upset. He was unemployed from the time that the center closed in the winter of 1939–40 until he got a W.P.A. job in the spring of 1941. The dizzy spells came back, and shortly before he got his job he had what his friends called a nervous breakdown. A doctor who had an excellent reputation in Eastern City examined him and was unable to find any organic causes to account for his condition. When I visited Cornerville in May, 1941, he was once again beginning to overcome the dizzy spells. He discussed his difficulties with me:

When I'm batted out, I'm not on the corner so much. And when I am on the corner, I just stay there. I can't do what I want to do. If the boys want to go to a show or to Jennings or bowling, I have to count my pennies to see if I have enough. If I'm batted out, I have to make some excuse. I tell the boys I don't want to go, and I take a walk by myself. I get bored sometimes hanging in Spongi's, but where can I go? I have to stay there. Danny offers me money, and that's all right, but he's been getting tough breaks. Last week he was complaining he was batted out and a couple of days later he offered me two dollars. I refused. I don't want to ask anybody for anything. Sometimes I say to Danny or Spongi, "Do you want a cigarette?" They say, "No, we've got some," and then I say, "All right, I'll have one of yours." I make a joke out of it, but still it is humiliating. I never do that except when I'm desperate for a cigarette. Danny is the only one that ever gives me money.

Before I got this W.P.A. job, I looked terrible. I eat here at home, but I can't expect them to buy clothes for me. I had one suit, and that was through at the elbow, and the cuffs had more shreds than a chrysanthemum. When I had to go to places, I kept my overcoat on, or else I carried it over my arm to hide the hole in the elbow. And I was literally walking on the soles of my feet. You think I like to go around like that?

Lou Danaro has been after me to go out with him. He's got a new Buick—a brand-new Buick. That's pretty nice, you know. He wants me to get a girl, and we'll go out together. But I won't go. I'd have to play a secondary role. No, that's what you want me to say. I mean, I wouldn't be able to do what I want to do.

Last summer, they asked me to be chairman of the Norton Street Settlement outing. I worked with the committee, and all that, but the night before the outing the whole committee was supposed to go out to the camp and spend the night there. That was a big time. But I didn't go. I didn't have any money. Next morning I saw them off on the bus, and I said I would be out later. I went around and bummed a couple of bucks and drove up with one of the boys. I stayed a couple of hours, and then I came home. The chairman is expected to be active at one of those affairs. He is supposed to treat people—things like that. They think I'm shirking my responsibilities, but it isn't true. It's the money.

I have thought it all over, and I know I only have these spells when I'm batted out. I'm sorry you didn't know me when I was really active around here. I was a different man then. I was always taking the girls out. I lent plenty of money. I spent my money. I was always thinking of things to do and places to go.

Doc showed that he was well aware of the nature of his difficulties, but understanding was not enough to cure him. He needed an opportunity to act in the manner to which he had grown accustomed. When that was lacking, he was socially maladjusted. If he had been a man with low standing in the group and had customarily been dependent upon others to originate action for him in set events, the dependence which resulted from having no money would have fitted in with the pattern of his behavior in the group. Since he had held the leading position among his corner boys, there was an unavoidable conflict between the behavior required by that position and the behavior necessitated by his penniless condition.

The type of explanation suggested to account for the difficulties of Long John and Doc has the advantage that it rests upon the objective study of actions. A man's attitudes cannot be observed but instead must be inferred from his behavior. Since actions are directly subject to observation and may be recorded like other scientific data, it seems wise to try to understand man through studying his actions. This approach not only provides information upon the nature of informal group relations but it also offers a framework for the understanding of the individual's adjustment to his society.

The story of Cornerville has been told in terms of its organization, for that is the way Cornerville appears to the people who live and act there. They conceive society as a closely knit hierarchical organization in which people's positions and obligations to one another are defined and recognized. This view includes not only the world of Cornerville but also the world of the supernatural. The picture becomes clear when one observes the way in which people symbolically represent their world to themselves.

The annual *Festa* of the patron saint reveals not only the nature of religious beliefs and practices but also the outlines of the social organization. Until the summer of 1940 the *paesani* of each town which had a sufficient population in and about Cornerville banded together for this celebration. Each *Festa* committee set aside a particular week end every year and selected a location for the construction of a street altar and poles to hold strings of colored lights over the surrounding area.

There were band concerts on Friday and Saturday nights, but Sunday was the day of the real celebration. In the morning the *paesani* attended a special Mass in honor of their patron.

The Mass represented the only direct connection of the church with the *Festa*. While it formed a part of the general religious life, the *Festa* was entirely a people's ceremonial.

Early Sunday afternoon all those who wished to participate in the procession—and anyone could take part—assembled before the altar. The committee accepted contributions from those members who sought the privilege of carrying the statue of the saint through the streets. In some of the larger processions several hundred people marched with the saint. There was the children's band and the fife-and-drum corps of one or of both Italian churches, in addition to one or two professional bands. Little children, dressed as angels, carried bouquets of flowers. A few of the men and many of the women marched carrying lighted candles. Some, particularly the older women, marched without shoes or even without stockings.

To the canopy above the statue of the saint were attached streamers on which contributions of money were pinned. Several of the women carried a large flag or sheet stretched between them to catch change thrown from windows. Others circulated through the crowd lining the streets to solicit donations. In recognition of the larger contributions, the professional band faced the house of the contributor and played the Italian national anthem. Upon passing each of the churches, the procession halted and the statue was turned toward the church, but no ceremonial followed.

The return of the saint to the altar climaxed the procession. The bands played, a string was pulled to release streamers and pigeons which had been imprisoned in a decorated box suspended over the center of the street. There was usually some declamation upon the life of the saint and his connection with the townspeople before the statue was replaced.

Sunday evening there was a final band concert, there were brief speeches by certain members of the committee, and usually a prominent politician expressed his respect for the religious devotions of the Italian people.

The *Festa* furnished the occasion for a great reunion of the *paesani* who had moved to other cities and even to other states. Thousands of people milled about the streets in the evenings. Vendors of ice-cream and other confections did a thriving business. The local barrooms and restaurants were filled with friends and relatives celebrating the occasion. All members of a family gathered in one house to eat and drink together. The *Festa* was a religious and social ceremonial and a sort of carnival at the same time. It was an elaborate affair entailing an expense up to $2,500 and receipts of a comparable amount.

I talked with members of the committees of various *Festas* to get an explanation of what it meant to them. One of my informants expressed it in this way:

The reason for the feasts is this. We want to renew and reinforce the faith of the people in God. We want to make ourselves disciples of Christ among the people. In this way we set a good example for the young. The child sees the *Festa* when he is growing up, and later he passes it on to his own children in the same way that it came to him. In that way we help to preserve our religion and keep it strong. Protestants pray directly to God. They say, "God knows us, he knows everything we do. Why should we not pray to him?" Yes, God knows everything, but we are weak sinners. Why should he grant us the favors that we ask? Instead we pray to some saint—to a person once a human being like ourselves, whose holiness and sanctity have been proven in order to make him a saint. We pray to this saint who is without sins: who has led such a pure life that he can take some of our sins off of our shoulders. We ask the saint to intercede for us and be our advocate before God. We are poor, little people. If we celebrated the feast of our saint once every twenty or thirty years, the saint would ask, "Who are these people that are calling upon me?" No, we set aside a day each year for our saint, and every year we celebrate the feast on that day so that the saint will come to know us as his people and will try to help us when we pray for his aid.

Some ignorant people think that the saint can perform miracles. That is not true. The saint can only ask God to perform the miracles. God is a God of Mercy. If the sinner prays to the saint, the saint stands in right with God, and God takes pity upon the sinner and forgives him his sins. That is the spiritual world. It is the same way in the material world except that here we are dealing with material things. If you drive a car, and the policeman stops you for speeding and gives you a ticket, you don't wait till you go before the judge. You go to the sergeant, the lieutenant, or the captain—some person of influence—and perhaps the captain knows your brother or some friend of yours. Out of friendship he will forgive you for what you did and let you go. If the captain won't listen to you, you talk to the sergeant or the lieutenant, and he will speak to the captain for you.

I inquired whether paying the captain to drop the matter was the same thing as giving money to the saint in the procession.

No, that's different. When you give money to the saint, you do it because you want to make the feast a success. You want to show your devotion to the saint. You make a vow that you will give a certain amount of money to the saint, or you will walk barefoot in the procession, or that you will carry the saint. You do that to show your faith. You cannot buy a favor from God. God is not influenced by money. You give that money to maintain your religious institutions. Of course, there are people that will not do things for you just for friendship. They are just after the material things.

It is true that the *Festas* are largely activities of the older generation, but nevertheless the view of society that they represent is fundamentally the same as that of the younger generation. According to Cornerville people, society is made up of big people and little people—with intermediaries serving to bridge the gaps between them. The masses of Cornerville people are little people. They cannot approach the big people directly but must have an intermediary to intercede for them. They gain this intercession by establishing connections with the intermediary, by performing services for him, and thus making him obligated to them. The intermediary performs the same functions for the big man. The interactions of big shots, intermediaries, and little guys build a hierarchy of personal relations based upon a system of reciprocal obligations.

Corner gangs such as the Nortons and the cliques of the Cornerville Social and Athletic Club fit in at the bottom of the hierarchy, although certain social distinctions are made between them. Corner-boy leaders like Doc, Dom Romano, and Carlo Tedesco served as intermediaries, representing the interests of their followers to the higher-ups. Chick and his college boys ranked above the corner boys, but they stood at the bottom of another hierarchy, which was controlled from outside the district. There are, of course, wide differences in rank between big shots. Viewed from the street corner of Shelby Street, Tony Cataldo was a big shot, and the relations of the corner-boy followers to him were regulated by their leaders. On the other hand, he served as an intermediary, dealing with big shots for the corner boys and trying to control the corner boys for the big shots. T. S., the racket boss, and George Ravello, the state senator, were the biggest men in Cornerville. T. S. handled those below him through his immediate subordinates. While Ravello refused to allow any formal distinctions to come between himself and the corner boys, the man at the bottom fared better when he approached the politician through an intermediary who had a connection than when he tried to bridge the gap alone.

The corner gang, the racket and police organizations, the political organization, and now the social structure have all been described and analyzed in terms of a hierarchy of personal relations based upon a system of reciprocal obligations. These are the fundamental elements out of which all Cornerville institutions are constructed.

The trouble with the slum district, some say, is that it is a disorganized community. In the case of Cornerville such a diagnosis is extremely misleading. Of course, there are conflicts within Cornerville. Corner boys and college boys have different standards of behavior and do not understand each other. There is a clash between generations, and, as one generation succeeds another, the society is in a state of flux—but even that flux is organized.

Cornerville's problem is not lack of organization but failure of its own social organization to mesh with the structure of the society around it. This accounts for the development of the local political and racket organizations and also for the loyalty people bear toward their race and toward Italy. This becomes apparent when one examines the channels through which the Cornerville man may gain advancement and recognition in his own district or in the society at large.

Our society places a high value upon social mobility. According to tradition, the workingman starts in at the bottom and by means of intelligence and hard work climbs the ladder of success. It is difficult for the Cornerville man to get onto the ladder, even on the bottom rung. His district has become popularly known as a disordered and lawless community. He is an Italian, and the Italians are looked upon by upper-class people as among the least desirable of the immigrant peoples. This attitude has been accentuated by the war. Even if the man can get a grip on the bottom rung, he finds the same factors prejudicing his advancement. Consequently, one does not find Italian names among the leading officers of the old established business of Eastern City. The Italians have had to build up their own business hierarchies, and, when the prosperity of the twenties came to an end, it became increasingly difficult for the newcomer to advance in this way.

To get ahead, the Cornerville man must move either in the world of business and Republican politics or in the world of Democratic politics and the rackets. He cannot move in both worlds at once; they are so far apart that there is hardly any connection between them. If he advances in the first world, he is recognized by society at large as a successful man, but he is recognized in Cornerville only as an alien to the district. If he advances in the second world, he achieves recognition in Cornerville but becomes a social outcast to respectable people elsewhere. The entire course of the corner boy's training in the social life of his district prepares him for a career in the rackets or in Democratic politics. If he moves in the other direction, he must take pains to break away from most of the ties that hold him to Cornerville. In effect, the society at large puts a premium on disloyalty to Cornerville and penalizes those who are best adjusted to the life of the district. At the same time the society holds out attractive rewards in terms of money and material possessions to the "successful" man. For most Cornerville people these rewards are available only through advancement in the world of rackets and politics.

Similarly, society rewards those who can slough off all characteristics that are regarded as distinctively Italian and penalizes those who are not fully Americanized. Some ask, "Why can't those people stop being Italians and become Americans like the rest of us?" The answer is that they are blocked in two ways: by their own organized society and by the outside world. Cornerville people want to be good American citizens. I have never heard such moving expressions of love for this country as I have heard in Cornerville. Nevertheless, an organized way of life cannot be changed overnight. As the study of the corner gang shows, people become dependent upon certain routines of action. If they broke away abruptly from these routines, they would feel themselves disloyal and would be left helpless, without support. And, if a man wants to forget that he is an Italian, the society around him does not let him forget it. He is marked as an inferior person—like all other Italians. To bolster his own self-respect he must tell himself and tell others that the Italians are a great people, that their culture is second to none, and that their great men are unsurpassed. It is in this connection that Mussolini became important to Cornerville people. Chick Morelli expressed a very common sentiment when he addressed these words to his Italian Community Club.

Whatever you fellows may think of Mussolini, you've got to admit one thing. He has done more to get respect for the Italian people than anybody else. The Italians get a lot more respect now than when I started going to school. And you can thank Mussolini for that.

It is a question whether Mussolini actually did cause native Americans to have more respect for Italians (before the war). However, in so far as Cornerville people felt that Mussolini had won them more respect, their own self-respect was increased. This was an important support to the morale of the people.

If the racket-political structure and the symbolic attachment to Italy are aspects of a fundamental lack of adjustment between Cornerville and the larger American society, then it is evident that they cannot be changed by preaching. The adjustment must be made in terms of actions. Cornerville people will fit in better with the society around them when they gain more opportunities to participate in that society. This involves providing them greater economic opportunity and also giving them greater responsibility to guide their own destinies. The general economic situation of the Cornerville population is a subject so large that brief comments would be worse than useless.

One example, the Cornerville House recreation-center project, will suggest the possibilities in encouraging local responsibility. The center project constituted one of the rare attempts made by social workers to deal with Cornerville society in its own terms. It was aimed to reach the corner gangs as they were then constituted. The lesson which came out of the project was that it is possible to deal with the corner boys by recognizing their leaders and giving them responsibility for action.

The social workers frequently talk about leaders and leadership, but those words have a special meaning for them. "Leader" is simply a synonym for group worker. One of the main purposes of the group worker is to develop leadership among the people with whom he deals. As a matter of fact, every group, formal or informal, which has been associated together for any period of time, has developed its own leadership, but this is seldom recognized by the social workers. They do not see it because they are not looking for it. They do not think of what leadership is; instead they think of what it should be. To outsiders, the leading men of the community are the respectable business and professional men—people who have attained middle-class standing. These men, who have been moving up and out of Cornerville, actually have little local influence. The community cannot be moved through such "leaders." Not until outsiders are prepared to recognize some of the same men that Cornerville people recognize as leaders will they be able to deal with the actual social structure and bring about significant changes in Cornerville life.

So far this discussion sounds much like the anthropologist's prescription to the colonial administrator: respect the native culture and deal with the society through its leaders. That is certainly a minimum requirement for dealing effectively with Cornerville, but is it a sufficient requirement? Can any program be effective if all the top positions of formal authority are held by people who are aliens to Cornerville? What is the effect upon the individual when he has to subordinate himself to people that he recognizes are different from his own?

Doc once said to me:

You don't know how it feels to grow up in a district like this. You go to the first grade—Miss O'Rourke. Second grade—Miss Casey. Third grade—Miss Chalmers. Fourth grade—Miss Mooney. And so on. At the fire station it is the same. None of them are Italians. The police lieutenant is an Italian, and there are a couple of Italian sergeants, but they have never made an Italian captain in Cornerville.

In the settlement houses, none of the people with authority are Italians.

Now you must know that the old-timers here have a great respect for schoolteachers and anybody like that. When the Italian boy sees that none of his own people have the good jobs, why should he think he is as good as the Irish or the Yankees? It makes him feel inferior.

If I had my way, I would have half the schoolteachers Italians and three-quarters of the people in the settlement. Let the other quarter be there just to show that we're in America.

Bill, those settlement houses were necessary at first. When our parents landed here, they didn't know where to go or what to do. They needed the social workers for intermediaries. They did a fine job then, but now the second generation is growing up, and we're beginning to sprout wings. They should take that net off and let us fly.

V. Social Problems and Social Control

16

Walter C. Reckless

THE DISTRIBUTION

OF COMMERCIALIZED VICE

IN THE CITY:

A SOCIOLOGICAL ANALYSIS

SEGREGATION AND PERSONAL DISORGANIZATION   The commercialized vice areas of the city represent a natural segregation of individuals on the basis of their interests and attitudes. They attract, on the one hand, persons who seek sexual excitement, and on the other, those who exploit sex as a business or profession. Indeed, the very development of vice areas is dependent upon the conditions making for personal disorganization, since under these circumstances the impulses and desires get released from the socially approved channels and consequently find an outlet in the pattern of vice.

Concerning the more or less temporary population of the vice areas it may be said that to a large extent the patrons of commercialized vice, and to a lesser extent amateur and clandestine prostitutes, fit into the category of dual persons who circulate between two conflicting social worlds, namely, a world of respectability in the residential neighborhoods and a world of disrespectability in the downtown districts. The former offers them a life of shelter and security according to the sanctioned definitions of society; the latter, a life of adventure and romance in the realm of the disapproved. Again, a large quota of the more or less permanent habitués of the commercialized vice areas consists of persons whose

Reprinted from *The Urban Community*, ed. Ernest W. Burgess (Chicago: University of Chicago Press, 1926), pp. 192–205.

demoralization has made them outcasts from respectable society, and also of those individuals who, growing up amid great neglect, have developed a disorderly, wild, unregulated scheme of life which makes them unfit to enter organized society without passing through a rather complete re-education.

THE MORAL AND GEOGRAPHICAL ISOLATION OF VICE   But vice is usually censored by the mores of the community. It is not merely defined as immoral; it is also conceived as pestilential. And its open patrons and entrepeneurs are relegated to a social pariah existence. Vice has, therefore, been forced to hide from the moral order of society in order to flourish.

Because of this moral isolation vice gets spatially separated from wholesome family and neighborhood life in the community. The moral attitudes operate as barriers to isolate geographically this peculiar form of human activity.

Accordingly, commercialized vice has assumed two characteristic locations in the community: one at the center, the other at the circumference. It is well known that the central parts of the city, because of the decaying neighborhoods, have very little resistance to the invasion of vice resorts. Furthermore, commercialized vice on the fringe of the city, lodged at inns, taverns, and roadhouses, meets with practically no opposition, since the *hinterland* of the urban community, due to its sparsely settled condition and its decadent rural culture, is really unorganized.

But the vice resorts are usually prevented from assuming this most central location. In the first place legitimate business such as large retail stores, financial establishments, sky-scraper office buildings, is able to pay the high rents necessary in the competition for space. In the second place the public generally exerts pressure to drive vice out of the community market, although, as will be pointed out later, a large part of it is able to evade suppression and surveillance through subterfuge and camouflage. But commercialized vice can assume a decentralized location without threatening its existence. The very urgency of its demand, namely, this desire for sexual thrill, means that patrons will seek the supply even in the most remote places of the city. In fact, the delay entailed in this pursuit adds to the intensity of the urge as well as to the excitement of the chase.

The central position of commercialized vice may be said to represent the natural, unimpeded play of economic forces. The decentralized or outlying location signifies, in the main, a reaction to political factors, namely, those of legal control and public suppression. However, rapid transit and the automobile have made these ordinarily remote sections readily accessible, and consequently commercialized vice has gone wth the tide of an outgoing pleasure traffic.

VICE AREAS RELATED TO THE NATURAL ZONES OF THE CITY

A study of the particular regions of the city in which commercialized vice flourishes will reveal more definitely the factors that determine the distribution and location of this activity throughout the community. In order to get an accurate picture of the exact regions in which commercialized vice exists, a spot map was made from the cases dealt with by the Committee of Fifteen of Chicago during 1922.[1] The vice resorts handled by this law-enforcing agency extended radially from the center into the surrounding residential areas, principally along the important traffic arteries. Transferred to E. W. Burgess' chart describing the natural organization of the city,[2] the commercialized vice areas as revealed by this spot map are found to be implanted upon the central business zone (Zone I), the zone of transition (Zone II) with its slums, immigrant and racial colonies, lodging- and rooming-house area, and the restricted residential zone (Zone IV), which includes apartment houses as well as single homes.[3] It may be said, therefore,

[1]   The year 1922 was selected to show the more recent tendencies in the distribution of vice in the modern American city. Ten years earlier, before public repression had produced its noticeable effects, the vice resorts, if plotted, would probably show a greater concentration in the near central regions and less dispersion into the more decentralized neighborhoods.

[2]   See chart in Park and Burgess, *The City* (University of Chicago Press, 1925) ; article by E. W. Burgess on "The Growth of the City," *ibid.*, p. 55.

[3]   In Chicago the rooming-house district of Zone II and the apartment-house area of Zone IV merge into one another on the direct south,

that commercialized vice areas represent a parasitic formation, since they thrive upon the natural organization of the city.

THE ADAPTATION OF COMMERCIALIZED VICE TO NATURAL AREAS   A closer examination of the Committee of Fifteen data in reference to the economic and cultural order of the city shows that this agency was dealing with assignation hotels in the central business district, brothels in the slum, and "immoral flats" in the high-class residential area. It is clear, therefore, that commercialized vice makes special adaptation to the type of neighborhood invaded. The peculiar conditions characterizing these regions in which commercialized vice is located constitute very definite factors in the distribution and segregation of this parasitic activity.

Prostitution, supposedly excluded from the center of the city, actually, however, is able to evade surveillance by certain camouflages. While the brothel type of prostitution in most instances cannot exist in the central business district, not merely because of its open, public character, but also because of its inability to command a site in face of competition from financial, retail, and wholesale establishments, the freer and more clandestine form of commercialized vice surmounts these obstacles. Streetwalkers have never been eliminated from the downtown districts. Moreover, the activities of the streetwalker in very recent times is not so easily distinguished from the rather wide-spread practice of making casual acquaintances. A large number of these clandestine prostitutes have access to the cheaper hotels, many of which are used for assignation purposes.

Prostitution is frequently an insidious adjunct to the downtown "high life," the social whirl centering about the restaurants, the

west, and north sides, a fact which is due primarily to the high value of land resulting from favorable locations and good transportation facilities. The zone of workingmen's homes (III) in Chicago is found largely on the northwest and southwest sides of the city, outside the lines of greatest mobility, and consequently outside the regions in which commercialized vice flourishes best. However, it is doubtful whether the vice resorts in any city can successfully invade Zone III because of the strong family and neighborhood organization found there.

cafés, the theaters. The existence of commercialized vice in the central business district is an inevitable part of the flux and flow of the region. Besides being a market place for thrill, the downtown district is a region of anonymity, where conduct either remains uncensored or is subject merely to the most secondary observation and regulation. Under such conditions personal taboos disintegrate and appetites become released from their sanctioned moorings.

But streetwalking and assignation hotels by no means exhaust the adaptations which commercialized vice makes to the central business district. It frequently insinuates itself under the protective coloration of massage parlors and bathhouses. In these instances the "vice interests" are exploiting a very natural relationship of bathing and massage to sexual excitement.

THE SLUM AS THE HABITAT OF THE BROTHEL   The area of deterioration encircling the central business district furnishes the native habitat for the brothel type of prostitution. All the conditions favorable to the existence of this flagrant, highly organized form of commercialized vice are to be found there. In the slums the vice emporia not only find very accessible locations, but also experience practically no organized resistance from the decaying neighborhoods adjacent. And, furthermore, they are located in a region where the pattern of vice is an inevitable expression or product of great mobility and vast social disorganization.

UNORGANIZED PROSTITUTION IN ROOMING-HOUSES   The rooming-house sections and, to some extent, the tenement districts harbor an unorganized form of prostitution. The freelance, clandestine prostitutes, unattached to brothels, resort frequently to furnished rooms as a place to live and "bring tricks." The landlords or landladies either demand high rents from them or require a special room tax on each service. Because of the great anonymity in these rooming-house areas the activities of these prostitutes go on relatively unnoticed and consequently undisturbed. Here again the location is one of proximity to the demand, for it is a matter of common observation that the rooming-house and lodging house areas quarter the hordes of homeless men in the community.

IMMORAL FLATS IN APARTMENT-HOUSE AREAS   Commercialized vice has recently invaded the livelier apartment-house districts of the city and has appeared at this location in the form of "immoral flats," "buffet flats," and "call flats." The presence of vice in this decentralized part of the city, such as in the rooming-house sections and even on the fringe of the community, is due partly to a reaction to public repression. But the prostitution which has fled the slum for the apartment-house area has materially changed its external dress. Commercialized vice in the apartment house, as a rule, seems to be much less organized and much more refined than it is in the brothel.

The immoral flats are really only accessible by taxicab or automobile, since they hug the boulevards rather than the street-car lines. They attract, therefore, a high-class patronage, a sporting element that does not subscribe to the cheaper entertainment provided by the brothel. The apartment areas in which this externally changed form of prostitution is found present a very inviting field to commercialized vice, not merely because of the lively and mobile character of these regions, but also because of the anonymity and individuation produced by the highly mechanized living conditions.

INDEXES OF COMMERCIALIZED VICE AREAS   Certain of the factors and forces that determine the distribution of vice throughout the community are reducible to indexes, which help to delimit, as well as explain, the distribution of vice in the city. It may be said that commercialized vice is found in those regions characterized by burlesque shows, rescue missions, crime and other major social problems, immigrant and racial colonies, disproportion of sexes, declining population, and high land values and low rents.[4]

THE BURLESQUE SHOWS   The burlesque shows of large American cities, if plotted on a map giving the distribution of vice resorts, would fall within the areas in which flourish the most open, public forms of prostitution. This part of the larger commercialized

[4]   For more detailed discussion of these indexes, see Walter C. Reckless, "Indices of Commercialized Vice Areas," *Journal of Applied Sociology*, January–February, 1926.

vice areas of the city is really the homeless man's playground, for, besides these cheap theaters, the brothels, saloons, gambling-dens, fortune-tellers, "dime museums," and lady barbers compete with one another in catering to the play and sex interests of the non-family men of the slum. The burlesque show, or "border drama," is symbolic of the fact that a veritable man's community, with all its characteristic patterns of disorder, exists at the core of the city.

THE RESCUE MISSIONS   It is well known that the rescue mission has pioneered among the brothels and vice resorts of the urban community. From a spot map showing the characteristic institutions of hobohemia in Chicago it is quite evident that these rescue missions are located on, or adjacent to, the notorious rialtos of the underworld.[5] In fact, the "church on the stem" has grown up to reclaim the "lost souls" of the city's slums, and consequently points to social forces at work in the community to counteract those making for demoralization.

CRIME AND OTHER SOCIAL PROBLEMS   The underworlds of vice and crime have usually been inseparable. The distribution of crime throughout the urban community portrays, in the main, the location of commercialized vice. A spot map of felony cases,[6] giving the place of the crime and the address of the criminal, which were reviewed by the Chicago Crime Commission during 1921, describes about the same territorial distribution for crime as the spot map of the cases dealt with by the Committee of Fifteen of Chicago in 1922 does for vice.[7] On analysis it appears that both crime and vice depend upon mobility and collections of people;

5   This map was prepared by Nels Anderson in his study of *The Hobo* (University of Chicago Press, 1923). It was not included in the first printing of the study.
6   The spot map of felony cases reviewed by the Chicago Crime Commission was prepared by Clifford Shaw, research fellow in the Department of Sociology at the University of Chicago.
7   There are certain discrepancies between the two maps. As would be expected, crime shows a somewhat wider distribution than vice. Furthermore, a large proportion of burglaries occur in the wealthier residential districts, which are usually free from commercialized vice.

both forms of activity are legally and morally isolated and consequently must hide in the disorganized neighborhoods in order to
thrive. It is also interesting to note that commercialized vice exists
in the same general regions of the city characterized by the distribution of the cases of poverty, divorce, desertion, suicide, abandoned infants.[8] Indeed, these problems, considered ecologically,
indicate the areas of greatest social disorganization within the city.

IMMIGRANT AND RACIAL COLONIES   Since commercialized
vice thrives amid the vast social disorganization of the urban community, the major part of which is localized in the slum, it is to be
expected that the underworld intrudes itself in the immigrant and
racial colonies. The relationship of Chinatown to the commercialized vice areas of American cities is too well known to need elaboration. It is only fair to say, however, that the assumption of the usual
parasitic activities by the Chinese in the Western World is probably
to be explained by their natural segregation at the center of cities,
as well as by their uncertain economic and social status.

The "black belts" of American cities have usually been located
in or adjacent to the vice areas, while the Negroes themselves in
face of limited occupational opportunity, have of necessity found
work as maids and porters in the vice resorts.[9]

Vice resorts are also found in the settlements of the most recent
foreign immigration, which must generally take over the most
undesirable sections of the slum in order to gain a foothold in the
community. But commercialized vice does not invade all immigrant settlements. Those like Little Italy and the Ghetto, with a
strong family and neighborhood organization, are relatively free
from prostitution.

Vice is more characteristic of the cosmopolitan areas of the
city, which represent a sediment of caught families and individuals
from the various classes and nationalities. Since group controls in

[8]   Observation based on a comparison of the distribution of these
social problems in Chicago as shown by spot maps prepared by the Department of Sociology at the University of Chicago.
[9]   See the report of The Commission on Race Relations, *The Negro
in Chicago,* pp. 342–43.

such regions have practically disintegrated, social life tends to be unregulated and often disorderly.

While burlesque shows, rescue missions, crime and other major social problems, immigrant and racial colonies are valuable as rough indicators of the location and ecological setting of commercialized vice, the disproportion of sexes, declining population, and the correlation of high land values and low rents more nearly approximate indexes as used in the scientific sense; for in the first place, they are capable of mathematical formulation, and in the second place, they reveal factors and forces fundamentally related to commercialized vice in the chain of causation.

THE DISPROPORTION OF SEXES   The drift and gravitation of innumerable casual workers, tramps, hobos, bums, into the twilight zone between the central business district and the area of deterioration surrounding it has stimulated the development of so-called "womanless slums," and consequently has created a very marked disproportion of sexes.

The disproportion of sexes, on analysis, discloses certain conditions which underlie the very existence of commercialized vice. Men's communities and "hobohemias" have ever been characterized by the presence of prostitution. Westermarck has shown that a primitive sort of prostitution existed in Easter Island, where the men greatly outnumbered the women.[10] Bloch, in his study of *Die Prostitution*, specifically states that the men's communities of classical antiquity, namely, the university towns and the military camps, provided a fertile soil for the activities of prostitutes.[11] According to Bancroft, vice ran amuck in the mining camps of California's Gold Rush when, in 1850, the female population constituted less than 2 per cent of the total in the mining counties.[12]

[10]   Citing Geiseler's *Die Oster-Insel* (p. 29), Westermarck makes the following statement: "In Easter Island, where there were many more males than females, some of the young women remained unmarried and offered themselves up to the men," *History of Human Marriage*, 3d ed., I, 137.
[11]   See *Die Prostitution*, I, 252.
[12]   See *History of California*, IV, 221–39, for account of rampant vice conditions; pp. 221–22 for statement of disproportion of sexes in 1850.

248   WALTER C. RECKLESS

To take a more recent example, attention has been called to the fact that commercialized vice is rampant in Pekin of the present day, where the male population amounts to 63.5 per cent of the total number of inhabitants for that city.[13]

The disproportion of sexes acquires greater significance as an index of commercialized vice when taken in connection with marital status. The homeless man is not merely footloose; he is usually unmarried. In his study of *The Hobo*, Nels Anderson makes the following pertinent statement:

Of the one thousand men studied by Mrs. Solenberger (1911), 74 per cent gave their marital status as single. Of the four hundred interviewed by the writer, 86 per cent stated they were unmarried. Only 8 per cent of the former, and 5 per cent of the latter, survey claimed they were married. The others claimed to be widowed, divorced, or separated from their wives.[14]

As a result of the personal disorganization incident to this detachment from family life the sex impulses seek outlets in the unapproved channels, not merely in prostitution, but also in perversion.

Furthermore, the homeless man of the city's slums usually suffers from sex isolation, due to his great mobility, his low economic status, and his unpresentable appearance. About the only accessible women are the lower order of prostitutes. The vagrant men of all time, because of their social-pariah existence and their resulting sex isolation, have of necessity subscribed to commercialized vice.

DECLINING POPULATION   The density of population is frequently used as a criterion to explain the major problems of city life. And, offhand, it would seem that this principle would apply to commercialized vice. For prostitution flourishes in the areas of highest density within the city, namely, in the slum, where this is great concentration, while it is conspicuously absent from decentralized neighborhoods with a comparatively low density. The general relationship can be shown by a transposition of the Committee of Fifteen data on a density base map of the city.

[13]   Gamble, Sydney David, *Pekin: A Social Survey* (New York, 1921), pp. 243–44.
[14]   *The Hobo*, p. 137 n.

But there are sections of the downtown environs which are outside the radial distribution of commercialized vice and yet are within the circle of the most thickly populated areas in the city. Certain immigrant colonies are cases in point. Foreign settlements are frequently protected against a wholesale invasion of commercialized vice not merely by virtue of their semiremote location, but also by a strong family and neighborhood organization. Furthermore, on the outskirts of the city commercialized vice is very often lodged at roadhouses, which flourish in the most sparsely settled regions of the urban community.

It is the type of community organization, rather than the density of population, that has the direct bearing on the presence and distribution of vice. This is the reason why declining population, rather than sheer density of population, is the more satisfactory index, since it points to a lack or a disintegration of community organization, and consequently to a condition in which commercialized vice can exist best. According to maps showing the comparative density of the census districts in Chicago, it was found that certain sections contiguous to the central business section revealed a marked decline in the number of inhabitants in 1920 as over against 1910.[15] These areas of declining population are precisely the ones which harbor the brothels, according to the Committee of Fifteen cases for 1922. Indeed, commercialized vice, as already noted, is merely one of the many symptoms of the intense social disorganization in these twilight neighborhoods at the core of the city, neighborhoods which are decaying in the inevitable transition from residence to business.

THE CORRELATION OF HIGH LAND VALUES AND LOW RENT

Indicative also of this transition and disorganization is the correlation of high land values and low rents which describes a condition of neighborhood deterioration in the slum area about the center of the city. It is known that high land values appear at the traffic centers. In fact, they are a product of mobility of population, which in turn creates a situation of social instability and flux—a

[15]   These maps were prepared by Nels Anderson, research fellow in the Department of Sociology at the University of Chicago.

setting in which the pattern of vice thrives. Furthermore, commercialized vice almost inevitably develops in these areas of great mobility which, after all, become the natural market-place for thrill and excitement.

The slum, which has ever sheltered the most blatant forms of commercialized vice, has generally been noted for its fluidity and kaleidoscopic life, and the high land values in this zone of deterioration certainly indicate this condition of great mobility and disorganization. The land here not only has a relatively high value because of its centralized, and thereby accessible, location, but also has a speculative value, due to the approach of business itself.[16]

The improved property in these mobile, decaying neighborhoods that are in direct line of business expansion is allowed to run down, to deteriorate, for upkeep generally results in a total loss to the owner, since business only ordinarily demands the site. These deteriorated dwellings of the slum, because of their undesirability, can command but very low rents.[17] It is unavoidable that the poor and vicious classes share the same locality in the city's junk heap.

The relationship of the distribution of commercialized vice to neighborhood deterioration and the value of the correlation of high land values and low rents as an index of the vice areas may be indicated by the following statement of findings:

By actual count in the city of Seattle over 80 per cent of the disorderly houses recorded in police records are obsolete buildings located near the downtown business section, where land values are high and new uses are in process of development.[18]

It is clear that the distribution of commercialized vice in the city comes about through the working of factors determined by the

[16]   This condition of relatively high land values in the zone contiguous to the central business district may be indicated by a study of the land-value data given for the entire city of Chicago in Olcott's *Blue Book of City Land Values.*

[17]   A map based on a field study of rents in Chicago by the Illinois Bell Telephone Company in 1921 shows that just surrounding the central business district there is a section of low rents, the lowest in the city.

[18]   R. D. McKenzie, "The Ecological Approach to the Study of the Human Community" *American Journal of Sociology,* XXX (November, 1924), 299 n [see this volume, pt. 2].

economic, political, and cultural organization of the community as well as through the operation of forces lodged in human nature. The segregation of vice into characteristic urban areas is, therefore, the result of a natural process of distribution rather than—as is so often thought—a sheer artifice of legal control.

The propositions expounded in the foregoing analysis are not presented in terms of absolutes, especially in view of the fact that the factual material for this paper was drawn from an intensive study of the growth and development of vice areas in Chicago.[19]

[19] See Walter C. Reckless, *The Natural History of Vice Areas in Chicago*, University of Chicago, 1925 (Doctor's dissertation).

They are merely working hypotheses which invite the challenge of future investigation.

17

Clifford R. Shaw and Henry D. McKay

MALE JUVENILE DELINQUENCY
AS GROUP BEHAVIOR

THE FIRST vital social contacts of the child are restricted largely to the intimate relationships within the family group. At an early age, however, the range of his contacts with other persons is extended beyond the narrow limits of the home. He begins to associate with children outside of the family and to engage in their various social activities. Through his participation in these activities, the child's intimate relationships with companions, play groups, and gangs are gradually developed.

The development of relationships with play groups outside of the home represents a significant enlargement of the child's social world. Through them he is subjected to the influence of an increasing number and variety of personalities, social activities, and moral norms. That these play-group relationships are important factors in determining behavior traits is indicated in the study of the life histories of both delinquent and nondelinquent boys. They are particularly important as a medium through which new social values are acquired and new attitudes and interests defined.

The tendency of boys to organize themselves into some form of social group is more or less characteristic of the social life in the deteriorated and disorganized sections of the city as well as in the outlying residential neighborhoods. Such groupings are usually

Reprinted from *National Commission on Law Observance and Enforcement Reports*, vol. 2, *Report on the Causes of Crime* (Washington, D.C.: United States Government Printing Office, 1931), pp. 191–99, 222–57.

spontaneous in origin and constitute a form of primary group relationship. While these groups are more or less universal in all sections of the city and possess many common characteristics with respect to the mechanisms of control within the group, they differ widely in regard to cultural traditions, moral standards, and social activities. In certain areas of the city the practices and social values of many of these groups are chiefly of a delinquent character. Frequently these groups develop persistent delinquent patterns and traditional codes and standards which are very important in determining the behavior of the members. Some of these groups are highly organized and become so powerful in their hold on members that the delinquent traditions and patterns of behavior persist and tend to dominate the social life throughout the area. . . .

Following these earlier studies, Thrasher, author of *The Gang*, made an extensive study of boys' gangs in Chicago. One important phase of this study pertained to the relationship between gang activities and juvenile delinquency. As a result of this study, Thrasher concluded that the gang, while perhaps not a cause of delinquency in itself, is an important factor contributing to the development of criminal attitudes and behavior. He states:

The present study does not advance the thesis that the gang is a "cause" of crime. It would be more accurate to say that the gang is an important contributing factor, facilitating the commission of crime and greatly extending its spread and range. The organization of the gang and the protection which it affords, especially in combination with a ring or a syndicate, make it a superior instrument for the execution of criminal enterprises. Its demoralizing influence on its members arises through the dissemination of criminal technique, and the propagation, through mutual excitation, of interests and attitudes which make crime easier (less inhibited) and more attractive.[1]

In order to secure a more exact measure of the extent to which juvenile delinquency is group behavior, a study was made of the relative frequency of lone and group offenders among cases of delinquent boys appearing in the juvenile court of Cook County.

[1]   Frederic M. Thrasher, *The Gang* (Chicago, University of Chicago Press, 1927), pp. 381, 382.

For this purpose an analysis was made of the records of all the boys who appeared in this court on petitions alleging delinquency during the year 1928. This analysis was made at the end of that year and took into consideration the delinquency record of each boy from the date of his appearance in the court as a delinquent. Thus, the group includes both the recidivists whose first appearances in the court had occurred prior to 1928 and many boys who appeared for the first time during that year.

Throughout this chapter a distinction is made between individual delinquents and offenders. The number of individual delinquents whose records we have considered in this study is 1,886 These individual delinquents were known by the juvenile court authorities to have been involved in 3,517 offenses. The number of offenders, as that term is used here, was determined by counting each individual delinquent as an offender for each offense in which he was known to have been involved. Thus, if 1 group of 3 delinquents was brought to court charged with 2 offenses, the number of individual delinquents would be 3 and the number of offenders 6. Likewise, if a boy appeared in court alone on three offenses, the number of offenders would be three. Thus, the total number of offenders involved and brought to court in connection with the 3,517 offenses was 5,480.

At the outset an analysis was made to determine the relative incidence of lone and group delinquents among the 1,886 boys included in this study. In this total number 1,402, or 74.4 per cent, were involved with companions in committing the offense for which they were first brought to court, while only 484, or 25.6 per cent, committed their first offenses alone. Furthermore, 124 of the 484 boys appeared in court as group delinquents on subsequent offenses. Thus the boys who always committed their offenses alone, according to the records, comprised only 19 per cent of the total 1,886 individual delinquents.

A tabulation of lone and group offenders was made also for the total 5,480 offenders. The tabulation showed that only 18.2 per cent of the total offenders committed their delinquencies alone. Thus, as many as 81.8 per cent were group offenders; that is, committed their delinquencies with one or more companions (see fig. 9).

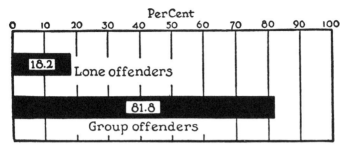

FIG. 9.—PERCENTAGE OF LONE AND GROUP OFFENDERS AMONG
OFFENDERS BROUGHT TO THE JUVENILE COURT

The distribution of the 5,480 offenders according to the number
of participants is indicated in Figure 10. According to this figure

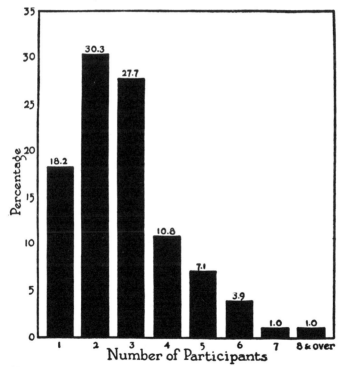

FIG. 10.—PERCENTAGE DISTRIBUTION OF OFFENDERS BROUGHT
TO COURT BY NUMBER OF PARTICIPANTS

it will be observed that the groups which have the highest frequency are those in which two and three participants are involved, the first comprising 30.3 per cent and the latter 27.7 per cent of the total number of offenders. As many as 10.8 per cent were involved in groups of 4, 7.1 per cent in groups of 5, and 3.9 per cent in groups of 6.

A comparison of the offenses charged against the lone and group offenders revealed that a much smaller proportion of the former were charged with stealing offenses than the latter. A disproportionately large number of the lone offenders were charged with offenses against the home and school. Among the total 5,480 offenders, 4,663 were charged with some form of stealing. Of these 4,663 stealing offenders only 11 per cent appeared in court alone, as compared with 89 per cent who were brought to court with accomplices[2] (see fig. 11). It is clear, therefore, that the fre-

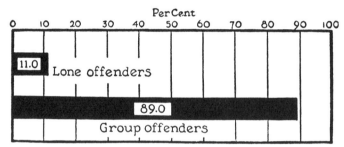

FIG. 11.—PERCENTAGE OF LONE AND GROUP OFFENDERS AMONG OFFENDERS BROUGHT TO THE JUVENILE COURT ON CHARGES OF STEALING

quency of lone offenders is greater among cases involving only stealing charges than it is for the juvenile court cases in general.

The distribution of the 4,663 stealing offenders according to the number of participants (see fig. 12) indicates that, as in the

[2]   In 1923 a similar study of lone and group offenders among cases appearing in the juvenile court of Cook County indicated that in a total of six thousand offenders brought to court on charges of stealing, 90.4 per cent committed their offenses in groups as against 9.6 per cent lone offenders. See "The Juvenile Delinquent," by Clifford R. Shaw and Earl D. Meyer, the Illinois Crime Survey (1920), p. 662.

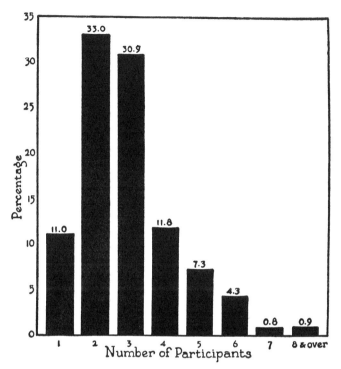

Fig. 12.—Percentage Distribution of Stealing Offenders Brought to Court by Numbers of Participants

case of the total 5,480 offenders, the groups which have the highest frequency are those involving two and three participants. The group involving two participants constitutes 33 per cent, and the group involving three participants, 30.9 per cent of the total number of stealing offenders. The frequency of groups involving either two or three participants is three times greater than the frequency for lone offenders. It is important to observe that the percentage of lone offenders is less than the percentage in the cases which involve as many as four participants.

As stated previously only offenders brought to court were taken into consideration in making the foregoing tabulations. A study of the records revealed that the 5,480 offenders had 3,004 alleged accomplices who for various reasons were not brought to court.[3] These two groups combined yielded a total of 8,484 alleged offenders of which 11.8 per cent were lone offenders, while 88.2 per cent were involved with companions (see fig. 13).

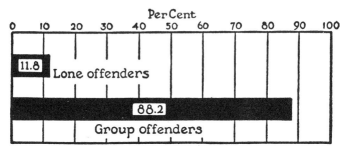

Fig. 13.—PERCENTAGE OF LONE AND GROUP OFFENDERS AMONG OFFENDERS KNOWN TO THE JUVENILE COURT

Here again the proportion of group offenders becomes even greater when the tabulation is restricted to those charged only with stealing offenses. In the total group of 8,484 alleged offenders, 7,393 were involved in some form of stealing. As many as 93.1 per cent of these stealing offenders were implicated with companions, as contrasted with the surprisingly low percentage of 6.9 for lone offenders (see fig. 14).

It should be borne in mind that these statistical tabulations have been restricted to offenders known to the juvenile court authorities. It is not assumed therefore that the relative frequency of lone and group offenders in the general delinquent population is identical with the percentages presented in this study. Obviously, not all of the boys engaged in delinquent activities are known to the court. Cases are not infrequent in which only one member of a group involved in an offense is apprehended and arraigned in court. In many of these cases the boy's loyalty to his group is so strong that he refuses to disclose the identity of his companions. It

[3] This group of alleged accomplices not brought to court was comprised chiefly of the following: (1) Persons alleged to have been involved but not apprehended; (2) persons apprehended but not brought to court on delinquency petitions because they were either above or below the juvenile court age limits for delinquents; and (3) boys who at the time of arrest were on parole or had escaped from correctional institutions and were returned to the institution without further court action.

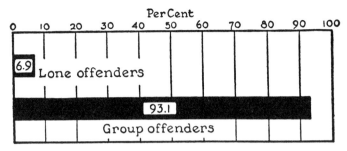

FIG. 14.—PERCENTAGE OF LONE AND GROUP OFFENDERS AMONG
STEALING OFFENDERS KNOWN TO THE JUVENILE COURT

seems probable, therefore, that the proportion of the offenders considered in this study who actually committed their delinquencies alone is less than the foregoing percentages indicate.

In many cases in which the delinquent boy actually commits his offense alone, the influence of companions is apparent. This point is clearly illustrated in the case of boys brought to court charged with stealing from members of their own family. In many such cases the theft, although the act of a single boy, clearly reflects the influence of companions. Frequently such thefts are planned by other boys and carried out at their instigation.

The findings of this study indicate quite conclusively that most juvenile offenses, at least those offenses charged against delinquents appearing in the juvenile court in Chicago, are committed by groups of boys; few by individuals singly. It is obvious that not all such group delinquencies are committed by well-organized gangs. While many of the delinquents may be members of such gangs, they usually commit their offenses in the company of only one or two other boys.

II

Excerpts from a limited number of case histories of delinquent boys [will] illustrate in a more vivid manner the activities and traditions of delinquent groups, and . . . draw attention to certain possible relationships between such groups and the origin and development of delinquent attitudes and behavior among boys.

. . . Cases of juvenile delinquency are largely concentrated in the deteriorated and disorganized areas adjacent to the central business district and the large industrial developments, and . . . in these areas various forms of delinquency and crime have persisted over a long period of time and have tended to become a part of the neighborhood tradition. To a very great extent these traditions of delinquency are preserved and transmitted through the medium of social contact within the unsupervised play group and the more highly organized delinquent and criminal gangs. In the deteriorated areas, where there is little organized effort among the citizens for combating lawlessness, these groups persist and tend to perpetuate delinquent and criminal forms of behavior. It is clear from the study of case histories that very frequently the boy's contact with the play group or gang marks the beginning of his career in delinquency. These groups, with their fund of delinquent tradition and knowledge, often become the chief source from which the boy gains familiarity with delinquent practices and acquires the techniques that are essential in delinquency. Many forms of delinquency require special skill and knowledge which are usually acquired through contacts with older and more experienced delinquent companions. Sometimes a group will specialize in a particular kind of delinquency and employ specialized techniques. In some of these cases it has been possible to trace the transmission of these techniques from one boy to another, from one group to another, and often from one neighborhood to another.

TRANSMISSION OF DELINQUENT TRADITION   The transmission of delinquent tradition through the companionship group is clearly illustrated in the case of Sidney. . . . His own description of his first delinquent experiences and his initial contacts with the delinquent group is given in the following excerpt from his life history. . . . Shoplifting was an established tradition among his companions prior to his first contact with them.

Case 1. It was at about this period that I began to go to school and I liked it. I had often asked my mother when I could start to go. When I finally went I was tickled to death.

Shortly after this I became acquainted with a boy named Joseph

Kratz, who lived a few doors from where I lived. Joseph was about four years older than I was and knew a lot. He knew so much about life and I liked him, so I made him my idol. At first he would not allow me to go places with him because I was so much younger than he was. But finally he allowed me to accompany him after school and we became fast friends. He proved to be very fast indeed; for one day while we were passing a fruit store he picked up an apple while no one was looking and continued to walk past the store with the apple in his hand. He performed for me in like manner quite a few times and nothing would do but that he must teach me to do the same thing. That was the first time I ever stole anything.

This fruit store had baskets, barrels, and boxes containing fruit and vegetables setting out in front of it, as the weather was still quite warm. He, that is Joseph, started to walk past the fruit store and as he came past the fruit store and as he came to a box of fruit he took some fruit and walked on. He motioned me to do the same thing.

I would walk behind him and as soon as he would pick up a piece of fruit I was supposed to do likewise. It took lots of practice and he had to set many examples before I could at last gain enough courage to follow suit.

Never a thought occurred to me as to whether it was right or wrong, it was merely an interesting game. The apple or orange didn't make as much difference as the getting of them. It was the taking them that I enjoyed.

On subsequent afternoons we made it our habit to pass this fruit store many times and steal various things. I found as much fun and enjoyment in grabbing a potato or an onion as to grab anything else. The proprietor soon discovered what was going on and in his endeavor to curtail further depredations on his stock began to keep a sharp lookout for our approach and to watch us closely as we passed. This only made the game more interesting and it began to require real skill to get away with anything. Often after this he would chase us for a block or two in order to teach us a lesson but he never did. This is when it started to get real good and you couldn't keep us away after that. The chases added spice to our little game.

Having heard of the Loop, with its many department stores full of toys, I craved to go there and to see what it was like. Joseph promised to take me there often but never did for a long time. Then one day he did. It was all arranged. I was to bum from school and go with him. On the morning we were to go he took me to a pool room that was not yet open, and merely made the fact known that we were to enter it by means of a hole in one corner of the plate-glass window.

The store faced a main thoroughfare and it was decidedly risky. It seemed a very interesting contemplation and held out possibilities of becoming even more interesting. Joseph wanted me to crawl in first but I lacked the courage. So he had to crawl in first himself. After he was inside he had to do a lot of coaxing and motioning in order to get me to follow him. I finally crawled through and we made for the rear, he leading. He went straight for the cash register and proceeded to rifle it. I had much rather have explored the cigar case. I got to my toes several times in an effort to peer into the cash drawer but Joseph cautioned me down with, "Sh! wait'll I get through." Finally he allowed me to help myself from the cash drawer. I couldn't raise myself high enough to see the whole cash drawer but I saw enough to let me know that they were all empty except one and that contained nickels and a few dimes. To my great chagrin he started to leave and we weren't going to explore the cigar counter. It looked like it contained many interesting things. We made hastily for the rear door and Joseph cautiously removed the bar and silently opened the door in order to peer out into the rear hallway. No one was there so we stole through to the side passage and thence to the street. With my hands in both pockets I commenced jingling the coins and made lots of noise walking down the street. I was reproved for this by Joseph for I was attracting people's attention toward us.

Finally I had my first visit to the department stores in the Loop. Joseph and two other boys had been shoplifting things in the Loop and making lots of money. They talked a lot about it, but had never asked me to accompany them. This day when they asked me to go to the Loop I was happy and knew what we were going to do. They took me through most of the big department stores and the 5 and 10 cent stores. I was greatly impressed by the sight I saw—the crowds and big stores. My chums stole from the counters but it was new to me, so I didn't try. There followed many more visits to the Loop and finally I began to steal little trinkets from the counters under my escort's tutoring. He knew the house detectives and spotted them for me and showed me how to slip things into my hat or put my hat on the thing I wanted to steal and then take it with my hat. We operated in different stores so the detectives would not spot us or get acquainted with us, so to speak. Within a few weeks I became an expert shoplifter. I lost interest in the companions of former days. I liked the new game of stealing I had learned, and it really was a game, and I played it with much zest and relish. I wanted to learn more about this new game and to indulge in it wholeheartedly, and I did this to the exclusion of all else. I forgot about school almost entirely. Compared to stealing and playing in the Loop, school life was monotonous and uninteresting.

Every morning the bunch would come past my home about school time. We left home at this time to make our parents think we were going to school. It was easy for me, for my mother was working and didn't know much about me. We would sneak a ride on the elevated railway, climbing up the structure to the station, to the Loop. After getting down town, we would make the round of the big stores. If we couldn't steal enough candy and canned goods for lunch, we would go without lunch. I did not know of anything else that interested me enough to go without a meal, but "making the big stores" did. I do not know whether a good thrashing would have cured me or not, as I never received one for stealing; just the ones my father gave me when he was mad. But anyway the shoplifting experiences were alluring, exciting, and thrilling. But underneath I kind of knew that I was sort of a social outcast when I stole. But yet I was in the grip of the bunch and led on by the enticing pleasure which we had together. There was no way out. The feeling of guilt which I had could not overbalance the strong appeal of my chums and shoplifting. At first I did not steal for gain nor out of necessity for food. I stole because it was the most fascinating thing I could do. It was a way to pass the time away, for I think I had a keener adventurous spirit than the other boys of my age, sort of more mentally alert. I didn't want to play tame games nor be confined in a schoolroom. I wanted something more exciting. I liked the dare-devil spirit. I would walk down between the third rails on the elevated lines in the same daring spirit that I stole. It gave me a thrill and thrilled my chums in turn. We were all alike, daring and glad to take a chance.

I became an expert shoplifter in time. I always followed Joseph. He would be walking in a store, me following, and take a ring or two from a counter or a bottle of perfume or a large carton of gum, stuff it into our belts under our coats, and leave the store. We would then sell the things to a fence. We could find fences who bought our goods; and then go to a show, buy something to eat, and there you are. I got so I could not only spot a house detective a mile away, but I could almost smell him. You can tell them by the way they act. If we did get caught —and we did several times—a few tears and a promise never to do it again would be enough to make him turn us loose, and sometimes he would just lead us to the door and tell us to stay out of there. Being little and very small for my age, it was easy to win the sympathy of the detective when we were caught. So on I went; you know when you get by with it once it makes it a little easier to get by with it the next time. I became cocky and self-confident and had a real pride in my ability to steal.

The practice of "jack-rolling"—picking the pockets of intoxicated men—is a form of stealing which frequently involves considerable specialized skill and technique. Various artifices are used to lure the victim to a secluded alley or vacant building where he is attacked and robbed. This form of stealing is particularly prevalent in the rooming-house section of the city, where the population is composed predominantly of adult unmarried males.[4] "Jack-rolling" and many of the special techniques associated with it are illustrated in the following case. This boy's experiences in delinquency prior to his contact with a group of experienced "jack-rollers" in the West Madison Street district at the age of 15 had consisted entirely of stealing from freight cars and vegetable markets and shoplifting. As indicated in his own story, his knowledge of "jack-rolling" was acquired through his contacts in the rooming-house district of West Madison Street.

Case 2. Going back to Madison Street, I found that my old job was taken, so I began to hang out at a pool room with a bunch of crooks. These crooks were young boys like myself, fifteen and sixteen years old, but they were more wise to the world and tougher. There were four of us who hung around together. The other three had been in St. Charles School for Boys while I was there, and that strengthened our faith in each other. I was looked up to as the hero of the quartet because I had done fifty-six months in St. Charles, more than all the others put together. They naturally thought I was one who had a vast experience and was regarded as one might regard the big social hit of society.

These lads had been "jack-rolling" bums on West Madison Street and burglarizing homes on the north side of the city. Knowing of my

[4]   Anderson, Nels, *The Hobo*, University of Chicago Press, 1923, pp. 51, 52.

long record, they asked me to join them, so I fell in with them. We formed "The United Quartet Corporation" and started to "strong arm" "live ones" (drunks with money), and to burglarize homes.

My fellow workers were fast guys and good pals. We were like brothers and would stick by each other through thick and thin. We cheered each other in our troubles and loaned each other dough. A mutual understanding developed, and nothing could break our confidence in each other. "Patty" was a short, sawed-off Irish lad—big, strong, and heavy. He had served two terms in St. Charles. "Maloney" was another Irish lad, big and strong, with a sunny disposition and a happy outlook on life. He had done one term in St. Charles and had already been in the county jail. Tony was an Italian lad, fine looking and daring. He had been arrested several times, served one term in St. Charles, and was now away from home because of a hard-boiled step-father. We might have been young, but we sure did pull off our game in a slick way.

So we plied our trade with a howling success for two months. Sometimes we made as much as two hundred dollars in a single day. But I had a weakness for gambling, so I was always broke. West Madison Street and vicinity was a rather dark section of the city, so it was easy to strong arm the "scofflaws." There were a lot of homosexuals and we played our game on them. We would let them approach one of us, usually me, because I was so little and they like little fellows, and then I'd follow him to his room or to a vacant house to do the act. My pals would follow us to our destination, and then we'd rob him. We made that part of our regular business. Two or three times a week we would pull off a burglary on the north side or on the south side.

It was springtime and we would go out to Grant Park during the day and lounge around and plan our burglaries. We always planned very carefully, and each pal had to do a certain thing. It was our absolute rule that if any pal did shrink from his part in the deal he would be branded and put out of "The United Quartet Corporation." We had a common fund for overhead expenses. If a pal had to take a bum to dinner so he could find out if he was "ripe" (had dough) or if a pal had to rent a room to take a bum into, supposedly for homosexual purposes but really to rob him, the expenses came out of the funds.

One day we were strolling along West Madison Street "taking in the sights," or, in other words, looking for "live ones." At the corner of Madison and Desplaines we saw a drunk who was talking volubly about how rich he was and that the suitcase he had in his hand was full of money. We were too wise to believe that, but we thought he might have a little money, so we would try. We tried to lure him into an alley to rob him, but he was sagacious even if he was drunk. He wanted to take me up to a room for an immoral purpose, but we decided that was too dangerous, so we let him go his way and then shadowed him.

He went on his aimless way for a long time, and we followed him, wherever he went. He finally went into a hotel and registered for a room. I saw his room number and then registered for a room on the same floor. Then we went up and worked our plans. It was not safe for all of us to go to his room, for that would arouse suspicion. One man could do the job and the others would stand by because they might be needed. But who would do the job? We always decided such things by a deck of cards. The cards were dealt, we drew, and it fell to my lot to do the deed. I was a little nervous inwardly, but did not dare to show it outwardly. A coward was not tolerated in our racket. Woe betide the one who shows it outwardly.

Putting on a bold front, I stepped into the hall and surveyed the field. Then I went to the drunk's door, my spinal nerves cold as ice. I tried the door and it was open, and that saved me a lot of work and nerve. The occupant was snoring, dead drunk, so the way was clear. I had a "sop" (blackjack) with me to take care of him if he woke up. I rifled the room, picked his pockets, and took the suit case in our room. With great impatience we ripped it open, only to stare at a bachelor's wardrobe. That was quite a blow to our expectations; but we dragged everything out, and at the bottom our labor was rewarded by finding a twenty-dollar bill. With the thirteen dollars I had found on his person and the twenty-dollar bill, we had thirty-three dollars— eight dollars and twenty-five cents apiece. We debated what to do. Since the job would be found out and suspicion would be directed toward us, it was decided to separate for a day or two, then we would not be caught in a bunch. We divvied up the clothes. I got a pair of pants and some other small articles. Then we separated.[5]

. . . The subject of case 4 lived during his infancy, childhood, and adolescence in one of the rooming-house districts which is notorious for its vice and extremely high rate of adult offenders.

[5]   From *The Jack-roller*, *A Delinquent Boy's Own Story*, by Clifford R. Shaw, The University of Chicago Press, pp. 96–98.

His career in delinquency began when he was twelve years of age and his record shows the following sequence of types of delinquent experiences: Petty stealing in the neighborhood, shoplifting, jack-rolling, picking pockets, and hold up with a gun. All of his offenses were committed in the company of other delinquents, most of whom were older than he. The case is presented because it shows quite clearly the manner in which the techniques involved in such a highly specialized form of delinquency as picking pockets are acquired through companionship groups.

Case 4. I started to go out of the house to play when I was six or seven years old and became a member of a group of about eight or ten kids of my own age, whose families lived on the block.

On Saturdays there was always a few kids that used to go up and down alleys and pick up bottles and rags and junk and take it over to the junk shop and sell it. At that time there was a certain kind of whisky bottle you could sell to saloons for a cent apiece. One time we got into an empty house and cut the lead pipe, pulled it out, and took it over to the junk man, who bought it. He also told us he would buy copper if we knew where there was any copper. . . .

Then there were some older fellows going to high school at the time. They were in first-year high at Wendell Phillips. I got in playing with these kids and started going down town and shoplifting.

Ed, "The Sheenie," O'Conner, and I decided to go down town, just because it was a place where we hadn't been taken to much, and we were like anybody else, curious to see those things. We bummed rides from cars on the boulevard and so got down town. Ed and Jack (The Sheenie) were both going to high school and had lunch money of fifteen or twenty cents. We took in nickelodeons and stole jackknives from five and ten cent stores and used to ride the moving stairways. We could always reach over and "hail a cake or piece of candy." Always stole enough food to satisfy our hunger. That was unknown to my people.

The first big thing I ever stole, I wanted a pair of hockey skates on shoes—Johnson racers, and I had been promised them for Xmas. We had an early winter that year and everybody was skating before Xmas, so I bummed from school one afternoon. I had saved car-fare from errands I had run. I and my friends went to the store in the sporting goods department. There I picked up a pair of Johnson racers that were in a box and I put my cap in my pocket, the box under my arm, and got in the elevator and went home. I hid my skates in the basement.

We did the same with them fancy gym shoes. Me and the Sheenie bummed from school one day and went downtown, and we were both basket-ball players, and some of the other fellows had a pair of good gym shoes that cost $4 or $5; so Jack and myself decided to get ourselves some. So we went in one of the department stores and each got ourselves a pair. Later, we went down and got several more pairs which we sold. . . .

I was sixteen when my mother died. I had graduated from school that summer. She died from an appendix operation. The fact of her death seemed to daze me for quite a while. I was moody, and seemed to be by myself more than I went around with the fellows, as one can understand.

And a month after her death, why, my father, rather than have a housekeeper, decided that he would send us to relatives, and an aunt took my sister, another aunt my brother, and an uncle wanted to take me. But I didn't seem to want to go. I didn't like to go to his house altho he had considerable more means than we did. He wanted me to go to high school. I figured I had about all the schooling I cared for.

Rather than living with my uncle, I got a room in a rooming house and started to hang out with the big guys. Two or three of us were on what they call "on the bum." When school started that fall, I had neither a job nor decided to go to school. The school authorities wired to our old address, enquiring why we were not at school. They were referred to my father by neighbors, who told them where my sister and brother was, but told them that he couldn't do nothing with me—that he hadn't seen me for a month altho he had looked high and low for me. . . .

I had been rooming with some people, and eating in restaurants, paying for my board and room every week with the proceeds of burglaries and jack-rolling. I had seen several of the older boys put what is known as "the arm" on a drunk, and later on when I happened to be walking down a street and I see a drunk, I always went to a pool room where they hung out, told them which way the drunk had gone and went with them not taking part in the actual robbery. I was always given all the way to $20 which I didn't know whether it was split or not. I didn't know just how much they got. Later I gamed up and took an actual part. . . .

Then we, these older fellows and I, started burglarizing stores. We could "close up" a store by one of us standing in the front, or across the street, and watch where the proprietor hid the bulk of the money. Then if he had a transom, one of us boost one into the transom and if we were successful in seeing where he put the money, he would get the money and climb out or go thru the back door. If not, we would enter thru skylights, saw bars to get in, and the three of us would search for the money. We did this for quite a while. It was always the same three of us who would go on a prowl. We would not pass up a drunk if we run acrost him in our looking for likeable stores. In the line of jack rolling I have got as much as $70; sometimes as low as $1.50 but as a whole I made fairly good money. During this time I was pinched a few times on suspicion of burglary and robbery, but they could never pin nothing on me. . . .

It was about that time that I had changed my place from where I lived to another, and there was two pickpockets rooming in this same place, which was a private family.

The people were very kind to me in several ways and had no idea, how I made my living, but often wondered. To satisfy them I told them I was working on a vegetable wagon.

When I first started living in the rooming house there I kept pretty much to myself. There were several other roomers that lived in this place. Outside of meeting them in the hall, and saying "good morning" that was as much as I ever had to do with them. I was living there about two months. I happened to be standing talking to some fellows on the corner, who were older than myself, and these two fellows come along and one of them stopped to buy a newspaper while the other came over to speak with the fellows I was talking to. I nodded to both of them. They called one of these fellows on the side and asked him who I was. They explained to him that they were living in the same place that I was, and I guess this fellow told them that I was jack-rolling and burglarizing stores, and would do anything for a dollar.

After they left, I asked this fellow who they called on the side, who they were and he told me that one of them was a well-known thief. At that time this thief had been in the business for sixteen years. The other man with him was a few years younger than the first, six or seven, I should say. Still about ten or eleven years my senior. Shortly after that I was coming up the stairs leading to the floor where I lived on, and one of them was coming in at the same time. He asked me into his room and asked me how business was. I complained of not making much money—we was having a siege of bad luck, and he asked me how would I like to work with them. Up until that time I had had several pickpockets pointed out to me, but I had never come in close contact with them.

I think I told him anything would be better than what I was doing at the time; so they made a "meet" to go out the next morning. I was of very little help to them the first few weeks. Later on I caught on to the game. It seemed to hold sort of a fascination for me. I can remember this one pickpocket had been married for a number of years, his wife also living there, and after being with them for some time he asked me how I would like to be able to "lift a poke" as good as he could. Him being the first one I had actually worked with, I was awed at his ability to pick a man's pocket without a person feeling it. I must say, in reference to this man, that he was one of the best in the "racket."

He first started to schooling me in a room in which he lived in how to pick a pocket. His name was Harry Pearson. I was with him for several months as his "duke man." During the course of these months he was giving me daily lessons. A pickpocket "mob" consists of three or four men. Generally three, sometimes five (what they call a "basket-ball team"). One is called "the stall." He is the man who is in front, slows up the victim's progress, and keeps him from turning. Then, "the wire" is the man who actually reaches in and picks the pockets. The "duke man" comes up on his left hand and covers the "wire's" hand while he is at work and covers him from the people standing back and the people on the side. A "duke man" always keeps his right hand at his side; so when the "wire" comes away from under "the mark's" coat with his purse or roll of money, he always hands it to the "duke man." The "duke man" puts it in his "left coat tail" (meaning his left coat pocket). The reason that the "duke man" keeps his right hand at his side in case of a "rumble" the wire pulls his hand away and there is always two hands there and the victim is undecided which one it was.

The reason that he always goes to his coat "tail" with the purse, in case the victim "blows" (meaning, feels his loss) and turns around and grabs the duke man, the stall and the wire know just what pocket to go to, take the purse out, and throw it on the floor.

The "sucker" is always satisfied when he sees his money. When I was with Harry P., I was his "duke man."

I worked with him for several months, and up until that time I had never stole a pocketbook myself, nor had ever tried. Still he was schooling me—different angles, how pocketbooks and rolls of money laid in people's pockets. While I was still working with him, he never worked on Saturdays. Saturdays seemed a day that the police were more active, and if they arrested you, you stayed till Monday.

On Saturday morning I decided to go downtown and do some shopping. I boarded an Indiana Street car at 31st, going north. While standing on the back platform the car got rather crowded. Some fellow was standing directly in front of me. I thought that this would be a good chance to try my ability as a pickpocket; so I started to work on him. I started working to get his pocketbook at 26th Street and finally got it at 18th. It was in the summer time, and how that man never felt me, I don't know to this day.

As soon as I had his pocketbook in my hand I got off the car, went in an alley, and opened it. There was $128.00 in it; so that I think the $128.00 is what really made a pickpocket out of me.

My intentions were when I started from home to go downtown to do some shopping, but after I stole that pocketbook, I boarded another street car and carried out my first intentions. After doing my shopping I decided to take in a show. While sitting in the show, I got to thinking of how I had picked that pocket; so leaving the show I went right out on State Street, and picked three more pockets that evening. The total amount that I got was less than $50.00.

Up till the time that I started picking pockets with Harry (Harry Pearson is one of the best-known pickpockets in Chicago, and has done several stretches for this crime. He had been in the business sixteen years when I hooked up with him), I hadn't given any thought as to when I would quit living the life that I was, or whether I'd continue. But after I found out that I could "take a poke," I decided that I would give that a whirl for awhile. Up to this time if anybody would have straightened me out, I believe that I would have done different, altho if I had my life to live over again I believe that I'd continue in the way I did.

I was about sixteen when I started picking pockets with Harry, and I had not been arrested as a suspect pickpocket, but I had once been arrested in between the time that I was stealing by myself in a "hot" car, and given thirty days in the Bridewell. Upon my release from the bridewell I kept right on picking pockets. I believe I was on that "racket" for three years before I had my first arrest as a pickpocket suspect. At that time Chicago was not policed on pickpocket suspects as well as it is now.

I worked State Street different times by myself and made barely a living. I didn't have the success that Harry had. Well, I worked at that for a while till I had confidence in myself, and thought I could support a troupe. By having a troupe makes it so much easier to pick a pocket. I didn't have confidence in myself that I could steal good enough to support a troupe, but after working alone for a while I decided to give it a whirl.

I asked two pickpockets who weren't working at the time and who were not very well known, to take a trip to Detroit with me. They were ascared to go out of town, not knowing nothing of my ability, and suggested that we work around Chicago for a while. After working with them a short time, we left town. I found the work very much easier having some assistance. There is different "offices" used by different sets of pickpockets.

The old-fashioned set seems to be used by the old-fashioned pickpockets, is of letting one another know when they have retrieved a man's valuables. When a "mark" is "clipped," you make a peculiar sound by sucking in the breath thru the lips. That signals to the "stall" that you have relieved "John" of his wallet, and you step right over to the next "mark."

Then, if the victim hasn't a pocketbook in his pants pocket or a roll of money, whenever the occasion may be, if it is on a train or at a convention, and the man looks prosperous enough, you would know that he had money some place. So it is then that they try what is known as an "insider," meaning that the man has his wallet in his inside coat pocket. This work, to take a poke from the inside pocket is altogether different. The "wire" has to be facing the victim. It is known to be a fact by pickpockets that if the victim will stand for what is known as a "throw," he can be beat. By a "throw" I mean putting a newspaper under the man's chin or by having a topcoat or short coat on your arm and holding that up under his chin. The "stall" is directly behind the "mark" in the position otherwise occupied by the "wire." The "duke" man is standing behind the "wire," bracing him with his body, if it is on a subway or a car or train, and a newspaper or coat shades his hand from working. He can unbotton three buttons on a "mark's" coat and reach in and take a man's pocketbook from inside his coat or even vest. The same thing goes for a stud or a diamond pin. I myself and several others that I have talked to find an "insider" as easy, if not easier, than a "prat poke" if the man will stand for a "throw." The average man, when you put a newspaper under his chin, he will brush it away, but anyone that will stand to have that paper laid under their chin can be beat, and most generally are.

Among pickpockets they always stay spread out, no matter where you may be. On a train, you stand by yourself, never "connecting." Working in the city, you never "connect," never stand talking to each other. While standing on a corner waiting for a street car to pull up one of the mob sees a "dick." Then we have what is known as a "works office." He reaches up and pulls with his right hand on the lapel of his coat—gets one of his companion's eyes, and then does this. That signifies that there is "heat." The other fellow passes that to the third, and so on, and when the car pulls up, you get on that "natural" —that is, you don't work. Once in amongst a crowd of people you do not steal one pocketbook or one roll of money, and then back out and wait for the next car. As soon as a man is beat, the "office" is given, and you step to the next. Sometimes they have as high as seven or eight or ten "stings" in one crowd.

After picking pockets for a period of years this young delinquent became associated with a group of adult criminals who were engaged in various forms of holdup with a gun.

I finally decided to quit picking pockets because it didn't pay enough. Besides I got in with a mob of stick-up guys who were making dough. I started working with this stick-up outfit who were preying upon gambling houses, union halls, and I learned their trade. I stayed at that for about three years.

Every gambling joint has "heavy men"—what are known as "floor men," and they are the "heat" in the joint. You have to be searched two or three times before you are allowed to enter the gambling house, and that way it is very hard to get up there with guns.

In order to stick up a gambling joint, the tip generally comes from a dealer or a hanger-on. Well, you then go up. Two of the mob, in which there are generally four or five, would go up and look the place over. The tipster would point out the "heavy men" who were unknown to us.

Now, in some of these places they only shake a man's person. They never bother with packages. So we got an idea if you took a suit box, put sawed-off shot guns in the suit box and pistols, one can could carry them in. But first a man would go up with a suit box with a suit in a laundry box and try it out a couple of times to see if it would work. And if they passed it up once or twice we would take a chance and go up. We never had a "rumble" before we got into a place by having the box examined.

Other places would check boxes and packages—they would take them off you. Lots of time if the place was prosperous enough we would "prowl" the joint after it closed up, and plant our stuff—guns, etc. Then come back the next afternoon and take the joint.

The main worry of this was you could never tell whether somebody had found the stuff. We always took the precaution first to examine all guns to see that they were loaded before giving the command that it was a stick-up.

As I said before, they was generally from one to three "heavy men," and they were already pointed out to us. If we were successful in getting a suit box in we would loiter around the place, always split out, and one man would go to the toilet and go in a booth and open the box, and we would all take turns of going in and getting our guns. The men who were going to use the sawed-off shot guns, of which there was always two, would be the last to go in.

Everybody would have their positions. The men would circle behind the "heavy men," so when the command was given they were always the first to go up because they didn't have no chance to reach for their guns.

One man would take the paying cages which consisted sometimes of two or three for race-horse bets. We would all spread out around the place, and when one man would give the order, that it was a stick-up, each one in the mob would echo the order singly. That was to let the people know that there was a number of us.

We would first relieve the "heavy men" of their guns. Most times you would find a gun or two in the pay window. Therefore, it was always a man with a shotgun that took care of them cages. After hoisting the place up we would chase everybody against the wall, facing the wall, with their hands up, chasing the cashier out of the cages. One man always had a sack or a brief case with which he went to the cages to gather the money. Everybody had a part in the drama, and it all went off like clockwork. It was a matter of routine.

Upon getting the "office" telling us that the cages were clean, all card tables, all boxes, all crap tables, we would then chase everybody from one side of the wall to the other and pick up all the money that was dropped. It was much easier that way than searching pockets. Sometimes we would look into their socks, just at random. We would not search individuals except those whose faces were familiar to us, and we knew the gamblers who would be apt to have rolls.

ACQUIRING THE DELINQUENT CODE   The foregoing cases illustrate the manner in which specific delinquent and criminal patterns of behavior may be transmitted through the intimate personal contacts within the play group and gang. These groups serve also as a medium through which the boys gain familiarity with the attitudes, standards, and code of the criminal group. As previously indicated, the ethical values of these groups often vary widely from those of the larger social order. In fact the standards of these groups may represent a complete reversal of the standards and norms of conventional society. Types of conduct which result in personal degradation and dishonor in a conventional group, serve to enhance and elevate the personal prestige and status of a member of the delinquent group. Thus, an appearance in the juvenile court or a period of incarceration in a correctional institution may be a source of pride to the young delinquent, since it identifies him more closely with his group.

The delinquent group, like all social groups, tends to develop its own standards of conduct by which it seeks to regulate and control the behavior of its members. It inflicts punishment upon those who violate its rules and rewards those who are loyal and conform. In the older delinquent and criminal groups there tends to be a definite hierarchy of social grouping, which ranges all the way from the petty thief to the gangster. Jack Black, who was a burglar for twenty-five years and published his autobiography under the title "You Can't Win," gives the following description of the code and social castes of the criminal group:

The upper world knows nothing about caste as compared with the underworld. Crookdom is the most provincial of small villages, the most rigid in its social gradations. Honors and opportunity are apportioned on the basis of code observance. There is no more caste in the heart of India than in an American penitentiary. A bank burglar assumes an air with a house burglar, a house burglar sneers at a pickpocket, a pickpocket calls a forger "a short story writer," and they all make common cause against the stool pigeon, whatever caste he comes from. He jeopardizes the life and liberty of his own, which is the great unpardonable crime in the underworld code. He is the rattlesnake of the underworld, and they kill him on the "safety-first" principle as swiftly and dispassionately as you would kill a copperhead. Respect for property in the underworld is as deep as it is in the upper-world. The fact that it is upper-world property which is involved makes no difference, for when property is transferred from the upper-world to the underworld it becomes sacred again.

The burglar who shoots his partner for holding out a lady's watch goes up in the social scale of the underworld. Like the clubman who perjures himself to save a lady's reputation, he has done the right thing in the sight of his fellows. Each is a better gentleman according to the code."[6]

This description by Black is amply confirmed by our detailed case-studies of delinquent careers. A few of the more common aspects of the code prevailing in delinquent groups, that are revealed in a comparative study of a large number of life histories of delinquents and young criminals are presented for illustrative purposes.

Since the young delinquent's most vital contacts outside the home are often restricted to play-groups and gangs whose standards and expectations may be greatly at variance with the standards of conventional society, it is not surprising that he has but little appreciation of the meaning of traditional norms and formal laws, and that he often regards the police and the school as influences inimical to his welfare. Efforts to suppress his delinquent tendencies by formal methods of education and discipline, especially when his delinquency is in conformity with the expectations of his group, often give rise to attitudes of rebellion and hostility.[7] He tends to assume these attitudes toward any agency—the school, the social settlement, the police, the court, the correctional institution—which seeks arbitrarily to impose the standards of society upon him and to prevent him from participating in the activities of his group.

[6] *Harpers Magazine*, CLX (February, 1930), No. 957, pp. 306–307.
[7] See E. H. Sutherland, *Crime and Conflict Process*, Proceedings of 58th Annual Congress of the American Prison Association, pp. 93–103.

Case 5. From the time I started to hang around with the older guys in the neighborhood. I learned to look at the police as my sworn enemies. All the guys in the bunch looked at them that way. The police were the only ones that interfered with whatever we wanted to do in the racket. The older guys knew all about the police, their ways, the third degree, and how to elude the police. I learned that the police always were to be shunned and avoided, at least those ones whose fingers weren't sticky for a little graft money. . . .

The first thing that I learned was never to trust any affairs of the racket to the police. Never talk to the police about your pals when you fall into the hands of the law. The best thing that guy could have said about you was "he won't talk," meaning that you wouldn't squawk on your pals when you got caught. I learned that a "rat" or "stool pigeon" was to be hated along with the police. . . .

If a criminal goes out to do a job, he won't be interfered with. If the police get in his way, he'll be shot. So the police and the criminal are on two sides of the fence. If one doesn't get the other, the other will get him. The criminal is to be caught and the police are to be avoided, escaped from, or bought off. Its natural for enmity to grow up between them. I knew from the time I was young not to trust the police, but to keep out of his clutches. That's the way all the guys in the bunch felt. . . .

Like conventional social groups, the delinquent and criminal group demands conformity to its code and ideals on the part of its members. Probably the most serious violation of the code of the delinquent group is for a member to divulge to the police the identity of his companions in delinquency. The contemptuous attitude toward the traitor is indicated in such opprobrious epithets as the "rat," the "stool pigeon" and the "squawker."

Case 7. The way I feel about it was that not only we but all the prisoners were not getting a square deal, except the "rats," who would sell their souls for a piece of tough horse meat.

Anybody who rats on a prisoner in prison is the lowest, most contemptible sneak on two feet. Hence they are called "rats." Of course, an allowance is given in some cases, but to make it your business to inform the "screw" (guard) about everything that is going on under the surface is not fair to prisoners. Because I feel that life is all a game and hard enough for some, like myself. Also, the prisoner has a slim chance against the rest of the world, and it seems unfair for a rat to spoil even that little chance. It only makes life harder for the prisoner, and he will have to remain in prison that much longer.

I believe that any game should be played according to the rules of the game. Violators of rules should be punished. Crime is a game, and therefore as a rat violates the rules or code by informing the "dicks" and the "screws" he should be punished. I think everyone will agree with me in my feelings about these low rats. All prisoners who are worthy of the name will agree with me.

In the laundry there are rats, and in every department of the prison. They are like vultures preying upon rotten things—noiseless, seeking information about the prisoners' conduct, and sometimes framing a trumped-up charge against a prisoner because he has a grievance against him or wants to win a favor from the guard. A prisoner could serve five years and be a rat all that time, and nobody but him and the guard would know it. But woe betide said rat if he is exposed. He is branded and shunned by the good prisoners and made miserable whenever they can make him miserable. When he is released there is always some one out to get him. In a few words, anyone who rats commits the unpardonable sin. The worst sin of the criminal world, and often the penalty is death. These rats are composed of dope fiends, petty thieves, and other similar low characters. A man with some manhood in him wouldn't stoop that low. The dirty, lousy, filthy vultures would knife a man when his back was turned. They are only born to be hanged. My feelings are always with the prisoners.[8]

Case 8. I was never given any lessons by any of the guys about keeping my mouth shut when arrested, but I knew how the fellows looked down on those that did talk when arrested. They considered them rats and shunned them. So when I was in the police station I figured, "the big guy don't squawk," and I didn't want to be looked down on by them, and so I would not squawk either.

Case 9. There are plenty of "rats" and "stool pigeons" in this reform school and every prison in the world. The prison world would run thousands of times better without those lousy "rats" and sure would decrease trouble. They sure would do a good deed if they got rid of those "rats" that are existing. No good criminal has any use for a "rat" and his presence. Most of them get "bumped off" or "taken for a ride" by the gang when they are caught up with. What they get in punishment from their gang they deserve and more yet. . . .

[8]   *The Jack-roller: A Delinquent Boy's Own Story* (The University of Chicago Press, 1930), pp. 111–113.

Case 12. After a man has violated the code he is almost always considered untrustworthy by those who know of his violation. Even if it has occurred through ignorance and inexperience and he has led an exemplary life in crime for years afterwards, he is always under suspicion, and is trusted only by personal friends who feel that he has lived down his indiscretion.

In cases where crimes have been committed by two or more persons, and one, with strong evidence against him, is arrested, he adheres to the code by refusing an offer of light punishment in exchange for information against his confederates.

It is the prevailing opinion that where a man makes a confession implicating only himself, he is not a violator of the code. . . .

It is a matter of great significance that there is a general tendency among older delinquents and criminals to look with disdain and contempt upon the person who engages in any form of petty stealing. Often he is distrusted and regarded in much the same manner as the "rat" or "stool pigeon." It is possible that the stigma attached to petty stealing in the delinquent group is one of the factors involved in the young delinquent's desire to abandon such forms of petty delinquency as stealing junk, vegetables, breaking into freight cars, stealing pennies from news stands, and to become identified with older groups engaged in larceny of automobiles, and robbery with a gun, both of which are accredited "rackets" among the older delinquents.

Case 15. In my racket, which was the auto racket, we wouldn't have a sneak thief of any kind. It takes guts to steal cars and we wouldn't trust our lives with a low piker like a petty thief. The way we looked at it was that if a fellow didn't have enough guts and ambition to do anything but jack-roll a poor old drunk man or snatch an old lady's purse was a coward and no good in a hot racket. A sneak thief is looked down on by all real criminals and is not trusted. Stealing junk and vegetables is all right for a kid, but it's not a man's job. . . .

Case 16. The prisoner in charge of the mangle that I worked on was Billy, a hardened criminal from Chicago. He was eight years my senior, and was in on a five to life sentence as a burglar and "stick-up" man. Billy took a great liking to me, mostly out of pity, and gave me instructions on how to get on in Pontiac, and how to get by with the police outside. He indelibly impressed two things upon my mind. First, never to trust anybody with your affairs in crime. You never know when a partner will rat you if he gets into a close pinch and finds it an advantage to "sell his soul" to the police. Billy would ask me questions about my rap and my past experiences, but he would not talk much about himself. He was old and experienced, and was different from most of the glib-tongued young crooks that I had known in St. Charles.

Secondly, Billy chided me for petty stealing. His idea was to "do a big job or none at all." Of course, he considered that I was just a kid and wasn't old enough to "do a job" like him. He figured that the dangers and penalty were about the same whether you did a little job or a big one, so you just as well chose the best. Besides, he said that there was some satisfaction in doing a real man's job, and that it was easier to pay the penalty for a big haul. That sounded reasonable to me, so I thought if I ever pulled another job it would be a big one or none. . . .

The antithesis of the petty thief is the "big shot," the person who has gained prestige and power in the delinquent group. Such persons are well known in the neighborhood and are often emulated by the younger members of the delinquent groups.

Case 20. How would you feel toward the King of England or the President of the U.S.A.? Well, the young crook feels the same toward the "big shot." The "big shot" is the ideal—the ultimate hope of every forward-looking criminal. So he is held in awe and respect.

Case 21. The big shot is respected by the criminals and honored for his power and brains to hold down a big job and have a number of gangsters under him and obeying his commands and orders. In every group of young crooks they mention things about the power of big-timers like Al Capone and many others of the well-known big-shot gangsters from Chicago or some other town or city. Some of the young fellows expect to work for some of these fellows and go into the racket on a big scale. I've never had anything to do concerning a big-shot myself, but I've heard plenty about them from fellows who know them and can see by their talk about the big-shots that they respect them.

Case 22. Every boy has some ideal he looks up to and admires. His ideal may be Babe Ruth, Jack Dempsey, Al Capone, or some other crook. His ideal is what he wants to be like when he grows up and becomes a man. When I was twelve years old we moved into a neigh-

borhood where there lived a mob of gangsters and big crooks. They
were all swell dressers and had big cars and carried "gats." Us kids
saw these swell guys and mingled with them in the cigar store on the
corner. Jack Gurmey was the one in the mob that I had a fancy to. He
use to take my sis out and that way I saw him often. He was in the
stick-up racket before he was in the beer racket and was a swell dresser
and had lots of dough. He was a nervey guy and went in for big stuff.
He was a mysterious fellow and would disappear sometimes for several days but always came back. He was looked up to as the leader of
his mob and anybody would be glad to be in his place.

He never talked to me about crime, but I secretly looked up to him
for his daring and courage. He was what a fellow would call a big hit
to me. I liked to be near him and felt stuck up over the other guys because he came to my home to see sis.

The foregoing cases have been presented to illustrate some of
the more common aspects of the social activities and standards of
delinquent groups. All of the cases presented are excerpts from the
life histories of delinquents whose cases we have studied in considerable detail over a period of several months. Thus it has been
possible in each instance to evaluate the boy's own statement in
the light of the total case history, which includes the usual clinical
findings, data from official records and from interviews with friends
and relatives of the subject. Only those cases in which the boy's
attitudes and the events which he describes were consistent with
the total case history have been presented.

It is not possible from the foregoing data to determine the
extent to which membership in delinquent gangs produces delinquency. It is probable, however, that membership in such groups
is an important contributing factor in many cases, since it is found
that very often the boy's contact with the delinquent group marks
the beginning of his career in delinquency and that his initial delinquencies are often identical with the traditions and practices of
his group. On the other hand, it is known that some of these groups
are composed of boys who are, as separate individuals, definitely
inclined toward delinquency. It is clear from these materials that
many types of delinquency are of such a character as to necessitate
the participation of two or more persons in their execution.

In conclusion it should be stated that the activities and social values of play groups and gangs among boys obviously reflect the traditions and social life prevailing in the larger communities. It is possible that the delinquent group is, therefore, a product of a neighborhood situation and should be treated as an integral part of these more general social processes.

These materials suggest, also, the great need for developing methods of group treatment in the field of delinquency, since it appears that delinquent behavior is in many cases a form of group activity.

18

Paul L. Schroeder, M.D., and Ernest W. Burgess

THE DEPRESSION

AS A FAMILY CRISIS

THE GREATEST DEPRESSION in the history of the United States has had no adequate recording by students of society. The social sciences individually and collectively failed, at the appropriate time, to collect the available data necessary for any accurate and systematic analysis of the effects of the depression upon social institutions and upon human behavior. Such is the sum and substance of the findings of thirteen research monographs[1] on "The Social Aspects of the Depression" recently prepared and published under the auspices of the Social Science Research Council.

The present study is one of the few shining exceptions to the prevailing unilluminated void of our knowledge of the effects of the depression upon the family. One hundred families, known before 1929 to the Illinois Institute for Juvenile Research, were selected for special interviews in 1934–35 to discover, if possible, the pattern of their reaction to the impact of the depression. The methods of research, the findings, and the conclusions presented in this book are of interest, among other reasons, because they present the joint work of a sociologist, Ruth S. Cavan, and a psychiatric social worker, Katherine H. Ranck.

Reprinted from the Introduction to Ruth Shonle Cavan and Katherine Howland Ranck, *The Family and the Depression: A Study of One Hundred Chicago Families* (Chicago: University of Chicago Press, 1938), pp. vii–xiii.

[1]   See, particularly, Samuel A. Stouffer and Paul F. Lazarfeld, *Research Memorandum on the Family in the Depression* (New York: Social Science Research Council, 1937).

This combination of psychiatric and of sociological viewpoints in the study was a recognition that the effects of the depression upon the family and its members were undoubtedly both psychic and social. In fact, the original plan of the study called for a short psychiatric interview with husband and wife, a procedure found to be not practicable with the limited resources available for the study.

That the adjustment of families to a crisis is both psychic and social this study clearly shows. Evident in the cases is anxiety, excessive worry, nervous breakdown, and suicidal thoughts or attempts, as well as changes in standards of living, in family roles, and in familial and personal objectives.

Because the number of cases in this study is small, few final definitive conclusions are reached. Nevertheless, several major points seem to stand out. Of these, three may be mentioned: (1) well-organized families met the depression with less catastrophic consequences than families that were already disorganized; (2) families and their members tended to react to the depression in much the same way as they had to previously encountered crises; and (3) the period of unadjustment and disorganization characterized by emotional strain which typically was manifest in the early stages of the depression generally was succeeded by a period of adjustment or maladjustment. Seemingly significant is the finding that the types of adjustment (including maladjustment) to the depression attempted by the families were much the same with both the well-organized and disorganized families but that the final outcome in terms of organization or disorganization of family life was different. Well-organized families, even when greatly affected by the depression, continued organized; unorganized or disorganized families became further disorganized. Adjustment seems to have been as much or more an attribute of family organization as of the degree of external pressure exerted by the depression.

In short, the adjustment of the family to the depression turned out apparently to be a function of the adjustment of the members of the family to each other. This conclusion, independently made, corroborates the generalization already reached by Robert C. Angell in his penetrating study of fifty families published under the title, *The Family Encounters the Depression,* namely, that the vulnerability of the family to the depression appeared to vary inversely with its integration and adaptability.

The concepts of families as organized or disorganized, integrated or unintegrated, and adaptable or unadaptable are more or less intuitively arrived at by a consideration of a number of characteristics of family life. They are at best only an attempt to denominate a resultant of factors interacting in the process of family life. None of these terms can explain why one family is organized or integrated and another family is disorganized or unintegrated.

Further progress, then, in the study of the effect of the depression upon the family is largely dependent upon the analysis of the structure of family relationships. Such a systematic analysis has not yet been attempted, but this study unquestionably indicates that it can only be satisfactorily made, if at all, by the joint effort of the psychiatrist and the sociologist.

In a forthcoming publication[2] the different aspects of the personality significant for marital adjustment have been differentiated as (*a*) interdependence of psychogenetic traits; (*b*) similarity of cultural backgrounds; (*c*) common interests, ideals, and ideas; (*d*) congruence of economic expectations and roles; and (*e*) harmony of response patterns. In any given family its unity, integration, and adaptability will be a resultant of the interaction of the husband and wife and of parents and children in these different aspects of their personalities. Temperamental traits, and especially their configuration, as fixed in the earliest years of childhood into "invariable reactive systems," have been defined and analyzed by psychiatrists as resultants of emotional aspects of family interaction. This precultural individual which Edward Sapir has named the "psychiatric personality" has been, and will doubtless continue to be, the central subject of attention of the research of the psychiatrist. The study of family interaction in terms of the social aspects of the person as the impress upon him of his cultural backgrounds, his interests, ideals, and ideas, and his economic expectation and status constitutes the field in which sociologists and cultural anthropologists

[2]   E. W. Burgess and Leonard S. Cottrell, Jr., *Predicting Adjustment in Marriage* (New York: Prentice-Hall, 1938).

have specialized. How psychological motivations and cultural conditions co-operate in integrating persons into the family structure
has become an imperative problem for further study, a problem
requiring the research techniques of psychiatrists and sociologists.

Angell's study indicates that flexibility and adaptability are
significant for the nature of the way in which a family adjusts to a
crisis like the depression. But neither his study nor this study provides a theoretical frame of reference for the analysis of the interplay of the psychogenetic and the cultural factors in the process of
integration. It is apparent that the rigidity or the flexibility of the
family may be psychological or cultural, or a combination of both.
At any rate, the elements of integration and of adaptability need to
be specifically defined and segregated.

In modern urban society the rigidity of the family structure has
lost the high value that it possessed in an earlier, predominantly
rural civilization. Even today the flexibility of family organization
is more desirable in the mobile and unstable situation of the city
than under the relatively more stable conditions of the agricultural
community. The greater instability and insecurity of urban life
makes all the more necessary research upon the factors making
both for the integration and the adaptability of the members of the
family in their interrelated functions and roles.

At present it is not feasible, perhaps, to conduct further significant research of the effect of the recent depression upon the
family unless to restudy groups of families already studied to ascertain their later reaction to the experiences of the depression. But
two closely related projects are feasible. It is always possible to
study the effect of sudden and severe economic reverses upon individual families even if these occur outside of depression periods.
Then, quite as significant would be studies in the effect of sudden
prosperity upon families and their members. The hypothesis could
be tested that under the impact of sudden prosperity, well-organized
families remain organized, and unorganized or disorganized families tend further to disintegrate.

Studies in the effect of economic conditions upon the family
comprise only one sector of family research. Such studies do show
the need for a fundamental analysis of the psychological and cul-

tural aspects of family organization. Research projects upon the interrelation of the family and the community, of the family in relation to leisure time, to education, to religion, and to child development, would undoubtedly show the same need of a more basic theoretical analysis of the mental and social elements in the integration of personalities within the family.

In a crisis the condition of strain placed upon an institution such as the family creates an unusually favorable situation to test the strength of its particular social structure and the relative value to its members of its various functions. This is especially the case at the time of a crisis such as a depression, where comparisons may be made with conditions in either the pre-depression or the post-depression periods or with conditions in both periods. Social scientists, it may be asserted, missed a unique opportunity during the past ten years for increasing our knowledge of the functioning of social institutions as affected by marked fluctuations of the business cycle.

The counterargument may be stated that the reason why sociologists and psychiatrists failed to make adequate studies of the effects of the depression upon the family lay in their lack of preparation for the task. They were not, and are not now, engaged in systematic and continuous research upon the family. They have neither the facilities nor the funds necessary. And this inadequacy, in turn, may be explained by the disposition of the public not to take the problems of the family seriously. Even intelligent persons consider their solution not as a subject matter for science and control but rather for common sense and trial and error.

In the field of other institutions, like government, industry, and education, systematic and continuous research has been carried on for decades. In the field of child behavior, institutes of child study and guidance are numerous; these, however, deal with the family only incidentally, although there is increasing recognition of the fact that many, if not most, behavior problems of children have their origin within the constellation of family relationships.

The findings of the present study show the value of the family as an institution for adjustment to a crisis. A series of further studies is desirable on the ways in which families of different types of organization meet other crises, social as well as economic. Studies commensurate with the problems facing the family in a period of social change and social disorganization need to be carried on within the perspective of all the relevant disciplines.

The problems of family life stubbornly refuse to be encompassed within the confines of any one discipline. They have their different, although at the same time related, aspects: biological, psychological, psychiatric, sociological, anthropological, historical, economic, home economic, educational, and legal. This complexity of the facets of the family is a great obstacle but at the same time a challenge to the planning of significant systematic research. Only the establishment of institutes of family research, bringing into one organization the different indispensable specialties, will provide the basic body of knowledge adequate for developing practical programs of assisting families to adjust to crises and to maintain their integrity under the changing conditions of modern life.

19

Ruth Shonle Cavan
and Katherine Howland Ranck

TYPICAL FAMILY REACTIONS

TO THE DEPRESSION

FAMILY LIFE before and during the depression has been
discussed chronologically and analytically. The family has been
presented at different stages: before the depression; in the period
of disorganization that accompanied the first realization of the
crisis; and in the process of adjustment. Types of family life, types
of disorganization, and types of adjustment have been differentiated. This breaking-down of the complexity of family life is necessary for an understanding of specific processes. But no process
exists in isolation from other processes, and every stage of a process
is but a link in a continuous chain. Two questions therefore stand
out: In one individual or in one family how have these different
responses to the crisis or these different types of adjustment been
combined? How has the disorganization been related to the pre-
depression situation, and how, in turn, has the readjustment been
related to the disorganization of the individual or the family? A
series of cases, as complete as the material available allows, is here
presented, selected to show the interrelation of parts and to illustrate different patterns of reaction. These cases in some instances
repeat excerpts given in the preceding chapters, but here the particular experiences can be seen in relation to the case as a whole.

In the attempt to uncover typical sequences, cross-classifications
were made of . . . four sets of classifications . . . (*a*) types of family

Reprinted from Ruth Shonle Cavan and Katherine Howland Ranck, *The
Family and the Depression: A Study of One Hundred Chicago Families*
(Chicago: University of Chicago Press, 1938), pp. 113–49.

organization prior to the depression (good or fair organization, good organization with the father in a subordinate position, conflict between parents and children, good except for the problem child, and disorganization); (*b*) types of crisis (contact with some relief agency prior to the depression, first contact after the depression, some other crisis more important than the depression, and no relief sought); (*c*) types of reaction to the crisis (normal worry, excessive worry, demoralization, family disintegration, depression outweighed by some other crisis, depression as part of earlier disorganization); and (*d*) types of adjustment (modification of functions of the family, changes in roles, and evasions—each with subtypes). . . . As a practical expedient it became necessary to simplify the classifications. Consequently, all families that had had good or fair organization prior to the depression, including those families in which the father held a subordinate role, were classified as being well organized. All other families were classified as disorganized. Table 12 shows, for these two groups, the total number of families with each type of crisis, each type of reaction, and each type of adjustment.

An inspection of the detailed work-sheets showing the interrelationships makes it possible to select certain general patterns that may indicate general trends. Thus, in the well-organized families there are few families who were on relief before the depression or in which some other crisis overshadows the depression. Two types of situation remain: necessity for relief after the depression, and ability to get along without relief. Normal worry or excessive worry are the characteristic types of disorganization of the group seeking relief; typical ways of adjusting are through modifications of family functions and roles or through evasions. The group that was able to forego relief tended either to feel no serious adverse effects, and therefore to have no real readjustment to make, or to exhibit normal or excessive worry, combined with a tendency to attempt adjustments in family functions accompanied by continued worry. In an occasional family that had been well organized prior to the depression there was excessive disorganization of some member.

In the families that were disorganized before the depression, more patterns are observable. In the group that had contacts with

TABLE 12

Type of Crisis, Disorganization, and Adjustment

	Organized Families	Disorganized Families
Type of crisis:		
Contact with relief agency before depression	4	14
First contact with agency after depression	12	13
Other crisis superseded depression	1	5
No relief obtained	31	20
Total number of cases	48	52
Type of disorganization:*		
Normal worry	11	11
Excessive worry	9	5
Demoralization		6
Family disintegration	2	3
Other crisis superseded depression	1	8
Disorganization		6
Reaction uncertain	8	4
Total number of cases	31	43
Type of adjustment:†		
Modification of functions:		
Adjustment without disorganization	12	6
Adjustment of activities in attempt to remain independent	22	25
Substitute activities	5	2
Increased unity of family	8	9
Adjustment through changes in roles:		
Changes in intrafamily roles	‡	‡
Acceptance of dependency	7	6
Evasions		
Refusal to face issue	7	7
Attempts to escape	5	10
Total types of adjustment§	66	65

* In addition, twelve organized and six disorganized families exhibited little or no disorganization, and five organized and three disorganized families accepted dependency apparently without much disorganization.

† In addition, ten organized and nineteen disorganized families had failed to make an adjustment at the time of the special interview.

‡ The shifts in intrafamily roles were so difficult of determination that no attempt can be made to give an exact number.

§ Many families exhibited more than one type of adjustment. Hence, the total types of adjustment exceeds the total number of cases.

relief agencies prior to the depression, the depression tends to be incidental to a previous or a concurrent crisis of some other sort, and the typical reaction to the whole situation tends to be continued disorganization, combined with refusal to face the issue, to "escape," and in some cases the acceptance of poverty and relief. The group that had its first contact with the relief agency after the depression began tends to become greatly disorganized in the crisis with excessive worry, demoralization, family disintegration, and the complication of other crises; the adjustment, although it contains attempts at modification of functions and roles, typically also tends toward evasions and the acceptance of relief, often with continued disorganization. The group in which some other crisis outweighs the depression tends to react with continued worry or demoralization. The group that received no relief either felt little adverse effect of the depression or reacted with worry or had the situation complicated by other crises; adjustments tended to take the form of modification of functions and roles, with some continued disorganization. It is characteristic of the families that were well organized before the depression that other crises do not complicate the situation; and of the families that were disorganized before the depression, that other crises either supersede the depression or complicate it in some way (many of these crises involve illness or death and suggest that ill health may have been an unrecognized factor in the disorganization that characterized the family before the depression).

Cases will be cited to illustrate the sequences outlined above.

1. *Families well organized before the depression that found it necessary to seek relief after the depression.* In the first case cited below, there is normal concern about the situation, a tightening of family bonds, attempts to meet the crisis both through modifications of functions and through evasions, with a final realistic adjustment.

The pre-depression situation. The Allen family in 1927 consisted of the father, mother, William, aged fifteen, and Thelma, aged seven. Mr. Allen was born in Chicago of Bohemian parents. He had an eighth-grade education and became an iron-worker, earning $55–$60 per week. Mrs. Allen was a German-American. The family was Catholic and had lived in a middle-class neighborhood since 1921, paying $40 a month rent for a five-room apartment.

William was mentally retarded and in a special room at school. His mother appealed to the Juvenile Court to have him placed in some institution where he could learn a trade, and the Court referred him to the Institute for Juvenile Research for examination. The Institute examination revealed a history of minor thefts and delinquencies, some in company with other boys, truancy from home, and recently more serious gang activities. He was accustomed to boastful lying and had become obsessed by an interest in sex. The parents had tried all types of punishment and continued to whip him. His difficulties seemed to be those of social adjustment rather than the outcome of any personality maladjustment; he was described as kind, helpful, cheerful, and affectionate. He always wanted to be doing something and was easily led. The parents seemed to be adjusted to each other, their only point of difference being the inability of the mother to save any part of the father's wages. They did not, however, understand the nature of William's difficulties.

William was in the Cook County School for a time, but at sixteen left school to find work, attending continuation school. He could not secure permanent work, but, through friends, found many odd jobs. According to his mother, as soon as he left school his behavior difficulties cleared up. From about 1928 to 1929 onward, therefore, the family may be considered as well organized.

The family took two newspapers, and the children had adequate play equipment. The father did not belong to any clubs but attended union meetings. The family rode in their car almost every summer evening, visiting friends, the parks, an amusement park, and the beaches; they rented a cottage in Wisconsin for several weeks each summer. In the winter they entertained their friends and went to many bunco parties. Mrs. Allen was a good cook and was in demand at the many birthday parties and weddings that they attended.

The crisis. After the beginning of the depression Mr. Allen's work became increasingly irregular. In 1930 he earned only $200; and in 1931, only $75. The family had saved $500, but this was lost in a bad investment. They had no other savings and no real estate.

Adjustment to the crisis. The parents were worried and made various modifications in family activities to meet the situation. They borrowed on their insurance policies, cashed in some policies, and practiced various economies. In 1932 they moved to a cheaper apartment, owing $210 rent. The car was sold, dental work was delayed, and cheaper food and clothes were used. Their many friends came to their assistance: a friend who worked in the stock yards brought them bacon and inexpensive cuts of meat; another friend gave them a dozen cans of macaroni; someone else supplied ice. A friend gave Mrs. Allen a coat that had been left at her house and never called for. Mrs. Allen's sister also came to her aid and, through an exchange of services, both benefited: Mrs. Allen mended for her sister, and the sister made clothes for her; the sister bought fruit, and Mrs. Allen canned all of it, retaining some for her work. Money was also borrowed from friends and relatives to the extent of about $900, and $90 was owed to doctors and for union dues.

The family dreaded the thought of the relief agency; but when unemployment continued and the resources of friends were exhausted, relief was sought, in March, 1932. The family received relief for a year and a half. Soon after relief began, they were requested by the landlord to move, and they secured a four-room flat for $15. The Allens were ashamed to be on relief—they were ashamed to check up to see why coal and groceries did not come as promised. Mrs. Allen hated to go to the stores, it seemed as though people "looked funny" at her. They made no requests of the relief agency except for actual necessities. Mr. Allen continued to seek work, and Mrs. Allen began to earn a few dollars a week by ironing. In 1933 William was given a C.C.C. appointment, and Mr. Allen began to find odd jobs. The family requested that relief be stopped.

A year later, at the time of the special interview, the family continued to live in the inexpensive apartment. All four members of the family lived at home. Mr. Allen was regularly employed as a laborer in a packing-house (not at his trade), earning $16–$18 per week; William had occasional odd jobs and gave all his earnings to his mother; Mrs. Allen continued to iron, although the doctor had advised her to stop because she was very much overweight and had high blood pressure; Thelma was in school and had become very resourceful in making over hats and clothes. The family still owed large sums to friends and relatives from the early period of unemployment, but extensive borrowing had ceased. Mr. Allen was very happy to have work, saying "I've got to keep my family together, and I'm willing to do any work for that." The family was managing to break even. Occasionally a few dollars were borrowed, but were promptly repaid. The family had given up many of the expensive good times of the pre-depression period but did not regret that they had, at that time, spent the money instead of saving it. Mrs. Allen said that "even now it is the parties that I go to that make me forget things, so that at the party I can be as happy as ever."

The Allens were pessimistic about the future and about improvement in work conditions, but Mrs. Allen said she had learned not to worry. "I have learned a lot about getting along without things; and as long as we all stay together, even if we live in one room, we're a lot better off than many families I know where the man drinks or there are lots of small children."

In the early period of the father's unemployment this family was characterized by a combination of modification in family activities to meet the situation and of evasions of a recognition of their need for relief. Their own resources and economies were not sufficient to tide them over, and they resorted to borrowing, attempting at the same time to maintain something of their old scale of living (as indicated by their failure to move to a cheaper apartment until requested to do so). When they were finally forced to apply for relief, the modifications of roles, as well as of activities, began, continuing after the father found work. The family has managed to keep its expenses down to about one-third of the pre-depression expenditures. The family, always rather well organized, has remained a loyal unit. The members are congenial and have common interests; they help each other. At the same time, friends and relatives have not only given material help but have included the Allens in their good times even when the Allens were without funds. . . .

2. *Families well organized before the depression that did not find it necessary to seek relief.* The first family is one in which the income was greatly reduced, the crisis was met by a modification of activities and interests, and a fairly successful adjustment was made.

Pre-depression situation. Mr. Farber, a Russian Jew, had a partnership in a dry-goods business. His income prior to the depression was sufficient for him to carry $30,000 insurance. The family owned no real estate but did own a car; rent of $65 per month was paid for a four-room apartment. The father was described as a quiet man, who found most of his satisfactions through his work. He was kind to his wife and two sons and "satisfied with his lot." The mother was more aggressive and very ambitious; she was especially ambitious for the school success of her older son, whom she also tended to protect. This boy was not, however, very capable with regard to his school work and was referred to the Institute for failure in school work. The father favored the younger son, a preference that hurt the older boy, who was very fond of his father. The parents were fairly well adjusted to each other; there were no serious points of conflict and no quarreling before the children.

The crisis. Business began to be poor in 1929, and in 1930 Mr. Farber began to borrow on his insurance, borrowing all that he possibly could. During 1930–32 he also borrowed from friends and used his business credit to the limit. In 1933 the family moved to a six-room apartment, for which they paid $40 per month. In the meantime the mother's parents had lost all their money and had come to live with them; the relationship between Mrs. Farber and her parents was complicated by the fact that she had earlier borrowed money from them to aid a sister and this borrowed money had been lost. In spite of their difficulties during this period, they also, from time to time, sent money to relatives.

The adjustment. During this period of low income the father spent most of his time at his place of business. The mother thought that he probably was greatly worried, but he was accustomed to working hard and making the best of everything. The mother threw herself energetically into club work and was especially busy raising money for a philanthropic organization. Their general feeling was that they were "doing much better and no worse than many others." Many of their neighbors were in actual want, and some of their relatives were much worse off.

The worst effect of the depression was not the restrictions caused by lowered income but the inclusion of the grandparents in the family. These grandparents were orthodox Jews of European background. The grandfather felt that he should hold the patriarchal position in the family. There was also considerable tension over the borrowed money. The father adjusted to the situation by quietly effacing himself and spending most of his time at his place of business. The mother adjusted herself without conflict. The greatest difficulty was experienced by the oldest son, who was none too well adjusted socially. This boy compared the grumbling and nagging of his grandmother to the grinding of coffee. He was a boy with no friends of his own age and few hobbies, so that he had little chance to escape from the home atmosphere.

Other shifts in the family relationships had taken place since 1928, although it is not clear that they have any relation to the depression.

The mother had relinquished some of her ambition for her older son. She found some satisfaction in club work; and she also tended to identify herself with the younger son, who was more successful in school work than the older boy. At the same time, she tended to identify the older son with her husband, whom she had come to regard as her intellectual inferior. The older son, in his turn, tended to accept the identification with his father. The mother admitted that she was no longer completely satisfied with her husband and wished she had waited longer before marrying (she was married when seventeen). Nevertheless, there was no evidence of any serious personal maladjustments or of impending family disintegration; rather, the members felt considerable unity and responsibility for each other, recognized the difficulties of the situation, and adjusted themselves as well as they could to the tensions involved in the "doubling-up" of families with somewhat incompatible views.

While the personal relationships remained much the same as time went on, the economic adjustment improved. In 1933 business increased, and by 1934 most of the business debts had been paid and many customers owed the firm money.

3. *Families well organized before the depression that suffered serious disorganization after the depression.* A fair picture of the experiences of the well-organized families would not be given if only those families were presented that made a fairly realistic adjustment of activities and roles without serious or permanent disorganization. While the minor forms of disorganization and a realistic adjustment are characteristic of the majority of cases, there are some cases in which serious personal disorganization occurred.

The first family is one that sought relief and eventually became reorganized through the acceptance of relief and through pride in the children.

Pre-depression situation. The Garfinkel family consists of the father, mother, and four children born between 1921 and 1930. The family came to the attention of the Institute for Juvenile Research in 1928 because the oldest boy defecated involuntarily but without physical cause for the lack of control. There was no misconduct or delinquency.

In 1928 the family was described as harmonious. The mother was fond of the father, who made a good living and was good to all of them. The father, in turn, said his home life was happy and that his wife was good to him. The sexual adjustment was satisfactory. The father assisted his wife in the home. There were some arguments over money and the discipline of the children, but the parents did not regard these as serious. The family maintained a kosher household; the father attended the synagogue on holidays. The mother was proud of her children, whom she had taken regularly to an infant-welfare clinic.

The social and recreational life was meager. There were no toys for the children in the home. There was no family recreation, and the parents never went places together. The father liked to have company come to the house to talk.

The father worked in cleaning and dyeing establishments. He held one position during all of 1928 and prior to that had been in one place for eighteen months. In 1928 he earned $40 per week, had $1,600 invested in bonds, and regularly saved to provide for any period of unemployment. The family lived in a four-room steam-heated flat for which they paid $48 per month.

The father in 1928 was described as a quiet, colorless man, healthy, and with no interest in drinking. He did not like to spend money but was generous with his wife. He liked to be with people and to talk with them.

The mother in 1928 was described as ignorant and emotional; she had little poise and laughed loudly before answering questions. The situation was complicated by the fact that she understood very little English.[1]

The picture of the family in 1928, then, is of a family with adequate income and the cautious habit of saving for short periods of unemployment, and with the parents adjusted to each other and proud of their children. The oldest boy was not adjusted but did not present delinquent behavior. The family life was barren, however, in that there was almost no provision for recreation.

The crisis. In 1929 the father began to experience long periods of unemployment and worked only about six months during the year. Wages had also decreased, and he earned only $14 to $20 per week when employed. His savings were soon used, and he began to contract small debts. The bonds in which he had invested $1,600 were valueless. This situation continued.

In 1931 the father applied for relief but was not granted it, as he was, at that time, receiving $10 per week from his union. In 1932 the

[1]   It is impossible to know how much of her seeming lack of poise was due to embarrassment at not understanding what was said to her.

father was granted intermittent relief whenever his earnings fell below a certain standard, and in 1933 the father was placed on work relief. Until the family became wholly dependent, the economic situation was precarious and the family had no feeling of economic security. They were neither self-supporting nor wholly dependent upon the relief agency. When the father's earnings were $17 or more for a few weeks time, the case was dropped from relief. When the father's earnings fell below this amount the family ran into debt and again applied for relief. The family moved to smaller and poorer quarters and paid less rent. In 1933 they paid $22.50 per month for two rooms; and in 1934, $10 for three rooms.

The father's caution in not spending money and in saving for unemployment, exhibited prior to the depression, developed into fear and a marked feeling of insecurity, which permeated the entire family and was most acute during 1930 and 1931, when the family had exhausted all its resources and had not yet been accepted as wholly dependent.

The father maintained a surface calmness, but his feeling of insecurity found outlet in great fears of bodily illness. He developed headaches and had spots on his body that "burned." He believed he had cancer and went from clinic to clinic, to be told in each that his only difficulty was nervousness.

The mother, recorded as having little poise in 1928, during the tension of economic reverses developed periods of excitement and confusion, aggravated also by high blood pressure. During one period the mother and children giggled so incessantly that little conversation was possible with or between them. When the financial condition became more stable, her excitement and confusion lessened.

The adjustment. In 1934, the mother was still worried about meeting the family expenses on the amount paid to the father for work relief, but there was none of the earlier fear of no income at all. The father also had lost his fears. The children seemed to be spontaneously happy, and the entire family felt pride in the achievements of each child. The children were all interested in school and had achieved such successes as appointment to the school safety patrol and a free scholarship to the Art Institute. The oldest boy was troubled with enuresis at this time.

In this case the family pattern of fear of insecurity, evidenced before the depression in thrift and careful savings, is exaggerated almost to the point of abnormality during the crisis of the depression. The emotional mother responded by exaggerated excitement and confusion; the timid father, by exaggerated fears. As the family became reorganized, the family unity found expression through pride in the accomplishments of the children. . . .

4. *Disorganized families having contact with a relief agency prior to the depression.* One more case may be cited, in which the family was on the verge of disintegration prior to the depression and in which the case workers have been a definite factor in the reorganization of the family. In this case there was no sharp crisis but a gradual process of disorganization and increased dependency upon the agency both for support and supervision.

Pre-depression situation. The background of Mr. and Mrs. Pana-suras must be understood in order to make clear the later marital diffi-culties. The mother had been a foster-child who lived with one family between the ages of nine and seventeen. The stories of the foster-parents and of Mrs. Panasuras do not agree as to what occurred then, but the girl left the foster-home, feeling unwanted. She worked in a restaurant, finding the work hard. When Mr. Panasuras, whom she scarcely knew, wished to marry her, she gladly accepted the offer. Mr. Panasuras is a Greek, who felt that he should be the head of his house-hold and that his wife should find herself fully occupied at home. His wife, on the other hand, desired the usual common recreational in-terests and wished to improve the appearance of her house in a way which seemed to her husband frivolous and extravagant.

Mr. and Mrs. Panasuras were married in 1921. During the next nine years six children were born. Mrs. Panasuras, physically frail, found herself unable to cope with the housework and the care of so many young children. She contracted syphilis from her husband and in 1934 was still receiving treatments for this disease. In 1930 she was sterilized.

Mr. Panasuras was a cook and, when working, made about $35 per week. He drank a great deal, however, stayed out late at night, and was quarrelsome. He went from one job to another.

In nine years the family lived in fifteen different places. Some were extremely undesirable. In 1927 the flat in which the family lived was "so situated in the rear that the garbage from a Greek restaurant, a barber shop, a grocery store, and several upstairs flats was deposited at the back door. There were no screens on the windows." Many of the moves were made because of evictions for nonpayment of rent.

Mr. and Mrs. Panasuras had failed to work out a satisfactory adjustment between themselves. Mr. Panasuras spent his free time away from home with his own friends. He ate his meals at his place of work. He therefore had little to do with the family. It was contrary to Greek mores for the wife to extend her life beyond her home, and he saw no reason why Mrs. Panasuras should need any freedom from her household duties or wish to go places with him. On various occasions he struck his wife, and each screamed and yelled at the other during quarrels. Mrs. Panasuras was ill much of the time and burdened with many small children. She had no assistance with her work and no household conveniences. The children were frequently dirty, underfed, and half-dressed; and the house was usually uncared for. In only a few entries in the record that extends over almost nine years are the children and the house referred to as being clean.

The children early became problems in the home. In 1927 there were four children in the family. The oldest child, aged four, was already unmanageable. He had violent spells of temper, bit and scratched other children, threw things, kicked, and swore. He had these spells whenever he could not have his own way. Much of his behavior duplicated that of his father. In 1928 he was placed in the Detention Home, then in an orphanage, then sent home. In 1930 he was placed in a boarding home. The third child, while in a sanitarium for treatment, spilled nitric acid on his foot and had to have his toes amputated. He received $3,000 as compensation for the injury. A guardian was appointed for him until he should be fourteen years old, and he was placed in a boarding home in 1928.

The crisis. In 1924 a relief agency had its first contact with the family, at a time when the father had burned his foot with boiling water and was unable to work for five weeks. This period of injury was followed by an attack of bronchial pneumonia and confinement for two weeks in the County Hospital. Mr. Panasuras applied to the agency after his recovery from pneumonia. He owed $180 for furniture and more for back rent. From that time on, the family came to the attention of this relief agency at frequent intervals. In addition to supplying material relief as needed, the agency attempted to work out some adjustment between Mr. and Mrs. Panasuras and to see that the children received better physical care. In 1930 Mr. Panasuras was able to contribute very little to the support of his family, and the relief agency became the chief means of support. The agency also assumed a more dominant place in the management of the family. In the summer of 1930 the three older children were placed in an institutional home, and the mother was sent to a camp with her two younger children for a month's rest. At intervals Mr. Panasuras continued to abuse his wife.

Adjustment. Mr. Panasuras was put on work relief in the fall of 1930 and was still on such work in 1934. During these four years he worked steadily, receiving his wages in cash. From time to time his wife reported that he refused to give her sufficient money for food. They continued to move frequently and to live in dirty and vermin-infested flats. A third boy had begun to run away from home, sometimes staying away as long as a week at a time. The parents requested that he be placed outside the home.

In spite of the apparent continuation of difficulties, the conditions in 1934 are superior to the earlier situation. One child had died, and with two others in foster-homes the mother found herself with only three children to care for. Moreover, she had the assurance that she would bear no more children. The operation and the fact of her sterility had, however, created some sexual maladjustment between husband and wife. The income, though small, was regular. The mother's own statement was that she "had it worse when he was making good wages."

This family will probably never be completely reorganized. The parents are unable to manage the children, and the difficulties between the parents seem to be deep seated and based upon differences in cultural background. Personal differences also enter in. Nevertheless, the shift from irregular earnings to complete dependence upon the relief agency did in some measure reorganize the family.

5. *Disorganized families that sought relief after the depression.* The case cited represents an unstable family that became rather severely disorganized and that failed to achieve a satisfactory reorganization. Some of the families in this group became reorganized financially and in personal relationships. In other cases, however, the family disintegrated.

The pre-depression situation. Mr. and Mrs. Bakaba are cousins. Both were Assyrians but spent some of their youth in Russia. The father learned the trade of bricklayer in Russia and came to the United States in 1913. Five years later his cousin came and they were married. Both regarded their respective families in Europe as having been in good financial circumstances and with good status in the community. They had a very strong feeling of loyalty to, and pride in, the family group in Europe. In fact, according to one report, the marriage may be interpreted as a manifestation of family pride and loyalty. When Mrs. Bakaba came to the United States, she landed in California and found herself without sufficient funds to come to Chicago, where she had relatives. She wrote to her uncle in Chicago; and he, together with her cousin, sent her money. This uncle was not able to support her and felt that it would be a disgrace for a woman of their family to work. The solution was her marriage to her cousin. Throughout the history of the case the family traditions are strong incentives to action.

The family lived in Cicero until about 1925, when they moved to Chicago to secure treatment for a sick child, which died. The peak of the father's employment was in 1923–24, when, for eighteen months, he earned $500 per month. At other times his earnings were about $300 per month. Jointly with his brother, the father bought an apartment building in Cicero, in the basement of which the Bakaba family lived. Although the mother had no assistance in the home and did the janitorial work in the apartment building, the family lived well, bought good clothing, saved money, and paid for the expensive illnesses of two children.

The crisis. The crisis in the family affairs was cumulative. After the family moved to Chicago, about 1925, the apartment in Cicero was managed by Mr. Bakaba's brother. Mrs. Bakaba was convinced that the brother defrauded them of their share of the income. As economic conditions became bad and the income from the flat decreased, she was more and more convinced of his dishonesty; and many heated quarrels took place between Mr. and Mrs. Bakaba over this subject. Mr. Bakaba maintained a protective attitude toward his brother, who was younger than he. As an older member of the family, he was impelled by family loyalty to give this protection. This source of conflict was not terminated by the foreclosure of the mortgage and the loss of the property about 1933, as Mrs. Bakaba continued to blame her husband for the loss of their investment.

Mrs. Bakaba's ill health also added to the family disorganization. Her ill health culminated in an operation (including sterilization) about 1929. After this operation she was weak, nervous, and complaining. One of her chief interests and chief topics of conversation was her various physical complaints. When she quarrelled, she became very much excited and could not stop quarreling, and at times struck her husband. She developed depressed moods and took a highly personal point of view of their economic difficulties, blaming her husband and her relatives for their loss of income. At one time she was removed from the home for a long period of rest in a convalescent home. The father reacted negatively to any suggestion of institutionalization for his wife because of her emotional instability. Such a step would be contrary to the family customs. One relative had had his wife confined, but she had attempted to kill her child; and unless his wide did something equally serious, he could not think of placing her in an institution.

Sexually, the couple had never been well adjusted. The wife complied with her husband's wishes from a sense of duty, and prior to the depression period had believed him unfaithful. After the operation the situation became more tense; and because of certain physical difficulties that followed the operation, the husband, as well as the wife, became dissatisfied.

The situation was further complicated by the behavior of one son, whose mentality was too low to permit the school success expected of him by the family. Truancy from home and school and continued enuresis had been his reactions to the conflict thus engendered and the resulting feeling of insecurity. A younger child was hydrocephalic and for a time added to the burden of the mother. This child was placed in an institution. The mother then worried about him and wished to have him at home. Toward the difficulties of these two children the mother again took a very personal attitude and blamed their condition upon her husband.

To this already unstable family situation the depression added further strain. The father lost his position in 1928 when he left his work to hunt for his son who had run away from home. He was unable to find regular work, and for three years had only short jobs. By 1931 he had no work and applied for relief. Later he was given work as an unskilled laborer on work-relief projects.

From 1928 on, the family suffered from lack of income and change in status. The family borrowed from the father's brother and also from the mother's brother until they could no longer supply money. Gradually the assets of the family disappeared. In 1929 the relief record states that "it is approximately a year since the father has been working steadily. It is the first time that he has ever been so completely down and out. Formerly he always had money in the bank and a small amount invested. He had paid a thousand dollars down on a lot but has had to lose that because of his inability to keep up with the payments. In the same way he lost his union card, valued at one hundred dollars, and five thousand dollars worth of insurance." The father was alternately discouraged when unable to find any work and elated when he secured work. When he could secure work at his trade, his earnings were good and he was able temporarily to pay rent and debts and to buy clothes for the family. But each time the work proved to be temporary in character, and soon the family was again without regular income. Eventually the father tried to secure any kind of work.

Both father and mother found it hard to face the fact of lowered income. The father repeatedly told the case workers of his former savings and bank account; both parents told of the wealth of their families in Europe; only with the greatest difficulty, after they were on relief, were they induced to move to an apartment with low rent. Their relationship with the relief agency was marked by continual complaints regarding the small amount of relief, coupled with a desire for personal attention from the case worker.

The mother was unable to see their difficulties in any but a personal light. She believed that the father had money but refused to use it to pay the debts or supply necessities. She quarreled with him, demanding to know what he did with the money.

The adjustment. Both parents exhibited a decided tendency to escape completely from the whole complicated situation, particularly during the period of first contact with the relief agency, when only partial relief was granted and the family was in actual want. Mr. Bakaba felt that the agency did not care whether or not they starved, and he became so discouraged that he did not care either. But he could not bear to see his family starve and thought of leaving home. At other times he talked of wishing to send his wife to Europe for a long visit with her relatives. Mrs. Bakaba also spoke of a desire to return to her mother's home. Mr. Bakaba thought vaguely of death; he did not consider ways and means of committing suicide, but he would say to himself, "I want to die right now." Several times Mrs. Bakaba attempted to commit suicide by turning on the gas.

The two organizing elements in the father's situation seem to have been his high sense of duty to his family, which prevented actual desertion, and his great faith in religion. Terming himself a "child of God," he related that "God had talked to him" in 1919 and that he had been religious since then. He did not attend any one church regularly but prayed three or four times daily. When his depression became very great and he thought of suicide, he found relief in prayer.

When the father was interviewed in 1934, the family had in some small measure become better organized. The father had been on work relief for about two years. The regularity of such work and the feeling of self-respect that it brings is usually an organizing factor. While the father did not expressly state that work relief had eliminated much of his discouragement, it is to be noted that he sought and secured work relief as early as possible and continued at it.

The mother still found her chief outlet in quarreling with her husband and blaming him for the various family difficulties.

In this case it is possible to see clearly the cumulative character of the crisis, until a point of great family and personal disorganization was reached.

6. *Families in which some other crisis took precedence over the depression.* Unemployability of the father, illness of the father, or death of the father are types of crisis found in the series. In the case presented, the death of the father was a crucial factor in bringing the family to the attention of the relief agencies.

Pre-depression situation. Before the depression Mr. Zinski worked as a laborer at a job that he had held since 1905. He received $45 per week, and with overtime occasionally received as much as $100 per week. The rent from the other flat in the house amounted to $37 per month. The family carried $3,000 insurance on the father and $500 on the mother and had invested $4,000 in a home upon which there were, in 1928, first and second mortgages.

Born in Poland, Mr. Zinski conceived his role as the dominant one in the household and exerted strict supervision over his children. He demanded instant obedience and allowed the children little opportunity for recreation outside the family. His wife aided him in this old-world pattern of control. As the older boys matured, they lied about their activities and eventually sought contacts outside the home. They did not do good work in school and became involved in serious delinquencies. By 1928 the two oldest boys had served sentences in a state correctional school, and a third son had been referred to the Institute for Juvenile Research because of displays of uncontrollable temper at school. The situation between the parents and older boys was very strained; the parents "hollered" at the boys for going away from the house, and they also objected to supporting the older boys, who failed to find regular work.

At the beginning of the depression, therefore, the family had an adequate income, the parents were adjusted to each other, but they did not understand the interests of American-reared children.

The crisis. In 1929 Mr. Zinski became ill and died. The mother received $3,000 insurance, and for almost a year her husband's employer paid the amount of his wages. With this money she paid the funeral expenses of $500, personal debts of the same amount, and $2,000 on the mortgage; the rest was invested in bonds, which proved to be worthless. The oldest son, who had worked from 1929 to 1932, was laid off; the second son had been unable to find steady work.

The adjustment. The family met the difficult financial situation by borrowing and by contracting debts. By 1932 they owed $1,000 to a relative and a total of about $600 to grocers, a butcher, and a milk company. It then became apparent that the situation could no longer be met in this way; and the family applied for relief, which was granted.

In 1934 the family was still on relief and was still very much disorganized. The two older boys merely ate and slept at home; they took no part in the family life, and the mother had no idea where they spent their time. One of these sons was openly antisocial in his attitudes and refused to work at a job paying $18 per week. He preferred to make an occasional holdup for a large amount. The other son had also been in difficulty, having been arrested for carrying a pistol. The third son had accepted responsibility for the family and worked at jobs provided by the relief agency. The mother was worried about these three boys; she felt that, if they had jobs, they would marry and settle down. They had no jobs and no spending money, and they wanted better food and clothes than could be provided.

7. *Families disorganized prior to the depression and not finding it necessary to seek relief.* The first case is one in which the depression had very little effect, either economic or psychological, upon the family.

Pre-depression situation. Mr. Russo, born in Italy, worked as a laborer earning $27 a week in 1928. A son earned about $15 a week in a garage. The family was buying a small home, of which they were very proud. There were two daughters, Esther and Martha, and a stepmother. The father had a "terrible temper" and adhered to the old-world conception of the status of the father as the absolute head of the family. The stepmother admitted that she was afraid of her husband; and Esther, who rebelled against the strict supervision, was in constant conflict with the father, who struck her when she disobeyed him. Esther attempted to live her life along Americanized lines and wished to go with boys. As a result of the conflict between her and her father, she became a truant from school and was suspected unjustly of sex delinquency.

The depression. There is no record that the depression presented a crisis. The son lost his job at the beginning of the depression. In 1935 he was in a C.C.C. camp. The father's work had been reduced to five days a week and his wages to $24 per week. He was, however, satisfied with his work and contemplated no change. Esther had married in 1931 and soon afterward died. Martha left school in 1933, after completing two years of high school. Unable to find work, she had adjusted herself to staying at home. The stepmother had given birth to a son in 1933, and this child was a source of pleasure to the entire family. The stepmother and Martha occupied themselves with the care of the house and a garden, while the father enjoyed carpenter work. Thus the family activities centered in the care and improvement of the home.

The adjustment. The adjustment between Martha and the father was fairly satisfactory. The father was reported still to be strict and irritable, but Martha was his favorite child and rebelled less than Esther had done. She was also permitted more freedom and went to shows, picnics—even dances—with girl friends.

The family found it necessary to economize; but this procedure presented no particular problems, as they always had economized and the mother had been accustomed to doing all the housework, including the sewing.

. . . Various factors that enter into the type of disorganization and adjustment of the families and their members have been discussed in the chapters on these subjects. It remains to emphasize the continuity of family life. It has proved difficult to take broad classifications, such as organized and disorganized families, and find definite differences in reactions or adjustment to the depression. But it is relatively simple in a given family about which data are fairly complete to find continuity in the process of family life. In fact, it seems probable that, if data were sufficiently complete about a family, it would be possible to predict with a fair degree of accuracy how an economic crisis would disturb the organization of the family and how the family would react and adjust to this disturbance. The ideals and traditions, the customs and codes of the family, and the personal attitudes and habits of its members continue through a crisis. They determine the vulnerable points of the family life and also the ways in which the family will react to a crisis. In general it may be repeated that the depression, as a social crisis, has tended to intensify the trends of family life already in operation. For example, in the Lind family one of the strong points in the family code was that it had no debts. When the depression had exhausted the cash reserves of the family, this abhorrence of debts offered a vulnerable point, and with the first hundred dollars of debt Mr. and Mrs. Lind both reacted with extreme worry and personal disorganization. Mr. Lind, who previously had become intoxicated occasionally, now began to drink more regularly. The reorganization came when the increase in debts was checked by relief work and the family could restore a semblance of its former independence. Relieved of this one great threat to its former symbol of self-respect, the family was able to adapt itself to the acceptance of relief and to resume the pattern of life developed before the crisis. Other cases indicate in like manner the place at which the depression may weaken the family organization, the accentuation of the previous trends toward unity or disintegration in the family (and toward integration or maladjustment of personality in the members of the family), and, when the crisis passes, the diminution of exaggerated reactions and a return to the pre-depression pattern.

It seems reasonable to presume that, if enough cases were available to account for all the possible combinations of factors, typical processes might be isolated. Such an analysis would have to take account of the family and the personal organization prior to the depression, the type of crisis, the way in which the particular crisis affected the previous organization of the family and its members, their immediate reaction, the way in which the effect of the crisis was moderated, and the final adjustment. With this number of general factors and the numerous possible subtypes under each, the number of cases in the present study has not made it possible to isolate exact sequences that would constitute typical processes. The following, rather general, typical processes may be suggested, repeated in part from the statement made at the beginning of this chapter and based upon the analysis of cases in this study:

1. Well-organized families that before the depression had maintained their independence and had avoided other serious family crises; reduction, but not complete loss, of income; adjustment in functions and activities to the lower level of income; little, if any, change in fundamental conception by the family of its status; little, if any, change in personal roles; trend of family life is continued without period of disorganization.

2. Essentially the same situation as in No. 1, except that some one member is seriously affected, perhaps through loss of employment (although the *family* income suffers only a moderate reduction), and this member tends to become disorganized or demoralized; when his employment (and hence his status and role) is restored, the disorganization or demoralization disappears and he resumes his former mode of life.

3. Families well-organized before the depression that suffered a great reduction in, or complete cessation of, income during the depression; worry, tending in some cases to become excessive; adjustments of functions and activities in accord with greatly lowered income; climax to worry when relief is finally granted; adjustment to relief agency and the new roles implied in the status of relief clients; resumption of employment at earliest possible moment and voluntary request that relief be stopped.

4. There are various modifications of the foregoing process; instead of, or accompanying, adjustments in activities to fit the lowered income, certain evasions may be made, such as excessive borrowing, contracting debts for goods and services, "nervous breakdowns," or refusal to see the financial situation; instead of accepting the new and temporary role as relief clients, the family or some member may resist submission to the control of the agency and become antagonistic to the case workers.

5. Families disorganized before the depression that suffered loss of income but not sufficient loss to necessitate relief; worry, with increased family disorganization; adjustment through modification of activities with a tendency toward evasions.

6. Families disorganized before the depression that found it necessary to seek relief during the depression; greatly increased disorganization, with a tendency toward disintegration of the fam-

ily; if the family did not completely disintegrate, a partial reorganization was effected.

A variant is found in those families in which the relief agency succeeded in giving the family a better organization than it had had before the depression.

7. Families that had sought relief before the depression because of a general state of disorganization and inability of the father to support the family; status of family little changed by the depression, and therefore family only slightly cognizant of the fact that there was a depression; continued disorganization.

8. Families that had sought relief before the depression because of illness or death of the father; depression plays only a minor role in comparison with the earlier crisis; status of family little changed by the depression.

9. Families in which the illness or death of the father occurred during the depression and family sought relief; the family crisis supersedes all other crises; relief is rationalized as the result of the illness or death, and relatively little loss of status is felt. This type differs very little from type No. 8.

10. Families either intermittently on relief before the depression or marginal, usually not well organized; thankful acceptance of relief (without much disorganization) as offering more security than their own efforts had brought.

These processes are suggestive rather than conclusive. The analysis of more cases undoubtedly would supply many variants and no doubt would add more independent processes.

Robert E. L. Faris

DEMOGRAPHY OF URBAN

PSYCHOTICS WITH SPECIAL

REFERENCE TO

SCHIZOPHRENIA

THIS PAPER is concerned with the make-up of the urban population in mental hospitals: What kinds of persons the patients are, what types of urban areas they come from, and what kinds of social life characterize those areas. Special attention is paid to social isolation as a possible cause of schizophrenia.

From a large scale study of *Mental Disorders in Chicago*, by the writer and H. W. Dunham, there emerge some very clear answers which may be typical of urban patients in general. Some parts of this study have been repeated in Providence, Rhode Island, with identical results. The details, which may be published soon, cannot be presented here, but some of the principal findings can be summarized. A most significant general finding is that different answers to the above questions must be given for the different types of mental disorders.

In answer to the first question concerning what types of persons constitute the hospital population, each index measured shows great differences for the different diagnoses. Omitting details, the true picture can be indicated by certain index figures. Age, for example, varies greatly in the different diagnostic groups. The peak age group for the senile psychosis, that is, the age group with the highest rate, is 75 years and over. The peak age group for general paralysis, manic-depressive, and alcoholic psychosis is 45 to 54 years. The

Reprinted from the *American Sociological Review* 3, no. 2 (1938) : 203–12.

peak age for paranoid schizophrenia is 35 to 44 years, and for hebephrenic and catatonic schizophrenia, 25 to 34. The range of ages as well as the peak age group also varies with each diagnostic group.

Marital status shows similarly great contrasts. In the same sample of cases, the ratio of married to single, taking single as 100, is, in the general paralysis group, 3.19, in the senile group 2.25, in the alcoholic group 2.07, in the manic-depressive group 1.82, and in the schizophrenic group .64. Some differences of marital status also appear between the manic and depressed types, between the types of schizophrenia, and in each of the schizophrenic types between the sexes.

Though no direct measure of economic status of these patients is available, it is possible to construct a serviceable index by using the median rentals in the areas from which the patients come. This procedure yields a symbolic monthly rental figure of $62 for the manic-depressive, of $39 for general paralysis, of $37 for paranoid schizophrenia, of $35 for senile psychosis, of $30 for hebephrenic schizophrenia, of $29 for catatonic schizophrenia, and of $23 for alcoholic psychosis. This represents a great spread of economic level, with the highest rental nearly three times that of the lowest.

Differences in nativity are also found. Though it is impossible to state the details, the outstanding facts are that the Negro rates are highest for senile, general paralysis, alcoholic psychosis, and catatonic and hebephrenic schizophrenia. The foreign-born group has the highest paranoid schizophrenia rate, and the native white group, which is lowest in most respects, has the highest manic-depressive rate, in which the Negroes have the lowest rate.

In these four respects, then,—age, marital status, economic status, and nativity, clear answers can be given, but different answers are indicated for each type of disorder. The selectivity of the mental hospital, then, is greater than generally known, but this selectivity does not appear if all cases are examined together, without division into types.

To the second question, concerning where these patients come from, a similarly complex answer is necessary. Again it depends on the diagnosis, and, in the city at least, very clearcut differences can

be shown. General paralysis, and paranoid and hebephrenic schizophrenia, mostly come from the central hobo, rooming-house, and
foreign-born and Negro slum areas. Senile psychosis cases come
from rooming-house and Negro areas, alcoholic from a broad
foreign-born slum area, and catatonic schizophrenia from more
restricted foreign-born areas. The manic-depressive rates are much
more widely distributed, but show a slight concentration in the
better class rooming house and apartment hotel districts.

Refinement of these area rates obtained by computing rates for
the different nativity groups by areas yields a very astonishing
result. For some of the diagnoses, it appears that the rates are high
for any population outside of the region in which that population
is in the majority. For example, although the schizophrenia rate for
Negroes is high, and schizophrenia rates in Negro areas are high,
the rates for Negroes are very high only for those Negroes outside
the Negro districts. The high rates are contributed by white persons
who live in these areas, where they constitute a small minority of
the population. Rates for native whites are low in native white areas
but are high in foreign-born areas, and rates for the foreign-born
are low in their own areas but very high in the Negro areas. The
rooming-house areas have such a heterogeneous population that no
group is in the majority, and the rates for all of these groups are
high there. In no case is the rate extremely high for any of these
groups in the areas in which they are in the majority. Schizophrenia, then (and this is true of several other psychoses as well),
comes mainly from hobo, rooming-house, and slum areas, and especially from those sections of the population in each area which
are in the minority for that area.

The answer to the third question, concerning the nature of the
social life in these high rate areas, might be expected to suggest
some causal connection between the sociological conditions and
the abnormal behavior. Even a casual inspection suggests that the
mobility, confusion, chaos, and personal isolation which are characteristic of these communities could provide only the worst sort of
background for mental health, but it is possible to describe the disorganization in more specific detail.

The hobo areas are inhabited by a drifting population of homeless and jobless men, many without family, friends, or even acquaintances, and without plans or goals. The informal social control of the type that is based on primary group life, and that enforcing conformity with folkways and mores is virtually lacking, so that there is no pressure to produce conventionality in appearance and behavior. Thus, completely free of the channels of approved social behavior, the behavior of the homeless man is free to drift in any direction his inner whims and outward influences may direct. When this drift has gone far, or when it takes a socially undesirable turn, society judges the man to be mentally abnormal, or delinquent, or both. Estimates vary, but the probable truth is that a high proportion of the older homeless men from these areas are deteriorated in behavior and mentality.

The rooming-house districts are also areas of high mobility and of anonymous life. There is no neighborliness, no gossip, no informal social control. Nobody cares what neighbors may think, for they pay little or no attention to one another. Here, again, the personalities are likely to become highly individuated and unconventional. Zorbaugh has described the loneliness of the rooming-house dweller and Cavan has shown the role of these chaotic conditions in producing the high suicide rates of these areas. These are also non-family areas, and substitutes for normal sex life in marriage relationships are provided by commercialized vice, by such institutions as closed dance halls, and by informal sex promiscuity and perversion. The relationship of this situation to venereal infection, and therefore to general paralysis rates, is obvious. It is also easy to see the difficulty of maintaining a normal and conventional personality in an area where the necessary social support is lacking.

The slum areas near the central parts of the city, inhabited by newly arrived foreign and Negro populations, also provide a mentally unhealthy background. These populations are new not only to this city, but for the most part to any large city, and are facing the task of adjustment from rural or village agricultural life to urban industrial existence. The old ways of life do not work and new ways are not easily learned. The assimilated and secularized Americans act in ways which appear strange, wicked, and incomprehensible.

Children who follow the American ways are also out of control. Where the population is heterogeneous, the neighborhood life lacks the intimacy necessary to social control. Free from the control either of parents or neighborhood life, the children may be controlled either by the criminal traditions of the gangs, or remain isolated and drift into eccentricity.

It must be admitted that many other features of life in these areas, though perhaps not so important, may still contribute to personal abnormalities. Among such conditions may be the insecurity of life, the low status of the slum dweller, and various by-products of extreme poverty.

From case studies, it is possible to show in still more detail the role of the community in producing abnormal personal behavior. It must be remembered that even in the highest rate areas, the psychotic percentage is a minority, so that whatever the community influences are, they do not so operate as to make abnormality universal inside their bounds. This fact indicates that the community influences are only a part of the complex of causes, although for some disorders, as indicated by the pattern of rates, nearly an indispensable part.

In the case of such a germ disease as general paralysis, an explanation is not difficult. It is known that the vice districts are generally located as conveniently as political conditions allow to the areas of high mobility, inhabited largely by unmarried persons. Here is the largest, though not the only, demand for commercialized prostitution. Residential distribution of persons arrested in vice raids and the distribution of venereal disease deaths coincide in showing the large patronage of prostitution in these areas. The distribution of general paralysis cases is essentially the same as these. Though the disease is a germ disease, some of the conditions which bring about the high rates in these areas are societal.

The high rates of alcoholism are also located in centralized areas although the pattern is not identical with that of general paralysis. The alcoholic psychosis rates are distributed similarly to those of arrests for drunkenness and of deaths due to alcoholism. These are among the immigrant groups and the lowest economic classes. The explanation of these distributions awaits fuller discovery of the relation between living conditions and alcoholism and the relation between alcoholism and alcoholic psychosis.

For the distributions of rates of senile psychosis, psychoneuroses, manic-depressive psychosis, and others, there is no available basis for explanation.

The distribution of the schizophrenia rates, however, offers a fascinating problem because of the neat distributions, sharp concentrations, and because there is no satisfactory organic explanation of the disorder. Case material furnishes a possible hypothesis that disorganized community factors, in combination with other factors, may be responsible for the abnormality.

The writer has suggested elsewhere that many, or most, of the typical symptoms of the schizophrenic may be viewed as a result of extreme seclusiveness due to isolation. Given a long, extreme absence of primary contacts with other persons, these various forms of eccentricity which are typical of the schizophrenic will develop. The *basic* cause of schizophrenia, then, will be whatever causes the isolation. The particular form the symptoms take must be explained by the special circumstances of the individual case.

The case studies show that community disorganization plays a part in producing isolation. It is not necessary to assume, as some have done, that the schizophrenics have a constitutional lack of sociability, or aggressiveness, or any other requisite for establishing normal social relations. It is found that a high proportion of schizophrenic patients have been at an early age normally sociable and that the forces which led to the isolation were only partly, or in some cases apparently not at all, within themselves but rather in their family and community relations.

In the typical sequence, the isolation process is not begun in community, but in family life. The great frequency of pampered, overprotected, spoiled children in the schizophrenic group has been noted by many observers. It is likely that the process begins here. This fact, however, is not connected, so far as we know, with community disorganization, nor is it sufficient to produce schizophrenia by itself. It is likely that in the better residential districts, overprotection of children is as frequent or more so, and yet these children may develop into normal adults.

The spoiled child who is able to play with other children usually has his selfishness and conceit eliminated by the action of the playmates. It is in communities where opportunity for such healthful social relations are more difficult to establish that the pampering may lead to a permanent isolation. It must be pointed out that the opportunities for intimate social relations among children may exist in the most disorganized areas. The delinquent boy gangs are composed of sociable members and furnish a reasonably normal background for mental health. The members of gangs are seldom schizophrenic. The schizophrenics are those who, because of the selfishness, pampering, and related traits, are excluded and perhaps persecuted by the gangs and hence become isolated. The data indicate that it is much more difficult for a pampered child to gain acceptance by the gang members in a disorganized neighborhood than in a better residential neighborhood. This difficulty of establishing normal social relations *outside the family* appears to be the community factor that explains the concentration of high schizophrenia rates in disorganized areas.

A typical sequence may be described as follows. A boy is pampered by his mother; she gives him so much attention that he develops superior abilities, neatness, and moral attitudes. He lives in a community where the majority of boys are rough and delinquent. At first he tries to play with them, but because of his neatness, precision of language, prudishness, and other traits he is teased and persecuted by the boys. Retreating to his mother, he is comforted and assured that he is much superior to those bad boys. This is easy for him to believe. As he accepts this evaluation of himself, he becomes even more conspicuous and is persecuted further by the rough boys. After repeated failures to gain their companionship, he may give up, stay at home, and amuse himself by solitary play or reading and get his only companionship from his mother, thereby increasing the damaging maternal attachment. After this retreat, his normally sociable inclinations may gradually disappear so that he begins to prefer his own company to that of others. This creates a vicious circle. The more he retreats, the more unacceptable he is to others, and the more they reject him, the greater his withdrawal. His withdrawal is not from "reality" but from social contacts with others. His behavior becomes less and less subject to that informal social control which preserves conventionality and thus becomes unconventional and incomprehensible to others. Because the communication in either direction is gone, he is just as unable to understand others as they are unable to understand him. His statements, reasonable enough to him, may appear as delusions to those who are unable to understand what is going on in his mind. The actions of others, reasonable to them, may appear to him as conspiracies directed against him, or fantastic in various other ways. For example, if he fails in his occupation, as is likely if cooperation with others is involved, he can not attribute this to any deficiency on his part, for his mother convinced him that he was superior to almost everyone. The only possible explanation of failure, then, is that others are working against him. He has some reason for this belief, as his unpopularity is visible; his only serious error is exaggerating the "conspiracy." However, since he fails so completely in so many things, it is easy to see how he can infer a giant and sinister plot directed against him. The balanced common sense that protects the normal person from such a conclusion comes from the intimate familiarity with the workings of human nature. The schizophrenic person has been unable to acquire this saving common sense because of his isolation.

In those communities, then, in which such conditions as extreme heterogeneity of types, mobility of population, secularization of ideas and individuation of personalities, are most prevalent, and where the person is surrounded by *other* races and nationalities, any person who, from pampering in infancy or any other cause, fails to establish normal social relations, finds it difficult or almost impossible to do so later. Because of the vicious circle effect, the longer the process goes on, the more hopeless the situation of the schizophrenic becomes. This may be the explanation of the apparently unfavorable prognosis in schizophrenia, especially for the older patients. There is no automatic process, either in normal society or in the hospital environment, which will reverse this process once it is well under way.

If the above interpretations are correct, a considerable portion of the mental hospital population is unpromising material for therapy. To reestablish cooperation and sociability will be most difficult with these patients, as it is necessary to reverse complex organizations of habits formed over a long period of years. Although it may not be impossible, mere kindly treatment and hopeful waiting will not do the work. What hope there is must lie in the newer, more active techniques of reeducation or in techniques yet to be discovered.

Perhaps the real hope will never lie in treatment of patients. If the disorganization of the community generates these forms of behavior, the relief that society desires is likely to wait on stabilization of these communities, whether it is done by the use of scientific knowledge or takes place automatically.